Social Welfare Pioneers

Social Welfare Pioneers

Herbert Stroup

Nelson-Hall Publishers **nh** Chicago

Library of Congress Cataloging-in-Publication Data

Stroup, Herbert Hewitt, 1916–
  Social welfare pioneers.

  Bibliography: p.
  Includes index.
  1. Philanthropists—Biography. 2. Volunteer workers
in social services—Biography. 3. Social workers—
Biography. 4. Social service—History. I. Title.
HV27.S85 1985   361.7'4'0922 [B]   85-13592
ISBN 0-88229-212-9 (cloth)
ISBN 0-8304-1164-X (paper)

Manufactured in the United States of America

10 9 8 7 6 5 4 3 2 1

The paper in this book is pH neutral (acid-free).

To my daughter and son-in-law
Trudi Ann *and* John Lawrence Kuczynski III

and to my grandson
John Lawrence Nicholas Kuczynski

Contents

Preface

In recent times, social work has grown remarkably in scope and appeal. Although its roots are grounded in antiquity, its present form makes it seem to be, in a large way, the product of our own day. Almost everyone at one time or another is touched by the branches of this growth. It seems that the growth of social service "from the cradle to the grave" will turn what once was the spontaneous and voluntary efforts of a relatively few persons (usually of the upper classes) into an immense activity of myriad professionally trained workers. Already social work has made giant strides in that direction.

One of the dangers in the relatively recent and somewhat hurried advance in the rise of modern social work is the possibility that social workers will lose sight of their foundations, the past out of which they have come. What is past is indeed prologue, and history throws its own peculiar light upon the actions and strivings of the present. It is well, therefore, for lay and professional people interested in social welfare work and its future to be well versed in its past.

The rapid growth of governmental services in our time has obscured the private or voluntary basis upon which social work rested. With anxious concern for governmental social services, some have tended to lose sight of the meaning and validity of the long history of social work that, along with other forces, has made possible the present strength of their interest. To these, as well as to others, the study of the history of social work is not only an anchorage against the winds and waves of present tempests but a beacon to guide them to a safe haven.

No completely satisfactory book on the general history of social welfare work exists at present. It is to be hoped that in time there will be many. Social work's history, however, may be approached in several ways. One way certainly is the usual and important method of the social historian. In his foreword to Frank J. Bruno's *Trends in Social Work* (New York: Columbia University Press, 1948), Shelby M. Harrison, former general director of the Russell Sage Foundation, says: "Much has been written on the development of our political institutions, our economic and industrial progress; our social history lags behind."

Another is that of the biographer. Several biographical attempts have been made to show the influence of individual personalities on the development of social work. A few of these are listed for the scholarly reader at the close of this book. Practically all of these volumes delineate the character and activities of particular individuals who have contributed to social work. Only a few attempt to assemble a number of "lives" in the effort to create a broader perspective. The present work is one answer to the need to perceive the historical meaning of social work in other than the terms of individual biography. Admittedly, it is less valuable than a more comprehensive analysis of each of the individuals portrayed; but many books exist upon which this book is based.

One of the stimulants toward the writing of this book was the excellent study by Professor Edith Abbott, *Some American Pioneers in Social Welfare* (Chicago: University of Chicago Press, 1948). From time to time I have made use of Professor Abbott's materials in my own classes in social work. In providing an account of the lives of ten of the leading social workers in recent history, there has been a necessary elimination of many details. No one should look upon the biographies presented in this book as giving each and every facet of the lives involved. Bibliographies at the end of the book are provided for those who wish longer and less condensed versions.

In selecting the ten lives presented, I carefully drew up a list of over one hundred potential subjects. For several dozens of these, I read one or more books to arrive at a judgment as to which persons might finally be selected. The decisions were not easy. One could wish that one were allowed at least two or three times the number of subjects included in the present book.

The persons presented lived in the nineteenth and twentieth centuries, and all ten are deceased. Although I recognize that the history of social work prior to these centuries contained many fascinating and helpful persons, I have tried to keep within the limits of the recent past. Not all of the special fields within social work are represented in this book, but many are; and the variety of the special contributions will become apparent as one reads.

It is difficult to place many of the persons included in this book within a single category or activity. Most of the historical contributors were talented along several lines; some along many. This fact raises an important question for the current training of social workers. Is the present-day education of social workers productive of as much variety in conception and action as is exemplified in the lives of social workers of the past?

As one might expect, there is a difference in the nature of the motivation that encouraged the earlier social workers compared to those of the present time. It may seem strange to some that the lives considered in this book so often were religiously motivated. Anyone with knowledge of the past should not be disturbed by this fact. Historically, social work has been the handmaiden of religion. These, then, in Beowulf's terms, are those "whom God sent the folk to befriend."

I am indebted in the preparation of this book to a number of libraries for their assistance: Brooklyn College; Central Research Collections Division of the New York Public Library; Hudson Park Branch, New York Public Library; Oberlin College; the Library of Congress; and the Y.M.C.A. Historical Library of the National Council, Young Men's Christian Associations.

I am indebted also to a number of organizations for their cooperation: National Council, Boy Scouts of America; Greenwich House; Hull House; the Juvenile Protection Association; the National Federation of Settlements and Neighborhood Centers; the Perkins School for the Blind; the Eastern Territorial Headquarters and the Metropolitan New York headquarters of the Salvation Army; the Shaftsbury Society of London; the Society of St. Vincent de Paul, Superior Council of the United States, St. Louis, and New York City; and the Women's International League for Peace and Freedom.

I am especially appreciative to the publishers of the books from which I have quoted. Some of the authors of these books were very close to the subjects whose lives are portrayed in this book. Some were relatives. So, I have depended upon these books not only for the quotations, but also for many facts and descriptions that are essential to the bibliographies.

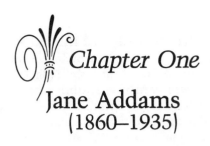

Chapter One
Jane Addams
(1860–1935)

A great professor without a university chair, a guiding woman in a man-made world, a brooding spirit of the mother hovering with gentle sympathy over the troubled sea of poverty, of weakness, of arrogance, of pride, of hate, of force and a great statesman without a portfolio.[1]

Jane Addams, the founder of famed Hull House, a pioneer in the settlement house movement in the United States, and the Nobel Prize recipient for peace in 1931, was born in a red brick house in Cedarville, Illinois, in the fall of 1860. Within the house lived busy people who knew moderate worldly success and who were secure in their homey integrity and virtue. The Addamses were a successful family.

Jane Addams claimed that her father was one of the most important influences on her life. Certainly he did make an incisive impression upon her. He came from English stock that had settled in Pennsylvania under the leadership of William Penn. He was born in Sinking Springs, Pennsylvania, in 1822, and while he was attached historically to the Quakers, he did not practice that religion after he left Pennsylvania and settled with his new wife in Illinois. In Cedarville, he attended two churches, each on alternate Sundays. He was a generous contributor to both churches, and he urged his family to be devoted and loyal to some church. But he did not talk much about his religious views. Once Jane asked her father, "What are you? What do you say when people ask you?" With a twinkle in his eye, he responded, "I am a Quaker."

"But that isn't enough to say," his persistent daughter replied.

"Very well," he added, "to people who insist upon details, as someone is doing now, I add that I am a Hicksite Quaker." Try as she may, Jane could not induce her father to explain further.[2]

John Addams was a man of strict conscience. When he was a member of the Illinois legislature, Abraham Lincoln wrote him about a certain measure: "You will of course vote according to your conscience, only it is a matter of considerable importance to me to know how that conscience is pointing."

Jane's father was one of the leading citizens of Cedarville and nearby Freeport. He won the financial respect of the people of both places because of his reputation as a shrewd and careful investor. He had come to Cedarville with about $3,000, and in time, he owned two thriving mills—one for flour, the other for wood. These he managed so well he was able to secure a dependable income that allowed him to devote some of his time to community improvements and to politics. In the winter of 1846, he was prominent in the organization of a convention in Rockford to urge the creation of a railroad to be called the Galena and Chicago Union. He worked with the convention until funds were obtained to make the idea an actuality.

In his work for the railroad, John Addams got to know many of the people in his part of the state, and this came in handy later when he ran for the state legislature. He was a member of the legislature during the Civil War and was a good friend of Lincoln. Jane Addams recorded the fact that the only time she knew her father to cry was on the death of Lincoln.

Sarah Addams, Jane's mother, was a devoted wife and mother. She, too, tended to idolize her husband. She was intensely interested in charitable activities, and it was her interest reflected through others after Sarah's untimely death that encouraged Jane to think of the poor. In the obituary written for Sarah Addams, the following line gives insight into the character of the woman: "Mrs. Addams will be missed everywhere, at home, in society, in the church, in all places where good is to be done and suffering relieved." No wonder that Jane felt the plight of the poor!

Jane's arrival into the family was a welcomed event. She was the eighth child. Her sister Martha died at sixteen; three of the other children died in infancy; only four reached maturity. In her autobiography, Jane Addams emphasized her "ugliness," but this view was contested by many who knew her in her youth. It is true that she was small, frail, and pigeon-toed, and had a slight curvature of the back, which caused her to hold her head slightly on a slant. Intensely introspective, she spent many hours debating her conduct. She was an avid reader and devoured many of the classics of Western intellectual tradition at an early age. In social activities she mirrored her father's behavior, being reserved and rather intellectual.

Sarah Addams died when Jane was only two, and her death was a severe blow to the family. Mary, the oldest daughter, assumed the female headship of the family, and life continued under her direction. John Addams was serving in the legislature much of the time and gave the children considerable responsibility. By the time Jane was eight, John married again. His second wife was Anna Hostetter Haldeman, the widow of a

Freeport miller. She had two sons: the elder was studying in Europe, but the younger son, George, came to live in the Cedarville homestead. Jane and George developed a close friendship.

George and Jane attended the local school in the village. George was mainly interested in "nature study," and while Jane had little regard for science, she was agreeable enough to help George in his various pursuits. Jane was chiefly drawn to Latin and English literature. One of her teachers was Samuel Parr, who later became a professor of Latin at the University of Illinois.

When she was not quite seventeen, Jane was graduated from the village school and looked toward college. She had hoped to attend Smith College in Massachusetts, but her father had different ideas. He wanted her to go to Rockford Seminary (later called Rockford College) for her basic college training and then to take advanced study abroad. He also apparently wished to have his daughter closer to home than she would be at Smith. Jane finally agreed to attend Rockford, even though she knew that it stressed "professing religion" more than she desired and it also did not award degrees.

About fifty students attended Rockford Seminary in 1877, and the cost for one year was about $300. Ellen Gates Starr, from Durand, Illinois, who later worked with Jane as a devoted friend and influential leader in her own right, was a member of the class of 1881, along with Jane. Jane was especially drawn to Ellen because of Ellen's appreciation of the beauty of religion. Jane was interested in religion, but more as truthful poetry than as dogma. Ellen was also witty, intellectual, and outgoing. The course of study at Rockford Seminary included Greek, Latin, natural science, ancient history, literature, mental and moral philosophy, and French. Addams studied music also in her first year, but gave that up because she felt she had no special talent, and substituted mathematics.

Perhaps as important as the courses she took was the discipline of student life that was imposed upon the student body by Miss Sill, the president of Rockford. Miss Sill, a Presbyterian, felt that people's lives should be run according to a definite plan, and she did not believe in wasting time. Even the walks that the students took were part of a plan engineered by

Miss Sill; she believed that a one-hour walk each day should be a part of every student's routine. In all pursuits she was methodical and painstaking. While Jane was not constituted to emulate Miss Sill, she did learn the value of organization and purpose.

Jane differed with Miss Sill on the subject of degrees. She believed that the seminary should become a college that granted degrees to its graduates. Her opinion was important, for she was the daughter of one of the trustees of the seminary (another reason Jane attended Rockford) and a man who was eminently successful in business and in politics. (It was said that John Addams had refused the Republican nomination for governor of Illinois.) Jane also created support for her idea by organizing a small band of students who agreed with her. In order to show the intellectual prowess of women, she delivered a commencement address in Greek—another sign to her that the seminary was ready to grant degrees. But she did not win her battle until the year after she was graduated, when the seminary became Rockford College. She was granted a degree at that time without further study.

Jane Addams was active in the social life of the college. She joined a newly formed association that discussed the latest scientific findings of the times and she had a reputation as a debater. In 1881 she was sent to Jacksonville as the seminary's delegate to the Interstate Oratorical Contest. There were nine contestants. One was Rollin Salisbury of Beloit College—a friend of Jane—and another was young William Jennings Bryan. Neither of these men won the contest, but neither did Jane, who finished "exactly in the dreary middle." After the contest, she induced a friend, Annie Sidwell, to remain long enough in Jacksonville to visit the state institutions for the blind and the deaf and dumb.

Jane turned her hand to literary enterprises during her college days. She early became connected with the *Rockford Seminary Magazine*, a student publication. For several years, she contributed articles, and in her senior year, she became editor-in-chief.

Seventeen students were graduated in Jane's class in 1881, and Jane was the valedictorian. When she was told that she would deliver an address at the commencement, she turned to the salutatorian of her class, who was her friend, and said,

"Nora, when we speak, we must say something." Her talk was serious, well composed, and thoughtful of the broader issues of the period. Indeed, throughout her life, whenever she was called upon to speak, she tried to "say something."

According to her own account, "It required eight years—from the time I left Rockford in the summer of 1881 until Hull House was opened in the autumn of 1889—to formulate my convictions even in the least satisfactory manner, much less to reduce them to a plan of action."[3] Rockford had opened many vistas of thought and action to Jane, and she did not know how she might consolidate them and begin a concerted effort toward the fulfillment of a consistent pattern of ideals. As an added factor in her confusion, her father died in the summer that she graduated. In his passing, she lost one of the most powerful influences in her life.

The death of her father increased Jane's determination to attend medical school. In the fall of 1881, she set out from Cedarville for Philadelphia to become a student at the Women's Medical College. For seven months she worked at her medical studies with considerable zeal and secured high marks for her efforts. But the strain was too much, and her health broke down, forcing her to return to Cedarville. At home, she tried to forget her health and her father's death by studying intensely. But, this course of action only proved more harmful to her health, and the following winter she was forced to spend about six months in bed.

In the spring of 1883, Addams was advised to spend some time in travel to relax and to regain her strength. Eagerly she planned a trip to Europe with her stepmother. After making a number of stops on their way east, the pair set sail on the *Servia* on August 22, 1883. One of the celebrities on board was novelist Henry James. In England they visited the places Jane had read about in her studies; but in her diary, she shows a preoccupation with the poor. One entry pertaining to Blarney castle reads as follows: "Owner said to have income of thirteen thousand pounds a year; ordinary man six shillings a week; could not kiss the Blarney stone, though the castle is very beautiful."

Leaving England, Jane and her stepmother traveled to the Continent, stopping for short periods in Holland, Germany, Austria, Italy, Greece, Switzerland, and France. They visited the great monuments of culture and spoke with leaders in many walks of life about their problems. Wherever she went, she noted the conditions under which the poor lived, sought solutions to their problems, and she studied. She was impressed by the "positivism" of Auguste Comte and thought for a time that it offered a compromise to the religious and social questions that puzzled her.

The two years that Jane Addams spent in travel were not to bring solace to her searching mind. She looked everywhere for comfort and singleness of purpose, but found none that satisfied and returned to the United States still perplexed as to what her life work should be. One insight she did gain during her trip through Europe was that learning is not enough. She saw that the practice of charity surpassed the acquisition of knowledge.

> I gradually reached a conviction that the first generation of college women had taken their learning too quickly, had departed too suddenly from the active, emotional life led by their grandmothers and great-grandmothers; that the contemporary education of young women had developed too exclusively the power of acquiring knowledge and of merely receiving impressions; that somewhere in the process of "being educated" they had lost that simple and almost automatic response to the human appeal, that old healthful reaction resulting in activity from the mere presence of suffering or of helplessness; that they are so sheltered and pampered they have no chance even to make "the great refusal."[4]

Despite what she said, Jane probably did not deserve the condemnation she brought to female college graduates. Through her European experiences, she saw clearly the need for "that simple and almost automatic response to the human appeal." Nor was she correct when she evaluated the lives of some of the women of her own and previous generations. Her generation of women possessed many notable leaders who contributed not only to acquiring knowledge but also to the practice of good will. But the impact of the idea of the need for social action had profound effect upon Jane's life, for it impelled her to discover a way that she could help the unfortunate.

Addams did not regain her health completely during her travels, so on returning to the United States, she spent a brief time in Cedarville. Then she joined her stepmother in Baltimore, where George was attending Johns Hopkins University. Jane helped her stepmother give parties and teas and other social functions, but she found no pleasure in her activities. In fact, she felt that the social occasions were a great waste of time and energy. She found the university men to be dull and uninspired, and she became depressed because she longed for work that would help people. In the summers of 1885 and 1886, she returned to Cedarville, the scene of her happy childhood. Here she tried to regain her lost composure.

She found a solution to her problems, at least for a time, in religion. Jane Addams joined the Presbyterian church when she was twenty-five, and her decision brought her great peace of mind. She was not interested in the dogmas of any particular religious group and did not wish a "canned" theology. Instead, she wished to be part of an on-going movement that stood for the humanitarian values that were so appealing to her and many others in her time. She felt that she owed membership to some Christian church; the Presbyterian happened to be the most suitable at the time. (She joined the Congregational church, now the United Church of Christ, when her life had become centered in Hull House.) In religion and humanitarianism, Jane Addams found a focus for her life—the service of the poor.

It was difficult for Jane to decide on the exact way to practice her new found faith. There were many possibilities. She already had had some experience applying her faith in everyday life. She had entered into a partnership with a young college man from Cedarville and bought a sheep-raising farm, but this she abandoned after she saw that the sheep were maltreated (at least to her way of thinking). She also maintained various personal philanthropies, for example, she gave $1,000 to Rockford College for books. She had been made a member of the board of trustees as her father had once been. And she helped several young men through college by paying part of their expenses. She also assumed responsibility for the care of the children of her oldest sister. (She wrote to Ellen Starr: "I am busy with the children. Esther [a niece] has been driving me crazy with questions about John the Baptist, and Weber [a nephew] has had his sled stolen, and is railing at the world with a power of invective that I have never heard equaled."[5]

In 1887, Ellen Starr decided to travel to Europe and urged Jane to join her. The idea appealed to Jane. She hoped not only to have a good time, but also to discover some means by which she might share her life with those in need. On December 14, 1887, she set sail from Hoboken, New Jersey, joined Ellen in Munich, and the two went on to Rome to spend the winter.

In the spring, Jane went to Madrid along with four friends. Their tour included a bullfight, and when her friends left the arena because of the brutality, Jane stayed to see five bulls killed. She was drawn to the activity because of its callousness and at the same time repelled because of her idealism. This seems to have been a significant experience in her life because the very next morning she approached Ellen Starr with the idea of establishing a "big house" right in the middle of "horrid little houses" as a means of bringing help to the poor. Ellen was enthusiastic about the idea, and from this experience, Hull House was conceived. Its birth had to wait until Jane and Ellen discovered the work of Canon Samuel Barnett in the East Side of London.

Toynbee Hall had come into existence only four years prior to Jane Addams' visit. Barnett was its first warden, or "head resident," and it was the first settlement house. Its staff was composed of university men, mainly from Oxford, who lived in the slums of London (Whitechapel) to learn conditions first-hand and to contribute to the improvement of life there with their own personal and financial resources. Toynbee Hall had already made its contribution to American life, for it was the model that Edward Denison (with the help of others) had used on the East Side of New York City in his founding of the University Settlement. It was this idea of the settlement house that Jane Addams also finally used. She believed that what Barnett had been able to do for the poor people of London she might attempt for the poor people of Chicago. She had found her mission, the purpose that she had struggled to find for so many years.

When Addams returned to the United States early in the summer of 1888, she immediately took steps to set her business affairs in order and to plan for her settlement. Until January of the following year, she was busy with preparations. She even took up bookkeeping in order that her idealism might be supported by practical methods. When she finally arrived in Chicago, it took her five months to locate a suitable house. She searched everywhere for the right place. She wanted to be in a section of the city where there was intense social and personal need and she needed a physically suitable house. The two were not easy to find in combination, but she found what she wanted one day, number 335 South Halsted, and she made up her mind to buy it.

Charles J. Hull, an early resident of Chicago, had built his house when the neighborhood was young. It was a two-story, brick house, set back from the street, and it seemed perfect as a settlement house. Addams' joy was complete when she learned that she could rent it and remodel it to suit the activities of a settlement.

On September 18, 1889, Addams, along with Ellen Starr, who helped her with the plans and activities, and Mary Keyser, who was responsible for the housework, took up residence at Hull House. Gradually, visitors from the neighborhood came to look in on the work in progress. Many of them could not understand how anyone would choose voluntarily to leave a pleasant environment to live on Halsted Street amid such poverty and need. Those who visited were often helped on an individual basis; others were interested in forming groups for the achievement of various ends.

In the first weeks of Hull House, Starr started a reading "party" of George Eliot's *Romola*. A group of young women came once a week to hear Starr read, and sometimes the members were invited to stay for a meal. The response of the neighbors was slow until they realized that the institution existed for them and that there would be no attempt to force any sort of views upon them that they did not like. Some initially considered Hull House as a "mission station" with the purpose of converting them. Others thought that there must be some "catch" to the House and its open door. But, in time, the word was passed among the residents of the neighborhood that Hull House stood for a genuinely humanitarian ideal.

The doors of Hull House were never locked, though Addams had two experiences with burglars who entered her room at night. On the first occasion, her nephew was asleep in the next room. Addams said to the man, "Don't make a noise." He was startled and started to leap toward a window. "You'll be hurt if you go that way," she said. "Go down by the stairs and let yourself out." And he did. The second burglar was an amateur. Addams told him to leave quietly and to come back the next morning at nine o'clock and she would try to get him some work. He met his appointment.[6]

During the first year, about fifty thousand individual visits were made to Hull House. Addams was acquainted with most of the people who came. Of course, she and Ellen Starr were not able to handle so many people and activities by themselves, so from time to time, women with ability and training volunteered their services to Hull House. Some had general interests and talents and others were able to help with specialized groups.

Addams spent time not only in Hull House but also visiting the homes of the neighborhood in order to interpret the work she was doing to those who had not heard of it or who were skeptical of its aims. She also was responsible for raising money to maintain the programs, as the funds that she (and the other residents) contributed were not sufficient to carry the whole burden. She was responsible, too, for the bookkeeping, and she actively studied the community, for she believed that social research is one of the important adjuncts to settlement work. All of these responsibilities kept her busy many hours of each day. Her physical condition at this time was much improved, and she found the strength for myriads of large and small obligations.

Hull House was a center for children's activities of various kinds. One of the first groups established was a kindergarten. In many instances, the children who came responded quickly to the programs arranged for them; but sometimes they adhered to special cultural ways learned in their homes. Thus, one of the principal goals of the kindergarten was to break down the social barriers that existed among children of different nationalities and races. In the main, the kindergarten was a success, as it not only helped the children to perceive the broader implications of their behavior, but also gave Hull House a way to establish relationships with the parents.

For older children, Hull House offered clubs and special interest groups. The staff discovered early that children like to form their own special groups and provide for their own leadership (with some direction from the staff). Some groups were formed around social relationships; other groups formed for an activity, such as sports, music, literature, painting, enjoyment of art, and discussion of current affairs. In time, the boys' activities became so numerous that a special five-story building was erected to house them.

On her first New Year's Day at Hull House, Jane Addams initiated a custom that became an annual tradition—the "Old Settlers' Party." Those who formerly lived in the neighborhood were asked to return to tell of their experiences. Some of the "old settlers" had risen in social status far beyond their beginnings, and their presence at the parties provided the people of the neighborhood with an incentive for their own advancement. The parties also gave an opportunity for "old settlers" to revive friendships. As the parties continued, former staff members who had been closely connected with the development of the House returned to renew old acquaintances.

Hull House was a refuge for individuals who had no other place to turn in time of trouble. One child, for example, was lodged at the House until he could return to live with his parents. His mother didn't want him because he had been born with a cleft palate. On another occasion, a new bride took shelter in Hull House because her husband beat her during their first week of marriage. Such cases of personal need were multiplied many times over in the course of the years. While Hull House was not conceived to be an agency that granted services to individuals on the same bases that other social casework agencies did, the staff could not ignore the cries of the suffering.

An investigation of the sweatshops in the neighborhood revealed to Addams and her co-workers that, especially in the busy season, the women workers paid little attention to their families. These women had to work long hours in order to make their small wages. Often, they were too tired to cook meals, even when they could buy the food. During the day, when their children were at loose ends, these women would provide a few pennies for their offspring to buy lunch at a candy store. In order to meet the needs of these families and others, Hull House began a public kitchen, which later became its Coffee House. The Coffee House was considered one means of centering the social life of the community so far as informal recreation was concerned; but, according to Addams, the fact that it did not offer beer made it somewhat less effective than the saloons.

Not all of the efforts of Hull House were directed at delivering services; Addams believed that people should be helped to help themselves as much as possible. The Cooperative Coal Association, which led a vigorous life for about three years, represented an attempt to help people help themselves through cooperation. The association helped families to finance their fuel needs at a saving. At one point before it closed, the association's gross receipts were between $300 and $400 a day. Dividends usually were given in coal rather than cash.

A further example of cooperation showed even greater success. A group of women who worked in a factory near Hull House went out on strike, but they were worried because they were unable to pay board and anticipated being thrown out of their rooms. At a meeting held in Hull House, one of the girls asked, "Wouldn't it be fine if we had a boarding club of our own, and then we could stand by each other in a time like this?" As a result, Addams investigated the possibilities of starting a boarding club. She found that the idea was basically sound, so she rented and furnished two apartments. After the first month, the women were able to assume the responsibility for the payment of the rent, and the club was a small success. By the time the third year had rolled around, the club had fifty members, who occupied all six of the apartments in the original building of the club. Afterwards, the Jane Club, as it was called, secured its own quarters.

The campaign for the Jane Club building aroused an issue that tested the ethical philosophy of Addams and her co-workers. When the needs of the club were made known, persons of means were found who were willing to have a share in the project. One man offered $20,000 to the building fund, but he had a reputation for underpaying the workers in his establishment and for other suspect practices. It was difficult for Addams to decide whether to accept or reject this generous offer, but in the end she told the man she could not take his money, knowing as she did of his reputation. Later she had some doubts about the practicality of her decision, but she never changed her rule, even though, through the years, it cost her considerable income for Hull House.

Over and over again, it was necessary for Hull House to provide services to individuals who came asking for immediate help. Hull House dealt with many categories of need. Addams felt especially responsible for women who had "gone astray" and who came to the House as one of the last havens available. Often, they were young and were living under intense economic and family handicaps. Addams tried to do what she could to give them shelter and to guide them toward a more stable life. Sometimes she felt her efforts were thwarted by well-intentioned people. In one instance she placed a woman in a job at a Sunday school of a church on the grounds that the new environment might aid her, but the church members learned of her background and refused to have her.

Hull House dealt with other cases of individual need. On occasion, women who had been deserted by their husbands came for information and support, and the House guided them to the existing welfare and court facilities in the city that could help them. The House also provided information for families in need of medical attention and other personal services.

Many people in the district required material support in times of unemployment and because of chronic poverty, but it was not possible for Hull House to meet all their needs. At times, the House did provide direct material assistance, but its funds were too meager for any sustained effort in this direction. The staff tried to tell individuals where employment could be secured or how changes could be made in employment in order to improve income, and sometimes budgeting advice was given. The Charity Organization Society and the Visiting Nurse Association had not been born in the earliest years of Hull House, but when they came into existence there was cooperation between them.

In the summer of 1895, Addams was appointed to a commission to investigate conditions in the county poorhouse. This commission was responsible to the mayor of Chicago and was formed because of rumors that the inmates of the poorhouse were badly treated. Neighbors of Hull House came forth to document these rumors with firsthand information. As a result of the study, Addams realized how inadequate the public measures were for the support of the poor and how lacking in responsiveness the governmental machinery and personnel were to the widespread problems of the poor. The resultant report helped define higher standards for poorhouses.

A kindergarten was one of the first features of Hull House; it met the needs of families who otherwise would have been unable to care adequately for their children. Addams also established a day nursery, one of the first in this country. It proved in its operation that daytime care of children is one way to offer support to poor families. The day nursery was first maintained in a little cottage on a side street near Hull House; later, the Children's House was established for the nursery and for other children's activities.

It was natural that, where there were so many social and personal problems, there would be discussions about the means for relief. Hull House early realized that its role in the neighborhood made it responsible not only for certain welfare activities, but also for discussions of means of changing the conditions that brought about the problems. For a time, Hull House offered public discussions of social issues. Experts in the various social philosophies and schools of thought were brought to Hull House to address large audiences. It was realized in time, however, that large meetings were not entirely adequate. Smaller clubs of men and women in which the individual members had an open opportunity to express themselves were then formed. These clubs taught a degree of tolerance to the members and brought to the realization of most that the problems with which they dealt were not capable of easy solution. No attempt was made to limit the kinds of social remedies that could be offered at these meetings.

One of the products of these meetings was the Hull House Social Science Club, which aimed to study social problems in a scientific manner. In some ways it was a parallel development to the modern social science of sociology. Through the club and the other meetings, Hull House gained a reputation for social radicalism. Wherever Addams went, however, she tried to make the point that the settlement, as such, maintained no particular opinion in social matters, but did believe that it had a responsibility to see that its neighbors had a chance to discuss all points of view.

Addams was aware that Hull House could not hold itself aloof from the labor conditions of the neighborhood. Many facets of this problem were attacked. A logical starting point was to oppose the use of children in the sweatshops of the area—surely the conscience of the community (mainly that of the employers) could be touched in regard to the conditions that adversely affected children. But this supposition was not entirely true. Employers were not responsive to the ethical claims of the director of Hull House.

The conditions that affected child laborers were as deplorable as they were common. Children as young as four years old helped their mothers in sewing. Some children were in poor health, and some were motivated to suicide as a consequence of the entanglements of early labor. One girl of thirteen, employed in a laundry at work that required the strength of a man borrowed $3 from a companion that she could not repay unless she told her parents and gave the companion a whole week's wages, so she committed suicide.

There was at the time no legal recourse against employing children in all sorts of work, since the existing child labor legislation pertained only to the use of children in mines. Mrs. Florence Kelley, one of the first residents of Hull House, became especially interested in this problem. She told the Illinois State Bureau of Labor of the conditions she found on visits through the Hull House part of Chicago and suggested that what was discovered there was probably in effect elsewhere. The chief of the bureau saw the need for an investigation and appointed Kelley as head of a special committee to undertake the research and make recommendations. The results of the committee's work became embodied in the first factory law in Illinois. The legislation regulated sanitary conditions and fixed fourteen as the minimum age for workers. In every way it helped to raise the standards of working conditions, and was especially beneficial in eliminating child labor—at least in its more formal and widespread form.

The passage of the factory legislation was not accomplished solely by the report of the committee appointed by the Illinois State Bureau of Labor. That committee provided the ideological instrument by which the legislation was achieved, but agitation and support were required from those who were affected by the conditions and from their friends. This meant that Hull House had to arouse public opinion not only in its own neighborhood but also throughout the city and, indeed, the entire state. The Trades and Labor Assembly, a central labor body in Chicago, was also interested in the legislation and used its influence. Representatives of Hull House, the Trades and Labor Assembly, and other interested organizations went to the state capital to lobby for the enactment of the legislation. Although it passed, it was only a beginning. Kelley was appointed as the first factory inspector, and with her worked a staff of twelve inspectors who helped enforce the law.

Chicago politics in the last decade of the nineteenth century were characterized by laxity and corruption. Since 1868, a broadminded citizen, Lyman J. Gage, had been trying to form a "voluntary association of citizens for the mutual counsel, support, and combined action of all the forces for good," and by 1893, he succeeded in creating the Civic Federation. Jane Addams had a principal share in its establishment and maintenance through the years of its effectiveness, and even the governor, Peter Altgeld, supported it. Among its membership ranked prominent persons of Chicago from various fields of activity: Cyrus McCormick, Marshall Field, Albion Small, Graham Taylor, and many others. The federation accomplished much good in Chicago and in Illinois. One of its main efforts was the attempt to employ arbitration in labor disputes.

Jane Addams was the secretary of the Civic Federation Committee on Industrial Arbitration, and under her guidance, a system of voluntary arbitration boards was sponsored by the state legislature. Governor Altgeld asked the legislature for "such legislation as will enable the parties to the dispute, alone or with the aid of a county judge, to select their own board in each case so that there may be no question about its impartiality, on the one hand, and no unnecessary salary paid on the other."[6] The legislature, however, turned down the request of the governor and appointed a standing board of three salaried members, one an employer, one a workingman, and a third who was neither. Massachusetts had such a board, and its success was fairly well known. But the board in Illinois did not function effectively because, where labor unions were strong, there was no willingness on their part to arbitrate disputes they felt they could win without arbitration. The same held for employers. The board failed mainly through disuse. Industrial relations were not yet ready for impartial arbitration.

The problem of garbage disposal illustrates Jane Addams' willingness to consider almost any problem affecting the welfare of her neighbors and her acquiescence to perform the most menial of duties. The Hull House Women's Club had reported that garbage collection procedures in Chicago were almost nonexistent. (This opinion, of course, was more widely held than just the membership of the Women's Club!) Every family in the neighborhood suffered. The collection of the garbage was given over to private companies on a contract basis, and this contract, like others, was a victim of political preferment and graft. In 1894, as a result of careful calculation, Addams made a bid for the business of collecting the garbage. Her bid was thrown out on a technicality, but due to the publicity that followed, Addams was appointed as the garbage inspector for the ward at an annual salary of $1,000. This was the only paid position she ever held. That the work was not easy is told graphically by Addams:

> The position was no sinecure whether regarded from the point of view of getting up at six in the morning to see that the men were early at work; or of following the loaded wagons, uneasily dropping their contents at intervals, to their dreary destination at the dump; or of insisting that the contractor must increase the number of his wagons from nine to thirteen and from thirteen to seventeen, although he assured me that he lost money on every one and that the former inspector had let him off with seven; or of taking the careless landlords into court because they would not provide the proper garbage receptacles; or of arresting the tenant who tried to make the garbage wagons carry away the contents of his stable.[7]

The complete list of Addams' political activities and nonpolitical efforts would be too long to include here. Indeed, many of her works extended far beyond the horizons of that neighborhood. Before she had lived her life, the entire world was aware of her humanitarian perspectives and zeal.

Addams became interested in the nationality groups that made up the neighborhood around Hull House. She was eager to have them come together to know each other, because she believed that some of the misunderstandings between peoples were due to the fact that there were no means for an interchange of cultural values. Addams did not believe that persons with foreign backgrounds should strive to lose their special heritage, but she also believed that, in some instances, the culture of the parents harmed their children. She knew that "the faithful child is sometimes ruthlessly imposed upon by immigrant parents who, eager for money and accustomed to the patriarchal authority of peasant households, held their children in stern bondage." She worked against such cultural restrictions, but there were more positive aspects to her activities with immigrants and their children. At first she provided space at Hull House for families and groups of the separate nationalities. Later she tried to bring the various nationalities together at one time. She was fairly successful in this, although there were many problems that militated against the full success of this idea.

By her travels through the Hull House neighborhood, Addams learned of the handwork of different ethnic groups. She realized that a collection of the various tools, especially those brought from the Old World, would represent an important and appealing collection. Therefore, she founded the Labor Museum, which at first consisted of one room in Hull House. In time, many rooms held the "story of work" as it was to be found in Chicago. One of the Hull House trustees, Julius Rosenwald, later founded the Rosenwald Industrial Museum, which carried Addams' idea much further than she was able to with the relatively meager resources of Hull House.

Juvenile delinquency was always a concern of Hull House. One of the strong reasons for the establishment of the House was to reduce the juvenile delinquency rates. By its manifold activities, the House provided a place in which boys and girls who might otherwise have been roaming the streets could assemble in peace and with sanction. Hull House stood as a symbol of constructive help to bewildered and needy young people. Addams was also interested in creating a juvenile court by which young offenders could be separated from hardened criminals in treatment and where steps could be taken at an early point to prevent the further development of criminal tendencies. She was not alone in this struggle. Mrs. James

Flowers, chairman of the Chicago Civic Federation's Department of Philanthropy, was the principal leader in the fight, and Addams gave Flowers every help that she could. Legislation finally established the Juvenile Court in Chicago on July 1, 1899, and a committee was appointed at the same time to see that the law actually worked. Julia Lathrop, a resident of Hull House, was the first chairman of that committee. The first probation officer provided by the law was Alzina P. Stevens, also a resident of Hull House. The juvenile court conception began in Illinois and spread to practically all of the states. Its worth has been proven over and over again.

The settlement house idea grew rapidly in Chicago as elsewhere. There was something about it so practical in its helpfulness, so genuine in its social concern, and so hopeful that persons from all ranks of society responded to it. Perhaps two of the most notable co-experiments in the settlement field in Chicago were the Chicago Commons and the University Settlement. Chicago Commons was established by Graham Taylor, who had come to the Chicago Theological Seminary in 1893 to open the first department in any American theological seminary devoted to the social interpretation and application of religion. He knew of the work that Samuel Barnett had done in London and also of Jane Addams' work in Chicago. He came to feel that the settlement was one of the best ways for expressing social Christianity. Therefore, he founded the Chicago Commons, which became in time one of the most notable of the settlements in the United States.

The University Settlement was founded by several persons attached to the University of Chicago. Albion Small, founder of the first department of sociology in an American university, was greatly interested in establishing a settlement. George Vincent and William Rainey Harper, also of the university, were co-sponsors with Small of the University Settlement. When plans were laid for its creation, the founding group looked about for a director, and they chose Mary McDowell, then a resident at Hull House.

The settlement house idea spread quickly through the United States. Today, there are more than eight hundred settlements, neighborhood houses, and community centers located throughout the United States. They are coordinated through the

National Federation of Settlements and Neighborhood Centers with national headquarters in New York City. The federation was founded in 1911 by Jane Addams and other pioneer leaders, and Addams served as its first president. The federation assists its members with the many and varied problems with which they are confronted as they seek to meet the changing needs of people living together in the urban centers of the United States.

Hull House had only two residents at its start, Addams and Starr. By the end of the first ten years, there were twenty-five men and women. Some settlements accepted only men or only women residents, but Hull House was a pioneer in the use of both. Some of the residents of Hull House achieved considerable prominence on leaving for other occupations. Ellen Starr achieved a measure of fame because of the work she did at Hull House. Julia Lathrop, like Addams and Starr, attended Rockford College. She was born in Rockford, Illinois, and spent one year at the college before she went to Vassar, from which she was graduated. After a period as resident in Hull House, she became the first head of the Children's Bureau of the United States government. Florence Kelley contributed to the development of Hull House with her own strong talents of leadership. She was mainly interested in protecting children, women, and labor generally from harsh employment and living conditions. Her work as head of the National Consumers' League represents thirty years of forceful social challenge for the common good.

The physical plant of Hull House also grew with the years. The original house was constantly busy with the life of the neighborhood, and almost the whole block surrounding Hull House was taken up with other buildings of the expanding settlement. Within the buildings were various specialized functions, some of which had been created for the first time in any settlement. As Hull House grew, it was no longer possible for Addams to assume full responsibility for its maintenance, so she arranged for a board of directors, which helped her in establishing policy and raising the money required for running the settlement. More and more, Addams became the executive of a large enterprise.

In 1901, Jane Addams became one of the central figures in the frenzied aftermath of the assassination of President William McKinley by Leon S. Czolgosz. Soon after the president had been killed and his assassin identified as an "anarchist," the federal government sent out a call to all localities to apprehend known anarchists. Quite a few people were incarcerated at that time, including Abraham Isaak, who was known by Addams to be "a quiet, scholarly man, challenging the social order by the philosophic touchstone of Bakunin and Herbert Spencer." She had met him once at Hull House some years previously when Prince Peter Kropotkin visited the settlement. When Isaak was placed in the jail under City Hall and not permitted to communicate with the outside world, the Russians of the Hull House neighborhood came to Addams to protest his treatment. The following day, a Sunday, Addams met with Mayor Dunne and asked that he not yield to the panic and that Isaak be given a lawyer. The mayor was unwilling to do this, but he allowed Addams to see the man. She reassured Isaak that he had friends who were working on his behalf. In time, a lawyer was secured, and Isaak was released, for he had no connection with the slaying of the president. Addams' stand for justice in this and other similar cases brought her to the attention of many who admired her for her courage.

After her work at Hull House had received popular acclaim, Addams was appointed to the school board and served in that position from 1905 to 1909. In her own estimate, she played "a most inglorious part" as a member of the board, that of the middle road between two extremes of philosophy, a "part" rarely well received. The "conservative" elements in the city claimed that she had sold out to the "radicals," while the "liberal" elements claimed she was responsive to the "reactionaries." Certainly, whatever her real contribution, she pleased practically no one. While she always included her position as garbage collector in Who's Who in America, she never mentioned her service on the school board. The issues that engaged the board are not relevant here, but it is important to see that Addams rarely was a "party" person. She liked to think things through to her own conclusions without feeling of obligated toward any person or group. On more than one occasion, her independent stand aroused public antagonism.

Participation in many responsibilities of social leadership greatly enhanced Addams' reputation nationally. She became the first woman president of the National Conference of Charities and Correction (now known as the National Conference of Social Welfare). In her presidential speech, she illustrated her broad humanitarianism, her deep patience with entrenched wrong, and her quiet optimism for the better world that she believed was shaping. In June 1909, Yale University presented her with an honorary doctor's degree, the first such degree ever offered a woman by Yale. Newspapers hailed her as one of the great women leaders. Smith College, to which her affections had early been turned, granted her a doctor's degree in the fall of 1909. In the procession with her was the mayor of the town, Calvin Coolidge. Many urged her to run for the U. S. Senate and other positions of public responsibility. Surely, she had achieved a popular acceptance that surpassed that of almost any other woman of her time. Her name became a byword for social welfare and social justice.

Jane Addams was a strikingly effective speaker. The oratorical flair she possessed in college was developed through years of experience. She was in demand as a speaker on many occasions and in many places, some far from home. Addams was also a writer of considerable power. She had always felt that research and writing were a part of the settlement house idea. At the end of the first five years of Hull House, Addams and the other residents published a book entitled *Hull House Maps and Papers*. The maps were taken from data gathered for the U.S. Bureau of Labor, and the papers treated various subjects of interest in the neighborhood. Later, when Addams was better known, she wrote articles and books that influenced many people. Her articles were found in such journals as *American Journal of Sociology, International Journal of Ethics, North American Review, Forum,* and *Atlantic Monthly*. Her books included *Democracy and Social Ethics,* 1902; *Newer Ideals of Peace,* 1907; *The Spirit of Youth and the City Streets,* 1909; and *Twenty Years at Hull House,* 1910. While all of her books were widely read, the most popular was *Twenty Years at Hull House*. In it Addams described her life in terms that were simple, appealing, and forthright. As in all her writings, she drew heavily on particular incidents, the sort that might well be forgotten by those less sensitive to people and their behavior.

In her writings, Addams commonly stressed the primary value of the home in shaping children's personalities. She believed that homelike qualities were to be cherished and furthered and that social institutions existed in large part for the full development and enrichment of the family. She did not make excessive claims for individual morality and independence, but believed that democracy entailed the restraint of individual tendencies for the benefit of the whole. She felt that democracy, in its basic sense of equality of opportunity, required much more social control than most people believed. Addams also believed that the virtue of a person is expressed to the degree to which that person is willing to contribute to the welfare of others, often at his or her own expense. Self-giving became a fundamental tenet of her personal philosophy, and in her own life, she exemplified the virtue.

In regard to the problems of youth, Addams stressed the view that some delinquency is due to a spirit of adventure that is basic to the growing-up process. She claimed that, in times past and in simpler societies, means existed by which children might express their need for adventure in relatively harmless ways, but that this was not true for our complex social order. "To set his feet in the worn path of civilization is not an easy task, but it may give us a clue for the undertaking to trace his misdeeds to the unrecognized and primitive spirit of adventure corresponding to the old activity of the hunt, of warfare, and of discovery."[8] The great need for the character development of youth, according to Addams, is the discovery and establishment of patterns of behavior that will be harmless or constructive while meeting the individual's need for adventure.

Addams was concerned with women's rights, an interest stemming from her days at Rockford College, where she met women who were convinced that they should have equal rights with men. The first step in the development of social equality for women was the winning of the right to vote. Addams used many of the traditional arguments in support of this cause, but she also suggested original ones. For example, she said that women needed to vote for the benefit of their children; it devolved upon women to defend the existing rights of children and to extend their advantages through political means. If women could vote, she declared, they would enter politics more actively and directly, and political participation on the part of women would increase family welfare. But Addams did more than argue about suffrage. She joined those organizations that were working toward the extension of the rights of women and played a leading role in several of them.

The presidential campaign of Theodore Roosevelt attracted Jane Addams, and to it she devoted her time and energy. She was a "progressive" by nature. She had few illusions about the "perfection" of Roosevelt, yet she knew that she must take sides in an imperfect situation. Even beyond the campaign, Roosevelt kept in touch with her, sometimes sending her newspaper clippings he thought she might have missed.

The Nobel Peace Prize was awarded to Addams and to President Nicholas Murray Butler of Columbia University in 1931. This prize was given her for her many years of devoted activity in the cause of peace. Jane Addams will remain as one of the most effective pacifists that the present century has known. Her message was not always well received, but she struck a chord for reason and ethics that has not been muffled to this day.

The source of Addams' pacifism is difficult to appraise. Some have suggested her Quaker background, but her Quakerism was casual at best, and she had no genuine or continuing contact with the Friends for the larger part of her life. The Friends with whom she was associated (the Hicksites), moreover, were not especially noted for their pacifism, as were the more orthodox Friends.

Probably the teachings and personality of Jesus had a considerable influence on her espousal of pacifism. Addams was not a traditional Christian. She found fault with many aspects of the work of the churches, and she never attained a great degree of theological astuteness. On the other hand, she was deeply impressed with the purely spiritual and social implications of the life and teachings of Jesus. Certainly her use of reason enabled her to achieve a pacifist position. Addams did on occasion refer to the rightness of the claims of the Gospels, but more often, she asserted that Truth itself was on the side of peace. She argued that war destroys more than human life, and she believed that national interests are never served by the waging of war. War does not alleviate intergroup tensions, according to Addams; it only intensifies attitudes of conflict.

Jane Addams was not an isolationist. She believed in international goodwill and mutual aid and that what happens elsewhere in the world is relevant to our own national and personal interests. Americans should cooperate, even at the cost of sacrifice, with all of the peoples of the world. Her lack of isolationist sentiment placed her in a different camp from those who advocated a hands-off policy in regard to the rest of the world.

Addams was a great admirer of Tolstoy, and especially liked his *My Religion*, which she reread many times during her life. Addams admired Tolstoy's religious philosophy and his insistence on practice. She believed that she had shared this philosophy by her activities at Hull House, as indeed she had. During her 1896 trip to Europe, she visited Tolstoy in Russia. It was a momentous occasion for Addams. Tolstoy, however, was critical of her. After he heard her description of Hull House and its activities, he took hold of her full sleeve and remarked that there was enough cloth in it to make a dress for a little girl. When he learned how she managed to support herself, he condemned her for being an "absentee landlord." This was disconcerting, and for a time Addams struggled with the insights Tolstoy had given her regarding her motivation in social work. She concluded that Tolstoy was "more logical than life warrants." Though she never lost her love of his teachings, especially his acceptance of nonviolence, she could not embrace all of his ideas.

Addams delivered a series of lectures at the University of Wisconsin in 1906, which were published as *Newer Ideals of Peace*. The volume was well received, although it provoked some to call her a traitor. She also was one of the featured speakers at the National Peace Congress held in 1907; she extended her ideas for peace at that congress. The congress of the following year increased her hopes that war was of the past and that peace had come in permanent form.

Her hopes were crushed with the start of the First World War. All of the gains that had been achieved were wiped away. Many of the peacemakers were saddened, and some turned to the war with a pathetic reversal of conviction. Addams felt all was not lost, since the United States had not yet entered the conflict. Among the women of the country, Addams took the lead for peace. In January of 1915, Addams was elected the chairman of the newly formed Women's Peace party. She also was the head of the National Peace Federation, which was organized to coordinate the efforts of many organizations working for peace in various parts of the country. The platform of the Women's Peace party was similar to Woodrow Wilson's "Fourteen Points."

In 1915, a meeting of women was held in Amsterdam, with representatives attending from twelve belligerent and neutral countries. The meeting was held to plan an international congress of women interested in peace, which was held at the Hague in April 1915. Jane Addams presided. Thus, she became the head of the Women's International League for Peace and Freedom. The assembled women advocated a Society of Nations, general disarmament by international agreement, and a series of proposals as the basis for a just peace. At the suggestions of Rosika Schwimmer of Hungary, two delegations were sent to the heads of fourteen governments and to the pope to present a concrete plan for an early peace: the creation of a commission of neutrals to offer continuous mediation to the belligerents. The delegations included Jane Addams and Emily Greene Balch (who was awarded the Nobel Prize for Peace in 1946 for her international activities, being the second woman ever to have received the award).

But, even these efforts were to no avail. The war came and spread despite the work of Addams and millions of others who supported various peace organizations. When war came, Addams protested against many of its events and requirements—conscription, for one. She castigated the failure of the national leaders to mediate peacefully the problems being fought over. She supported conscientious objectors. Nothing that she did or said, however, was taken as an offense by the great bulk of Americans, and certainly she and her ideas were well received, under the circumstances, by the political leaders in Washington.

After the war ended, Addams helped arrange for the second meeting of the International League, which took place in Zurich. Representatives of sixteen nations were present, including those of the conquered countries. Addams again was the head of the meeting. While the league did not influence the making of the peace at every turn, it did make itself felt throughout the world as a moral force. The league met annually six times before Miss Addams resigned as its president in 1929. In that time she had created an effective instrument of maintaining goodwill on an international basis. It was largely because of her work with the league that she was given the Nobel Prize for Peace.

The Women's International League for Peace and Freedom continues today its historic purposes. Its international head-quarters are in Geneva, although it has "national sections" in many countries, including the United States. It conducts special missions (to China, the Middle East, Africa, and elsewhere), publishes a quarterly on the subject of its activities and the cause of peace, and maintains international summer schools. The league also raised money through its sections and members in many countries to erect an apartment house for the resettle-ment of thirty-two refugee families in the town of Spittal-Drau, Austria. This international memorial was dedicated to Jane Addams in the summer of her centennial in 1960 and is known as the Jane Addams Refugee House.

The closing of the war and the meeting of the league gave Addams a chance to rest. A trip around the world took her nine months, and when she returned, she was welcomed as a hero. Once back home, she began her work again at Hull House. In the 1920s, she devoted considerable time and effort to the problems of her neighbors, especially immigrants and their children. Her work, however, was not without strain, for she was sixty years old in 1920.

Addams did not support the Prohibition Amendment during the 1920s. She believed that the problem of alcoholism should be met through education. She also did not believe in the use of force to change personal behavior. Some of her friends were surprised that she did not champion Prohibition, especially since she had been so close to the negative results of alcoholism in the Hull House neighborhood, but she remained steadfast in her conviction that legislation was not the means to solve the problem.

In 1929, when Jane Addams was sixty-nine, Hull House held a fortieth anniversary celebration of her leadership. At the celebration were outstanding citizens from many different places and walks of life. Some previously had been residents of the neighborhood. Others were related to Addams in her world-wide activities for human betterment. All gratefully added their thanks to the celebration.

In February 1931, Addams was voted one of the twelve

"greatest living women in America" by a popular women's magazine. In the same year, she attended the fiftieth anniversary of her graduation from college. Her words of practical wisdom were remembered by the graduates that year. In October 1965, Jane Addams was honored by being included, along with Orville Wright, Oliver Wendell Holmes, and Sylvanus Thayer, in the New York University Hall of Fame for Great Americans.

Addams died on May 21, 1935. She had been suffering for some years with several maladies; her heart was weak (which curtailed work in the latter years), and she had cancer. As the hearse containing her body moved through the streets of Chicago, a policeman stopped traffic and spoke to the driver.

"Is it her?" he asked, respectfully.

"Yes," said the driver.

"She goes in peace," said the policeman.

She was buried in Cedarville where, in her childhood and youth, she had known peace.

Hull House continues to serve its neighborhood in Chicago today, although the neighborhood and the House have greatly changed from the days of Jane Addams. The new urban campus of the University of Illinois is a principal factor in the neighborhood, and Hull House has been restored to its original size physically, the third story, for example, having once been removed. Jane Addams' agency of social welfare remains as a vital monument to her life's efforts to serve the poor of many backgrounds in the middle of a vibrant city.

Chapter Two
Robert Baden-Powell
(1857–1941)

What Is a Boy Scout?

A scout! What fun he finds in hiking into the woods! He tells North from South by the stars, or East from West by the shadows.

He can talk to a brother Scout across a river by signalling. He knows the principal trees and birds and animals that he meets. He knows which are poisonous weeds or reptiles. He can find his way as did the Indians and pioneers before him.

If matches are forgotten, he laughs and proceeds to kindle a fire by rubbing sticks together or by striking steel on flint. The fire once started, what good things he can cook out there in the open!

He keeps himself physically fit. He avoids poisons of alcohol or tobacco. He guards his tongue from loose speech or boasting or sacrilege. When he speaks of anyone he tries to speak well of him.

His Scout "Good Turns" to someone each day make him many friends—for the way to have friends is to first BE one. His motto is "Be Prepared" and he thinks through in advance what he would do in fire or storm.

When someone is injured he is ready to help him with his First Aid knowledge. He always tries to be a useful citizen. He helps his community.

Another big thing a Scout enjoys is camping—there he finds fun in game or swim—finds new friends in woods and other fellows—and there among the trees, or under God's silent stars, or by the camp-fire's ruddy embers, he dreams out his great *tomorrow*.[1]

Robert Stephenson Smyth Baden-Powell,

founder of the Boy Scout movement, was born in London on February 22, 1857. Robert was only three years old when his father died, but there can be no doubt that the memory of his father, as it was preserved by his mother, made a deep impression on him and his career. His father, the Reverend H.G. Baden-Powell, was a scholar and scientist of note, being Savilian Professor of Geometry at Oxford University from 1827 until his death in 1860. In 1824, he had been elected a member of the Royal Society, a mark of distinction for a man of his field. His specialization was optics and radiation, and he worked with famed Sir John Frederick William Herschel.

The Reverend H.G. Baden-Powell was a man of broad interests. While geometry was his specialty, he also studied natural history. He believed that science, in its broadest connotations, should have an established place in the university.

In religion, Robert's father was a liberal. As a man of science, he believed that there was no need to deny the essential validity of scientific findings. But he also felt that there was no reason to assume that science was contrary to religious truth. He sought a compromise or union of scientific and religious outlooks. His stand was not popular with either scientists or religionists. Scientists felt that he was "giving in" to religious requirements, while religionists felt that he held his religious beliefs with tongue in cheek.

With Benjamin Jowett, Mark Pattison, and William Temple, the Reverend Baden-Powell contributed to *Essays and Reviews,* a publication that was judged heretical by the Established Church of England. Only his death prevented him from being brought to public trial as a destroyer of the faith. Nothing, however, was further from his true intent.

Robert's mother, Henrietta Grace, was one of the daughters of British Admiral William Smyth. The Smyth family traced their descent from Captain John Smith of colonial fame. During the American War of Independence, the admiral lost considerable land in America, especially in New Jersey, because he refused to be disloyal to Great Britain. Admiral Smyth devoted most of his time to charting the Mediterranean; his nickname, appropriate to his chief distinction, was "Mediterranean Smyth." He, too, was interested in science. As a researcher in astronomy, he won a fellowship in the Royal Society, and he was a founder and charter member of the Royal Geographical Society.

When Henrietta Grace married the Reverend Baden-Powell, she acquired a ready-made family. He had been married twice before, and both wives had died. His first wife had borne no children. The second union produced two daughters and a son. Henrietta became the stepmother of these three children; at the time of her marriage the eldest was eight and the youngest three. In time, she bore ten children, seven of whom survived infancy.

A month after the last child was born, the Reverend Baden-Powell died. His death left Henrietta with the responsibility for ten children. She was a woman of considerable talent, however, and succeeded on a moderate income to raise her children successfully. Not only did she manage the household, but she was able to take part in voluntary hospital work in the poorer sections of London. She was also a painter; some of her work may still be seen in the Cardiff Public Library in Wales. Mrs. Baden-Powell strongly supported the fuller education of girls, and found time to work for the Central Committee of the Women's Education Union.

Robert's earliest education consisted not so much of reading books as of walks in the company of his mother and brothers and sisters throughout the countryside. Early, he learned to love nature, as did his father before him. He was able to identify the various plants encountered as they hiked, and throughout his life he enjoyed adding to his storehouse of knowledge of the out-of-doors.

The moral atmosphere of the Baden-Powell home was set by his father. Robert was not indoctrinated into the full confession of the English church, but, on the other hand, there was a strong emphasis within the home on ethical values. The good life took the place of correct theology in the Baden-Powell household, and Robert came early to understand the importance of "doing justly." After his eighth birthday, he wrote the following "Laws for me when I grow old":

I will have the poor people to be as rich as we are, and all who go across the crossings shall give the poor crossing sweeper some money and you ought to thank God for what He has given us and He made the poor people to be poor and the rich people to be rich and I can tell you how to be good. Now I will tell you. You must pray to God whenever you can but you cannot be good with only praying but you must try very hard to be good.

> by
> R. S. S. Powell
> Feb. 26, 1865
> Robert Stephenson Smyth Powell[2]

This brief statement shows clearly how morally centered young Robert was. The degree of "socialism" inherent in his "Laws for me when I grow old" somewhat shocked his grandfather, the admiral. But his insistence on the rights of the poor and the responsibilities of the rich were fast becoming a fashionable subject for English Christians of the time. The preaching of Charles Kingsley illustrates that very clearly. There is also implicit in the "Laws" that Robert devised an emphasis on works in contrast to faith. He was not taught to distrust faith, but to use it as a means of strengthening action; it was action that finally counted.

The professor's children got to know a number of famous people, largely through the reputation of their father and the interests of their mother. Robert knew British novelist William Makepeace Thackeray, and John Ruskin was a frequent visitor at the Baden-Powell home. Once, when Ruskin found Robert painting, he gave him some pointers. Robert's mother worried because Robert painted sometimes with his left hand and sometimes with his right. Ruskin told her not to worry but to allow him to develop the use of both hands, and throughout his life, Robert remained ambidexterous. To entertain friends, he sometimes would draw two pictures at the same time, one with each hand.

The time quickly came in Robert's development when the instruction of the household had to give way to more formal efforts. He first was placed in a Dame's School in Kensington

Square, London. In 1868, he transferred to Rose Hill School, Tunbridge Wells, the school his father had attended. After a year at Rose Hill, he received scholarship offers from the Fettes and Charterhouse schools. Fettes was in Scotland, and it was rejected because it would have removed Robert too far from his family and because the family had no Scottish connections. Charterhouse was the older and perhaps better school and had educated some famous Englishmen, including John Wesley, Thackeray, Joseph Addison, and Richard Steele. Robert spent two years at the Charterhouse in London before it was moved, under the influence of Dr. William Haig Brown and by an act of Parliament, to a more spacious location in Godalming.

Dr. Brown had a strong influence on the lives of the members of Charterhouse; he has sometimes been called the second founder of the institution—so great was his effect on the school. He had the gift of individualizing his students. He did not require the same of all, but parceled out to each the study and discipline that met the specific and unique needs of the person. In that sense, he might be accused of having no genuine theory of education; more basically, he strove to assist the greatest possible development of each child in terms the personality and background of the child suggested.

Dr. Brown believed that a minimum of discipline was desirable for the proper growth of students. The story is told that once, when he came upon two groups of students who were hurling stones at each other in one of their "wars," he stood silently watching the evolving strategy of the combatants until it occurred to him that one side could rout the other if it could pass through a certain door to introduce an outflanking movement. This idea he quickly told the students. But the door was locked. Dr. Brown took a key from his pocket and unlocked the door. The ruse worked, and the "enemy" was promptly defeated.

Dr. Brown also believed in various kinds of "societies" for the students. He urged them to form groups that represented their interests. Some groups, however, represented doubtful and superficial interests, such as the Druids Club, which Braden-Powell helped to found. It lasted for three years. Each member had a special name; Robert was Lord Bathing Towel. One of the club's rules illustrates the activities of the group: "Any brother not producing a song or speech (within a minute after being called on), the latter in length not less than five minutes, or one yard, shall be fined a bottle of lemonade." Despite such rules, or perhaps because of them, the Druids were a happy group.

Baden-Powell was described by one of his fellow students as a "a boy of medium size, curly red hair, decidedly freckled, with a pair of twinkling eyes that soon won friends for him." The last part of the statement needs to be qualified somewhat in the light of other evidence that suggests that Robert was rather shy. He made friends more easily with the older members of the staff than with the boys around him. He was not friendless, but he was not the most popular boy in the school.

Robert was not a brilliant student, although that was not expected of him. One of his school evaluation forms suggests that he could probably have done better work than he did. Robert, however, was more interested in outdoor activities. He took an active part in sports of all kinds and found great satisfaction in them. He also loved the campus on which the school was situated and the surrounding countryside. It was here that the rudiments of scouting were encouraged—as Baden-Powell later recognized. In many ways, it was the supreme contribution of the school to his education. Many years later, he wrote of the meaning that the outdoors had for him at that time:

Why, ... it was only the other day—it can't be fifty years ago—that I was learning to snare rabbits in the copse at the "new" Charterhouse, and to cook them, for secrecy, over the diminutive fire of a bushman. I learned, too, how to use an axe, how to walk across a gully on a felled tree-trunk, how to move silently through the bush so that one became a comrade rather than a interloper among the birds and animals that lived there. I knew how to hide my tracks, how to climb a tree and "freeze" up there while authorities passed below forgetting that they were *Anthropoi*— being capable of looking up (or was it perhaps that they were real *Men* who refrained from looking up knowing that they would discover one?).

And the birds, the stoats, the water voles that I watched and knew?

Those things stand out as if they were of yesterday. Cricket? Footfall? Athletics? Yes, I enjoyed them too; but they lied long ago,

they were only a memory, like much that I learned at school. It was
in the copse that I gained most of what helped me on in after life to
find the joy of living.[3]

The time Robert spent at home was devoted mainly to
sailing. This interest was encouraged by his eldest brother,
Warrington. They began with the building and operation of
small boats, and once they worked on a collapsible boat. In time,
they concentrated on larger and more seaworthy vessels. One of
their boats, a ten-tonner named *Koh-i-noor,* took them along the
coasts of England and Scotland and even to the shores of
Norway. Robert learned to assist his brother with the problems
of sailing and became, in time, a well-trained boatman.

Hiking was also a favorite activity of Robert. Of this activity
he later wrote:

Much as I liked these boating expeditions, I liked tramping ones
just as much. In the holidays we used to walk through countries
like Wales and Scotland, each of us carrying a bag on his back and
sleeping out at night wherever we might happen to be.

Generally we would call at a farm and buy some milk, eggs,
butter, and bread, and ask leave to sleep in a hay-loft if it was bad
weather. Otherwise, in summer time, it was very nice to sleep in
the open alongside a hedge or a haystack, using hay or straw or old
newspapers as blankets if it was cold. In this way we got around a
lot of splendid country, where we could see all sorts of animals and
birds and strange flowers and plants, of which we took notes in our
log; and we had to make our way by the map which we carried, and
at night we used to learn to find our way in the dark by using
different sets of stars as our guide. We made sketches of any old
castles, abbeys or other buildings that we saw and read up or got
someone to tell us their history.

When we got to any big town we used to ask leave to go over
one of the factories to see what they made there and how they
made it, and we found it awfully interesting to see, for instance,
how cloth is made from sheep's wool, how paper is made from logs
of wood, iron from lumps of stone, china from bones and flints
powdered up and mixed in a paste and then turned on a potter's
wheel, how furniture is made, how engines work, how electricity is
used and so on.

In this way we got to know something about most trades and

learnt to do some of them ourselves in a small way, which has often come in useful to us since.[4]

When Robert reached the age of nineteen, he had to decide on a career. This was not easy; his forebears had shown talent along many lines. Most of his brothers were interested in law and finally became lawyers of some distinction. The family thought that Robert should talk the matter over with Benjamin Jowett, master of Balliol, Oxford University, and his father's friend. Jowett reported that Robert was not quite up to "Balliol form," that is, to a first-class, advanced education. This decision was fateful in many ways, for it directed Robert's thinking away from more schooling.

But his future had already been decided. He had taken an open examination for an army commission without much hope that he would qualify. When the results were announced, Baden-Powell had taken second place for cavalry and fourth for infantry, this in competition with about seven hundred men. For some of those who passed the examination, further training at Sandhurst was required, but for the first six, nothing further was asked. They were immediately given their commissions. In fact, their commissions were antedated two years as a reward. Baden-Powell became a sub-lieutenant in the 13th Hussars, a regiment stationed in India. On October 30, 1876, Baden-Powell set sail for India to take up his new duties with the army.

For eight months after he arrived in India, Robert spent his time in garrison training at Lucknow. After this, he was declared ready for his officer's position. The position did not offer enough income for Robert to take his place in the society of the officers, for his salary was only about $500 a year. For the most part, officers were sons of rich families and went into the army to honor their family name and to secure a rather leisurely social existence. Baden-Powell was not of their category. He did not feel that he was obligated to honor his family simply through his work in India; moreover, he always enjoyed travel. He also was not looking for an easy time.

The social status of the Baden-Powell family was relatively high, but their financial assets were not great. After a short time in India, Baden-Powell wrote to his mother that he had given up smoking in order to save money. Perhaps in compensation for his lack of money, as well as for other reasons, Baden-Powell spent a great part of his time in perfecting his knowledge and skill in military affairs. He took everything quite seriously.

One of his interests, carried over from his student days, was sports, especially polo and pig-sticking. The work of soldiering was not strenuous, and soldiers looked for divertisement in sport. He did rather well in sports, as records kept by his friends indicate.

When not busy in his job or in sports, he spent his time in theatricals. The soldiers spent much of their free time on dramatics, and worked in all aspects of the productions. The talent that Baden-Powell had for painting was soon utilized on stage scenery. He was excited with this new medium for artistic expression and devoted many hours to it. On occasion, he also filled in as an actor.

In 1878, Baden-Powell was ordered back to England for a period of recuperation. There he visited his old friends and his family. He spent some time at Hythe taking a musketry course, which he passed with flying colors, and pursued his interest in the theater. He saw some Gilbert and Sullivan productions and sketched their scenes during the performances. These he carried back with him to India in 1880. He immediately interested his fellow soldiers to produce some Gilbert and Sullivan light operas. Baden-Powell, himself, took the role of Deadeye in *H.M.S. Pinafore.*

The military and political situation had changed somewhat, making the army more important. The British resident at Kabul (now the capital of Afghanistan) and his staff had been massacred the previous year. Lord Roberts, chief of the British Army in India, routed the Afghans at Charasia. He then began a three hundred mile march from Kabul to Kandahar. At the time that Baden-Powell came back again to India, the army under Roberts was under march, and Baden-Powell was ordered to Kokoran. The task of catching up with his comrades was not simple, although Baden-Powell's love of the outdoors enabled him to enjoy the long journey by horseback through strange surroundings.

When at last he rejoined his regiment, he was given a job of drawing maps of the battle site at Maiwand. These he did with such care that the commanding officer complimented him personally. However, because of his map assignment, he secured no first-hand battle experience. The closest he came to this occurred on the withdrawal of the British troops when he accidentally shot himself in the leg. This necessitated his spending time recovering at Quetta (now in Pakistan).

Some of the soldiering Baden-Powell did in India came very close to Scout work as it was interpreted at a later time. Even the military ventures of the regiment called for skills that were appropriated in part by the Scouts when they came into existence.

In 1882, Baden-Powell became the adjutant to the regiment; he served four years in that capacity. In 1883, at age twenty-six, he was made a captain. By 1884, however, the work of the regiment was almost completed, and it was ordered back to England. Baden-Powell took a six-month leave for a hunting trip with five companions in Portuguese East Africa (now Mozambique). This trip increased his ability to cope with the problems of rough, outdoor living.

During the two years spent with his regiment in England, Robert continued his military life somewhat as he had in India. He still was interested in the entertainment of the troops and devised additional leisure activities for them, and also turned to writing. In 1886, Robert went to the Continent for a protracted visit, and his younger brother, Baden, accompanied him. Robert had heard that the Russians had perfected an observation balloon and a searchlight, and he wanted to investigate these developments. When they arrived at Krasnoselye, where the balloon was located, they disguised themselves by donning Russian clothes. For some days, they took long walks into the territory surrounding the location of the balloon. One day, they saw the balloon in flight, and noted its exact place in the countryside, then waited until the attendant soldiers left the balloon to eat. They approached the balloon, got into the observation car, and made notes of many of the details. This established a pattern for their observation of the searchlight by night. They assumed a bolder approach to this problem and walked right into the station, saluting anyone they thought needed to be saluted.

One day they learned that the czar himself was coming to

see the balloon. Nothing could stop Baden-Powell from gaining a glimpse of the ruler. The occasion was a success until Baden-Powell made the mistake of failing to salute the carriage of the czar as he passed. He was immediately arrested and taken to St. Petersburg for questioning.

In St. Petersburg, Baden-Powell was put in a hotel room, his passport was taken, and he was placed under open arrest. A sentence of five years in jail was possible for his offense. With the help of a German agent, however, Baden-Powell and his brother (who had joined him in St. Petersburg) were able to escape on a boat to Germany. There Baden-Powell inspected army maneuvers and observed the battlefields of the Franco-Prussian War.

In 1887, Baden-Powell's uncle, General Henry Smyth, was appointed commanding officer in South Africa, and he asked that his nephew be appointed as his aide. At the time that Baden-Powell set sail for Natal, the natives had insurrected against their British-appointed district chiefs. One of the first responsibilities of the Britishers was to rescue one of the chiefs, Pretorius. When the British landed, they went into action directly, marching fifty miles in two days. It was on one of these marches that Baden-Powell heard the Zulu chant that he later adopted for the Boy Scouts.

In his South African career, Baden-Powell conducted numerous spy campaigns. He was most effective in getting through broken country to pick up information in an informal manner. His scouting habits were of considerable advantage in this work.

When he returned to England in the summer of 1889 for a short leave, he met Sir Francis de Winton, who had been appointed to run an investigation of Swaziland (now Botswana). Sir Francis had heard of Baden-Powell and wanted him to help with the study. Baden-Powell gladly spent some time in helping Sir Francis gain the information.

The year 1889 also saw the publication of Baden-Powell's *Pig-Sticking or Hog-Hunting*, which described in a detailed and somewhat scholarly fashion an activity that fascinated many military men. According to the commentary supplied by Baden-Powell, "pig-sticking" was helpful to the development of the "soldier's eye" (that is, the activity was supposed to train the soldier for quick, accurate hand-eye coordination).

Baden-Powell's career in South Africa came to a close in 1889, when his uncle was transferred to the island of Malta, and he took his nephew with him as aide. Malta bored Baden-Powell. He was used to rougher living and was uninterested in the social life of a British officer in this "civilized" place. So he turned his attention to the welfare of his troops, establishing a series of entertainments and a soldiers-and-sailors club, where the men could rest and enjoy themselves.

Baden-Powell continued his spying activities for his personal preoccupation and enjoyment. He was appointed as an intelligence officer for the Mediterranean area for this purpose and traveled to many places about the Mediterranean in search of military information. Usually, he went as a Britisher who was interested in collecting butterflies. This simple occupation acted as a successful disguise, and no one questioned his aims. Baden-Powell was especially talented for this purpose not only because of his scouting skills but also because he was an excellent sketch-book artist. Wherever he went, he drew pictures of what he saw and of the personalities that impressed him. On his spying trips, he would make accurate, usable notations in the form of disguised nature pictures. On one occasion, he sketched all the military emplacements of a defensive position in the form of a butterfly. A code of symbols referring to the markings on the back of the supposed butterfly gave him a record of each military factor.

After he had achieved considerable gains for the British Army through his work with the troops and his spying expeditions, he decided to return to the 13th Hussars, then stationed in Ireland. Taking up his new duties in 1893, he saw service on several occasions in Ireland.

In 1895, Great Britain had need of him once more. The Ashanti in the Gold Coast region of western Africa had long been hostile, but in 1895, a new uprising occurred, and it was decided that Baden-Powell would be suited to the type of militia work that the situation entailed. He was sent to head a native contingent. The British had tried unsuccessfully to live at peace with the Ashanti, but their efforts, both peaceful and warlike, failed. It was felt that the only permanent solution would be the outright military conquest of the Ashanti. Local troops were chosen for the main part of the task.

Baden-Powell landed in Cape Coast (now Ghana) with instructions to try to raise a levy of local manpower. Then he was to march through the land of the Ashanti until he captured the important city of Kumasi. With the cooperation of six local tribes (not Ashanti), he succeeded in organizing 861 natives, divided into companies of from 20 to 30 men each. A "captain" was appointed over each company. The companies were assembled according to tribe, and the chief of each tribe was directly responsible to Baden-Powell.

After the men were secured and organized, the march to Kumasi began. Several scares came to the expedition, but no real difficulty. In January 1896, Baden-Powell and his men succeeded in capturing Kumasi and subduing the chief and the men of the Ashanti. The trip back to the coast took only seven days. The cost in lives was practically nil, but almost 50 percent of his officers and men perished later of fever.

As a reward for his work with the Ashanti, Baden-Powell was promoted to the rank of brevet-lieutenant-colonel. He was at the time only thirty-nine years old. Upon his return to England, he went directly to Belfast to rejoin his regiment, but in several weeks' time, he was given another special assignment, this time to Matabeleland (now Zimbabwe). There had been a history of unrest in this region for some time, but in March 1896 there was a great uprising. The natives set fire to the villages of white traders and miners and assaulted many of them. The British fought valiantly to defend their stronghold, economically as well as militarily. Baden-Powell was among those sent from England to provide help. He worked under Major-General Sir Frederick Carrington as chief of staff, which gave him recognition for his previous work and his capacity at the type of warfare that was required in Africa. After landing in Africa, the reinforcements traveled 557 miles and reached the besieged whites at Bulawayo just in time to save them.

As chief of staff, it was Baden-Powell's duty to plan the military action. He was able to wage a successful campaign in part because of his knowledge of the African natives and of the type of warfare that was demanded. Often while preparing for a phase of the campaign, he would take himself to the hills in his old capacity of scout and discover for himself the conditions that he would have to meet in battle. On several occasions, he was complimented by high officers on the accuracy of the maps that he drew as a result of his reconnoitering. The difficulty in Matabeleland was not of major importance and peace was soon established. The noted British trader Cecil John Rhodes had a major part in the formulation of the terms of peace. The campaign taught Baden-Powell many things about the importance of scouting in connection with the army. In his account of the Matabeleland affair, he wrote regarding the importance of scout methods in such warfare, noting that a few downtrodden blades of grass may lead to significant military encounters, that the presence of women and boys could be told by the nature of the imprints of sandals, and that the drinking habits of the natives told of their travels. He was quick to notice the smallest details and was able, on the basis of his scouting experience, to advance his military objectives.

By Christmas of 1897, Baden-Powell was on his way back again to England, this time in the company of Cecil Rhodes. On board ship, Baden-Powell was called upon on several occasions to enliven the passage with his wit and songs.

Upon his return to England, he rejoined the 13th Hussars and was rewarded for his African services with a promotion, this time to the rank of brevet-colonel. Within his own regiment, he now held a higher rank than his commanding officer. Within a short time, however, he was given the command of the 5th Dragoon Guards, then stationed in India. It was not easy for him to leave the regiment with which he had served for twenty-one years. When he arrived in India in April 1897, he wrote to a friend:

> Behold me, arrived all well and comfortably settled down into my new billet in my old station. It always feels as if I had been away from it for twelve months instead of twelve years. I am delighted with the Regiment; it is certainly a very fine one, and in good condition all round. When I have set things en train I shall run up for a few days to see the Baker Russells at Naina Tal in the hills.[5]

In his new command, Baden-Powell worked on several principles that he had tested in his previous experience. For one, he required a great deal of work from his men. He believed that work was the answer to many problems in personal relations. He led his men in ways that would give them a sense of responsibility. He did not try to manufacture work for them, but he did seek to have every man busy.

Another principle was providing sufficient and attractive entertainment for his troops, so he set up a refreshment room. Although he was opposed to hard liquor, he did permit the men to have beer.

After two years as the commanding officer of the 5th Dragoon Guards, he was recalled to England. Upon his arrival he learned that he was to take up new duties in South Africa as commander in chief, Northwest Frontier Forces. He was to organize two regiments of mounted infantry, and in the event of war he was to organize the defense of the Rhodesia and Bechuanaland frontiers. His chief responsibility was the recruitment and training of two regiments of men. His headquarters were established at Mafeking.

The situation in South Africa quickly changed, for the Boers were mobilizing to battle with the English. Several months after Baden-Powell's arrival in South Africa, war was declared, and the Boers laid siege to Mafeking with nine thousand men. Baden-Powell's command totaled 1,251. The town was without natural defenses, so Baden-Powell ordered artificial defenses to be erected. Although the town was under siege, Baden-Powell believed that he could accomplish more by clever attacks of a minor sort against the Boers than by a continuously passive resistance. In time six thousand of the Boer soldiers were withdrawn from operations elsewhere; even so, the garrison of Mafeking was outnumbered. There was little to do but wait. The forces headed by Baden-Powell were especially short of artillery, and the food situation also became serious.

In April 1900, two events occurred: the Boers increased their forces by another thousand men, and Queen Victoria sent a telegram to Baden-Powell that read: "I continue watching with confidence and admiration the patient and resolute defense which is so gallantly maintained under your ever resourceful command." Relief finally came when two thousand reinforcements arrived. The Boers were routed, freeing the town and

Baden-Powell and his men. The siege, which had lasted for 217 days, was called a victory for the British by the commanding general of the area, Lord Wolseley. He wrote to the queen asking that Baden-Powell be raised in rank to a major-general as a reward for his skillful handling of the situation.

As a result of his activity in the Boer War and his promotion, Baden-Powell became popular with many people throughout the world, especially in Great Britain and the United States. Many boys wrote him idolizing letters; some told him their private woes. To his admirers, he always wrote words of tested advice. His epistles to various boys make interesting reading, for they show how sensitive he was to their needs.

Prior to the official close of the Boer War, Baden-Powell was asked by the high commissioner to organize a constabulatory for the maintenance of law in South Africa. The task was not easy. For one thing, Baden-Powell had to decide what kind of men he wished to recruit. Because of his high standards, it was not always easy to find the proper men. He also had a high estimate of what was required of a soldier, and this discouraged some from joining his forces. But the fame of Baden-Powell was also an attraction, and men came from distant places to join up with him.

As the organizer of the constabulary, Baden-Powell had to decide on many details. For one, he was responsible for designing the uniforms for his men. He liked a full brimmed hat, and chose khaki for the color of the uniform, which was somewhat like that used by the Boy Scouts today, although there were major differences. He was also responsible for selecting horses for his men, bringing them from Australia. The actual training program for the men was a major and time-consuming responsibility.

Baden-Powell took a most active part in all things connected with his job. By 1901, one year after he started to organize the constabulary, he had trained ten thousand men. But this kind of supervision took a heavy toll on his health. Exhausted, he was ordered home to England for a six month rest. The physician in charge wrote to Baden-Powell's mother as follows:

> I venture to write to tell you that I have long hoped that he would not work so hard. He would get fever of a severe enough type to lay

most men up in hospital, but he would go on working. What our General went through at Mafeking was again enough to lay most men up for a considerable time: and all this on the top of the organization of such a corps as this, 10,000 strong, was more than human endurance could stand. About a month ago an undoubted attack of influenza came on. It was followed by bronchitis: so I would not take the responsibility, and was only too glad to have a medical board and recommend the General for six months' leave. Of course he didn't think he required so long, but though his brain power is phenomenal, his body cannot go on at full tension forever.[6]

He did not look for additional honors on his return to England, but on all sides there were crowds to welcome him. King Edward VII wrote, asking to see him about the campaign he had directed in the Boer War and made him a companion of the Order of the Bath. Several cities invited him to celebrations in his honor, and he laid the foundation stone for the War Memorial Cloister.

In the immediately succeeding years, he was connected with official life in one capacity or another. In 1904, he established the Cavalry School at Netheravon, and in 1905, he began *The Cavalry Journal*, a publication about training cavalry soldiers. In 1906, he went with the duke of Connaught on an official tour of South Africa. Hardly another man could have been as helpful on such a trip. On the way home, he visited several other territories and countries and, as a result of his experiences, drew up the popular book *Sketches in Mafeking and East Africa* (1907). During all this time, he was the inspector-general of the British Army, a post he resigned in 1907. With his resignation, he was nominally retired at half pay. While he was later to return to soldierly duties, he turned at this time to a new project—the development of an experimental camp at Brownsea Island, which led to the Boy Scout movement. The camp provided Baden-Powell with the experience necessary to prove to himself and "his boys" that camping was a very real possibility on a large scale.

Using the work at Brownsea as a prototype, Baden-Powell began to encourage boys in London and wherever else boys showed an interest to organize local groups, or troops, of Scouts.

The newly formed groups were informal in their organization and drew their inspiration from Baden-Powell. Their existence acted as a stimulus to the creation of other groups. It would be difficult to point out another group or movement of the nature of the Scouts that grew so quickly. Within a period of two years, through the patient and skillful leadership of Baden-Powell, the movement was a success and required full-time leadership.

Within two years of Baden-Powell's resignation as inspector-general, a rally was held in the Crystal Palace in London and ten thousand Boy Scouts attended. It was clear to Baden-Powell that he had to make a decision between the army and the Scouts for the major work of his later years.

In 1910, he resigned his last connection with the army, his territorial command, and purposed to spend full time in the energizing of the Boy Scout movement. Richard Burton Haldane, the secretary for war, accepted his resignation with regret, but added, "I feel that the organization of the Boy Scouts has so important a bearing on the future that probably the greatest service you can render to the country is to devote yourself to it." Baden-Powell's reply was, "I was not built for a general. I liked being a regimental officer in personal touch with my men."

It is difficult to say precisely who really founded the Boy Scout movement. There are several persons who have claimed the foundership. Dan Carter Beard had much to do with the organization of the Scout movement in the United States, and some persons think of him as the founder of the international Scouts. Others, in one way or another, have issued a claim to the establishment of the movement. Baden-Powell was aware of the difficulty of saying who exactly should take credit for the Scouts. One of his letters, written to a man who claimed to be the founder, was kept in his office with the following notation upon it: "Note for Office to keep in case of revival of arguments later when I am dead. R.B-P. 17.12.13." It reads as follows:

> This man is the 4th to claim that he invented Boy Scouts. I have no recollection of his scheme for training boys which he says he sent to me in 1905—but he may have sent it and I may have written to express my interest in it: it did not in any case make a great impression on me. My idea of training boys in scouting dates from 1897 when I applied it to young soldiers in the 5th Dragoon

Guards, having for years previously found the good of developing the man's character before putting upon him the dull routine training then considered necessary for a soldier.

The possibility of putting responsibility on to boys and treating them seriously was brought to the proof in Mafeking with the corps of boys raised by Lord Edward Cecil there in 1899 and led me to go into it further.

When I came home from the War in 1902 I found my book *Aids to Scouting* being used in schools and by Boys' Brigade Officers, etc., for teaching boys. As this had been written for soldiers I re-wrote it for boys (after having an experimental camp in 1907). I did not then intend to have a separate organization of Boy Scouts, but hoped that the B.B. and Y.M.C.A. would utilize the idea. However, such a large number of men and boys outside these organizations took it up, that we were obliged to form a directorate to control it.

The movement grew up of itself. In 1910 I had to give up the Army to take charge of it.

The idea of the dress of the Scouts was taken from a sketch of my own dress in Kashmir in 1897, in every detail, including hat, staff, shirt, shorts, neckerchief, belt knife, rolled coat, etc.

The badge was that which I used for Scouts in the 5th Dragoon Guards (since adopted throughout the Army). It was taken from the sign of the North Point of the compass as shown on maps as guide to their orientation.[7]

This letter points out what is a fact: it is extremely difficult to say when Baden-Powell initiated the Boy Scout movement. In a sense, his early home training was primarily responsible for his scouting ideas. The year 1910 is used as an official founding date, because it was then that Baden-Powell resigned from the army to take full-time charge of the Scouts. But certainly there was a Boy Scout movement in spirit, if not in fact, before then.

The experimental camp that Baden-Powell instituted on Brownsea Island was one of the important steps in the growth of the movement. To this setting, for a period of several weeks, he brought twenty boys from various strata of English life to test the scouting ideas he had developed over a lifetime. The Boys' Brigade, an organization founded by Sir William Smith, similar to the Boy Scouts, aided him in the location of the site for the camp, in obtaining the boys and in the equipping of the camp.

This camping experience was an attempt to standardize and test Baden-Powell's ideas on camping. The experiment worked out so well that Baden-Powell enlisted the financial aid of C. Arthur Pearson, a publisher, to carry his scheme forward for the next year. Pearson, with vision, accepted the responsibility; he also agreed to publish a weekly paper, *The Scout*. The original headquarters (supplied by Mr. Pearson) consisted of one room on Henrietta Street in London.

The publication of *The Scout* greatly encouraged the growth of the movement. Boys throughout England were attracted to the magazine because it was sponsored by Baden-Powell, and they eagerly tried the many suggestions and plans that he contributed to the magazine. The idea of scouting took hold; people everywhere were drawn to it. Throughout England, local groups of Scouts were established. Usually, they called themselves "Scout Patrols," in reference to the patrol basis of organization used in the Brownsea experiment and later. Other organizations interested in youth took part in the strengthening of the Scout movement; for example, the national headquarters of the Y.M.C.A., approached by Baden-Powell, contributed to the spread of the Scout idea. Several new camps were established at this time, one in Chile, the first foreign Boy Scout organization, by Baden-Powell while he was on a trip to South America.

The writings of Baden-Powell were of inestimable value in the stimulation of the Boy Scout movement. He was able, through his experience in the army in other lands, to describe the essentials of scouting to boys in a fashion that encouraged them to join the movement. He demonstrated the romance of the Scout's life. He was imaginative enough (and practical, too) to know that boys would respond to the thrill and excitement of outdoor life. He also was skilled in instructing boys in the arts of outdoor living. Those who read his writings learned methods that had never occurred to them before. They were willing to study his writings and to test his ideas in practice because he called upon them to learn something new and interesting. Reading signs, knowing plants and their purposes, signaling by various means, cooking on an open fireplace, and many other essentials to the scouting concept were appealing to boys. The fact that the boys were called upon for action also increased the attractiveness of the movement.

Baden-Powell realized the importance of group spirit. He asked that the Scouts form small patrols, consisting of six to eight boys, which could be conjoined into a troop that gave a further sense of comradeship. But the primary relationship for the individual boy was to the patrol. The patrol, or small group, organization of the Boy Scout movement has been one of its most successful features, for it has encouraged boys to share closely in the lives of others.

Baden-Powell believed in positive appeals to the moral character of the Scouts. Other youth movements have been based upon a negative philosophy of character growth. The Woodcraft Indians, for example, established by Ernest Thompson Seton, had a set of "laws" of a negative nature. "Don't rebel." "Don't kindle a wild fire." "Don't make a dirty camp." These statements also were surrounded with appropriate punishments.

The Boy Scouts have never included this negativism within their movement. From the beginning, the Scout regulations have been positively stated and have not included penalties. The Scout Oath implies this constructive philosophy:

> On my honor I will do my best—
> To do my duty to God and my country,
>   and to obey the Scout law.
> To help other people at all times.
> To keep myself physically strong,
>   mentally awake, and morally straight.[8]

This oath is taken by Scouts when they join the movement. The twelve Scout Laws also express the same orientation to character development:

1. *A Scout Is Trustworthy*
   A Scout's honor is to be trusted. If he were to violate his honor by telling a lie, or by cheating, or by not doing exactly a given task, when trusted on his honor, he may be directed to hand over his Scout badge.

2. *A Scout Is Loyal*
   He is loyal to all to whom loyalty is due, his Scout leader, his home, and parents and country.

3. *A Scout Is Helpful*
He must be prepared at any time to save life, help injured persons, and share the home duties. He must do at least one "Good Turn" to somebody every day.

4. *A Scout Is Friendly*
He is a friend to all and a brother to every other Scout.

5. *A Scout Is Courteous*
He is polite to all, especially to women, children, old people and the weak and helpless. He must not take pay for being helpful or courteous.

6. *A Scout Is Kind*
He is a friend to animals. He will not kill nor hurt any living creature needlessly, but will strive to save and protect all harmless life.

7. *A Scout Is Obedient*
He obeys his parents, Scoutmaster, Patrol Leader, and all other duty constituted authorities.

8. *A Scout Is Cheerful*
He smiles whenever he can. His obedience to orders is prompt and cheery. He never shirks nor grumbles at hardships.

9. *A Scout Is Thrifty*
He does not wantonly destroy property. He works faithfully, wastes nothing, and makes the best use of his opportunities. He saves his money so that he may pay his own way, be generous to those in need, and helpful to worthy objects. He may work for pay, but must not receive tips for courtesies or Good Turns.

10. *A Scout Is Brave*
He has the courage to face danger in spite of fear, and to stand up for the right against the coaxings of friends or the jeers or threats of enemies, and defeat does not down him.

11. *A Scout Is Clean*
He keeps clean in body and thought, stands for clean speech, clean sport, clean habits, and travels with a clean crowd.

12. *A Scout Is Reverent*
He is reverent toward God. He is faithful in his religious duties, and

respects the convictions of others in matters of custom and religion.[9]

The Boy Scouts, as conceived by Baden-Powell, have always stressed individual responsibility; no one should mistrust a Boy Scout. A Scout should be told what his honor is and then be held to it. The interpretation of his honor to a large degree is the right of the individual. Baden-Powell makes this point clear:

Once the Scout understands what his honor is, and has, by his initiation, been put upon his honor, the Scoutmaster must entirely trust him to do things. You must show him by your action that you consider him a responsible being. Give him charge of something, whether temporary or permanent, and expect him to carry out his charge faithfully. Don't keep prying to see how he does it. Let him do it his own way, let him come a howler over it if need be, but in any case leave him alone and trust him to do his best.

Giving responsibility is the key to success with boys, especially with the rowdiest and most difficult boys.

The object of the Patrol system is mainly to give real responsibility to as many of the boys as possible with a view to developing their character. If the Scoutmaster gives his Patrol Leader real power, expects a great deal from him, and leaves him a free hand in carrying out his work, he will have done more for that boy's character expansion than any amount of school-training could ever do.[10]

Baden-Powell originated the merit badge system, which is still an important part of the Boy Scouts. This particular feature was experimented with during Baden-Powell's experience with the 5th Dragoon Guards. He found that the incentive of his troops increased if they had a grading system based upon an exact formula. By 1910, first and second class badges were set up with appropriate rules for their achievement. The rules have changed somewhat, but the principle has remained.

In the beginning, no special clothing was used by the Scouts, but as the movement grew, Baden-Powell designed a uniform that would be serviceable to the tasks of the Scouts. He decided

that they needed clothes that would permit maximum movement, and he devised the shorts that the Scouts have made so
popular. This innovation does not appear as being novel in our
day, but, in the time of Baden-Powell, wearing shorts in public
was looked upon as a breach of the mores. It was characteristic of
Baden-Powell that, once he saw the need for something, he
allowed nothing to deter him from its use. Scoutmasters, at first,
were not regulated in clothing as closely as the boys, but, in
time, orders that required a particular dress for them were
issued.

The orders and regulations initiated by Baden-Powell were
severely tested by the corporate experience of the Scouts.
Whenever some part of the organization seemed to be unwise or
impractical, it was discarded.

The Boy Scouts were a decided success within the first few
years of their official creation. Baden-Powell remained as the
main leader of the movement, but he could not care for all of the
many duties that came his way. He placed the general direction
of the movement in an executive committee, of which he was
chairman. This committee was composed of men who devoted
themselves to the building of the movement: Sir Edmond Elles,
C.C. Branch, Colonel Ulick de Burgh, Sir Percy W. Everett, and
H. Geoffrey Elwes. These men established the policy for the
national organization. Under them were county councils with
county commissioners in charge. District commissioners were
appointed under the county commissioners, and these had
contact with local organizations. The hierarchy of leadership
believed that its function was not to impose a system of thought
and activity upon local scoutmasters. The chief responsibilities
for the success of the movement rested upon the quality of
leadership found in the local organizations. The scoutmaster
was given considerable freedom in his choice of a program.

Baden-Powell's time was devoted mainly to the general
supervision and stimulation of the movement. He made local
inspections, not in a true military style, but with the idea of
encouraging units to take pride in themselves. He also lectured
on the meaning and organization of the Boy Scouts. The
speeches he gave helped establish a clear picture in the minds of
most of his countrymen as to the aims and accomplishments of
the movement.

His services extended beyond his own country. In 1910, he was invited by the czar of Russia to discuss the founding of the Boy Scouts in that country. In the summer of that year, he traveled with a group of Scouts to Canada and the United States. The Scout movement had already been introduced to these countries some years previously. Everywhere Baden-Powell went in the New World, he found signs of the success of the movement.

As the movement spread, prominent people came to its support and increased its popularity. Lord Roberts, a field-marshal and a British hero of the day, was one. He said:

> I like the idea and I think it may have good results. Boys are very receptive and would enjoy the delights of such training if it were carried out in a satisfactory manner. Good instructors would be needed and I suppose a certain amount of financial assistance would be required. I am sure that it would be better for the boys to spend a day in bicycling in the country near the large towns and learning to Scout, than to waste their time—as so many of them do—in looking on at games in which they are not sufficiently skilled to take part themselves. I hope your scheme may be given a fair trial.[11]

From the beginning, the Boy Scouts have been accused of being a militaristic organization. The movement might seem on the surface to be an inculator of military virtues, but such is not the case. The use of a uniform cannot of itself be termed militaristic. There is no genuine parallel between the ranks in the Scout organization and military stratification. The failure of the Scouts to incorporate specific military practices is conspicuous; Baden-Powell always opposed the inclusion of a great amount of drill work in the Scouts. In his book *Scouting for Boys*, he mentions two reasons for his resistance to military drill for boys within his movement:

(1) Military drill gives a feeble, unimaginative officer something with which to occupy his boys. It saves him a world of trouble; (2) Military drill tends to destroy individuality, whereas we want, in Scouts, to develop individual character. . . . Our aim is to make young backwoodsmen of the boys, not imitation soldiers.[12]

Here, in unequivocal language, the chief Scout outlined his distaste for militaristic features.

Certain qualities that are encouraged by the Boy Scouts *may* lay the basis for the military life. For example, the Boy Scout learns group cooperation. This quality can be helpful in wartime, but it is equally valuable in time of peace. There is nothing in group cooperation of itself to favor war. And so with other qualities nourished by the Boy Scouts. In fact, there is real reason to assume the Scout movement has more significance for the establishment and maintenance of peace than it does for war.

The boys who early were attracted to the Boy Scouts were quickly followed by their sisters. At the mass rally at the Crystal Palace in 1909 were some "Girl Scouts." It was clear to Baden-Powell and his co-workers that an organization similar to the Boy Scouts would have to be set up specifically for girls. By 1909, about eight thousand girls had already registered with the Boy Scouts. With the need apparent, Baden-Powell proceeded to organize the Girl Guides, an organization for girls that was modeled closely after the Boy Scouts. In the United States, the counterpart to the Boy Scouts is the Girl Scouts, but in England, it still is called Girl Guides. Baden-Powell's sister, Agnes, led the Girl Guides. She published the *Handbook for Girl Guides* in 1912, which accomplished for the Girl Guides what *Scouting for Boys* did for the Boy Scouts. Both books were extremely influential in publicizing the scouting movement.

In 1912, the Boy Scouts were legally incorporated. The same year, the Scout Farm at Buckhurst Place in Kent was established. This school trained boys in agriculture with the hope that they would leave England for the colonies. The outbreak of the First World War, however, brought that school to an end.

In 1912, Baden-Powell began a world tour that brought him into communication with the growing Scout movement in the dominions, the colonies, and the United States. It was on this trip that he renewed his acquaintance with Olave St. Clair Soames of England, whom he had known in London several years previously. She later was to become his wife and the chief of the Girl Guides.

After their marriage, Mrs. Baden-Powell helped her husband greatly in his work. They had three children—Peter, born in

1913; Heather, in 1915; and Betty, in 1917. There can be no doubt that Baden-Powell was strengthened and inspired by his family. He was a devoted husband and father, even though his duties frequently took him away from home.

The Wolf Cubs made their first public appearance in June of 1914, when Queen Alexandra inspected eleven thousand Boy Scouts of London. The Cubs had been needed for a long time, for the leaders of the scouting movement realized there was need to differentiate between the boys over twelve and those under. The Wolf Cubs were organized to take care of boys from the ages of nine to eleven. They were modeled on the general Boy Scout pattern and were made a part of the same organization. The Cubs soon became very popular, and in time there were many thousands of young boys within the ranks.

Just before the outbreak of the First World War, the Boy Scouts began an endowment campaign. They had been able to secure funds from interested citizens to carry on their work effectively, but they needed more money for expansion and for improvement of the permanent program. During the first six months of the campaign, Baden-Powell spent almost all of his time speaking at different places. About $500,000 was raised, but the campaign had to be called off when war broke out.

When war came, the Boy Scout organization was put under considerable strain, but it managed to survive and to contribute heavily to the national life of the various countries which were engaged in the war. National allegiance and service were cardinal principles of the movement. In England, as elsewhere, the Scouts acted as messengers. They patrolled railway lines and bridges, helped in hospitals, collected waste materials that could be converted to war purposes, and took part in a host of other activities. The Sea Scouts, developed as another branch of specialized scouting, contributed to the effort; some thirty thousand young men took part in the patrolling of the coasts of England during the war period.

When war started in 1914, Baden-Powell had been retired for four years and was only fifty-seven. He was considered for a position of command in the army, but it was concluded that the role that he filled in leading the Boy Scouts was more valuable than any position he might fill in direct relation to the war. He was called upon in many ways to help informally. Because of his contribution through the Scouts to the alleviation of the problem of juvenile delinquency (which is always a serious wartime condition), he received the thanks of persons of high governmental rank.

The Scout movement came out of the war with increased strength, but it also was faced with the problems of an organization that has undergone a period of rapid expansion. The ten years following the war can be termed the years of consolidation. The gains the movement made in membership prior to and during the war were outstanding. After the war, there were problems with consolidating the organizational gains of the past. The movement needed to give more attention to the quality and training of its leadership. In the beginning, the leadership was highly spontaneous and voluntary. After the war, it became more professionalized. Baden-Powell realized that training courses should be set up for scoutmasters and other officials.

Another problem of the postwar period was that of older boys; they required special consideration. The Rover Scouts were the result. Older boys were not interested in badges, so these were eliminated. According to Baden-Powell, the Rover Scouts did not need a definite program of activities but an ideal that they could seek to attain. He believed there were three aims to the Rover Scout movement: service to the self, service to the Scouts, and service to the community. While these ideals are found also in the other branches of the Boy Scouts, in the case of the Rover Scouts, they were stressed as general guiding principles. The second objective also lent itself to the training of scoutmasters.

Baden-Powell wrote books for each of the subgroups within the Boy Scouts. His first volume, *Scouting for Boys*, had been written for the general body of Scouts. His second book had the Wolf Cubs specifically in mind: *The Wolf Cub's Handbook*. His third, *Rovering to Success*, dealt with the particular problems of the older Scout.

In 1918, the Boy Scout movement was ten years old. Baden-Powell had planned for a large jamboree to celebrate the occasion, but the war did not permit it. In 1920, however, the first jamboree was held in London and about six thousand Scouts from all over the world attended. At the end of the jamboree,

Baden-Powell was elected the Chief Scout of the entire world. An international committee and bureau were established with the help of an American, F. F. Peabody. The continuance of the committee and bureau was dependent financially in the later years upon another American, Mortimer Schiff. The committee and bureau were created to handle the international problems that resulted from the complicated organization and extension of the movement. It received the full support of Baden-Powell.

As the Boy Scout movement expanded and became a vital force in social affairs in England and other countries, efforts were made by various groups to swing it behind other social programs: political, religious, and economic. Every group thought, "How nice it would be if the Boy Scouts were on our side." Baden-Powell was approached on many occasions by representatives of organizations, but he steadfastly refused to allow the Boy Scouts to become the arm of any other interest. In fact, Baden-Powell was nonpolitical throughout his career. Like many military men, he felt that politics was a lot of "hot air." Once, when Lord Roberts suggested that Baden-Powell run for Parliament, he wrote, "Delighted—which side?"

Baden-Powell also had difficulties with religious groups. Each sectarian faction wanted the Boy Scouts to be on its side exclusively. To each one, Baden-Powell patiently showed how detrimental and illogical such a position would be from the viewpoint of the Boy Scouts. He did not refuse the sanction of the churches; he willingly permitted local Scout organizations to be sponsored by churches. He was unwilling, however, to sign up in an exclusive way with any one denomination. He tried to get all interests represented on the council of the Boy Scouts.

Jamborees were found to be a popular activity. They were held every four years, each time in a different country to help bring together Scouts from many lands. At the Jamboree of 1929, termed the Coming-of-Age Jamboree, Scouts gathered from thirty-one parts of the British Empire and from forty-one nations. The jamboree lived up to its name; the Scouts had a wonderful time, despite occasional mud and rain. Baden-Powell was honored in several ways for his effective leadership, and the king conferred a peerage upon him in recognition of his services to the nation. Baden-Powell decided he should take the title of Baden-Powell of Gilwell, the location of the major training camp for Scout leaders. The Scouts themselves presented him with a Rolls-Royce car and trailer. This became affectionately known as the "Jam-Roll." To the jamboree came many distinguished people and leaders from all sections of public life, including the Prince of Wales. The leading Roman Catholic and Protestant leaders also took active roles.

Despite the many duties that Baden-Powell had, he always found time to develop his first interest, outdoor living. By carefully organizing his time, he was able to take hikes into the rural sections of England. Often he combined business and pleasure by camping while en route to some meeting or other.

In time, Baden-Powell found that he should no longer attempt to head up the Scout movement; his office should be held by a younger man. But the membership and officers would not permit him to resign. They knew his value as a cohesive symbol of the widely scattered movement.

In 1934, at the age of seventy-seven, Baden-Powell undertook a world tour, which included a jamboree in Australia. In 1936, he went to South Africa to work out some of the problems that had arisen there in regard to racial discrimination in the Scouts. On his eightieth birthday, he was in India, celebrating with the 13th Hussars. But, due to his advancing age and his strenuous life, the pace could not be maintained.

He died on January 8, 1941, an old man, but one who had lived a full and fruitful life. The twenty-eight decorations and orders and the seven honorary degrees that had been granted him by universities in several countries could not in themselves measure the affection with which the people of the world viewed him. His body, by his request, was buried in Nyeri near Mount Kenya, a place he had admired in his earlier life.

Baden-Powell's spirit is epitomized by his statement to the World Jamboree held in Holland in the summer of 1937:

> The Emblem of our Jamboree is the Jacobstaff. This was the instrument by which the navigators in old days found their way across the seas. Let it also for us today be an instrument of guidance in our life. It is the Cross which for all who are Christians points the way; but it is also a cross with many arms; these are held out to embrace all creeds. Those eight arms, together with the head and foot of the emblem, remind us of our ten Scout laws.
>
> Go forth with this emblem to spread the spirit of goodwill. . . .

Now the time has come for me to say good-bye. I want you to lead happy lives. You know that many of us will never meet again in this world. I am in my eighty-first year and am nearing the end of my life. Most of you are at the beginning and I want your lives to be happy and successful. You can make them so by doing your best to carry out the Scout Law all your days, whatever your station and wherever you are. I want you all to preserve this badge of the Jamboree which is on your uniform. I suggest that you keep it and treasure it and try to remember for what it stands. It will be a reminder of the happy times you have had here in camp; it will remind you to take the ten points of your Scout Law as your guide in life; and it will remind you of the many friends to whom you have held out the hand of friendship and so helped through goodwill to bring about God's reign of peace among men.

Now good-bye. God bless you all.[13]

Chapter Three
Samuel Barnett
(1844–1913)

In the minds of many people he lives as a social reformer,
as an active Poor Law administrator, as an ardent educa-
tionalist, but he was all these things and many more,
because his one never-sleeping desire was to help people to
live their lives in relation with God. Had we not made the,
to us, momentous decision, standing opposite St. Jude's
Church that day in the rain, and had his work lain in a
parish where conditions were normal, I doubt if his mind
would have turned in the directions it did. He would then
have followed the inclination of his spirit, and taught the
people religious truths. It was because they were living
under circumstances which precluded them from receiving
such truths, that he poured his whole life's force into
improving conditions. The walls of degrading and crippling
environment hid from many the light of truth. "Throw
down the walls," he cried.[1]

Samuel Augustus Barnett, founder of the settlement house movement, was born on the morning of February 8, 1844, in Bristol, England. It was a happy and rather successful family into which Samuel was born. His father, Francis Augustus Barnett, owned a foundry, the chief product of which was iron bedsteads, the first to be manufactured. The couple had been married five years before the birth of Samuel, the first son. Another son, Francis, was born two years later.

Samuel's grandfather, Mr. Gilmore, owned cargo ships that traveled all over the world. He had a marked influence on the upbringing of young Samuel, teaching him many of the ethical values that were apparent in his later life. For example, Mr. Gilmore, who owned considerable property that he rented, made it a principle never to accept more than 5 percent profit on these investments, believing that amount—but no more—to be justified. Whenever he earned more than 5 percent, he turned over the proceeds to the renters on a profit-sharing basis.

Samuel easily learned the responsibilities of the privileged to the less fortunate through the example set by his grandfather, and he also learned how to share in other ways. On one occasion when the family was sitting in their garden, they heard some unusual noises, so Samuel and his brother went to investigate. When they returned, they reported that they had found some boys stealing apples and had chased them away. The old man asked, "Did they get any?"

"No, we drove them away," the boys responded.

"Then let us go and give them some," was the advice of the grandfather.

No wonder Samuel was constantly alert throughout his life to the needs of the poor, understanding his responsibility to them to an unusual degree.

According to the testimony of his mother, Samuel never quarreled with his younger brother. They were inseparable companions, standing up for each other's rights with great loyalty.

Samuel's father was not attracted to learning. Though he read Charles Dickens and had an almost phenomenal remembrance of *Pickwick Papers*, his literary tastes went no further.

The boys studied under tutors, and until he was sixteen, Samuel had never studied formally outside of his own home. He passed the Cambridge junior local examination in 1858, and, in 1860, passed the senior examination. Samuel had wished to enter the ministry of the Church of England, but pressure was put upon him to turn his attention to business, since his father's lucrative iron works might depend upon him some day. Samuel resisted such suggestions, believing that he was destined for religious work.

When Samuel was sixteen, his parents felt that he needed to live with a tutor (a "crammer") so that he would be prepared for advanced education. At the tutor's home, Samuel lived with other boys, many of whom had failed in their formal studies or were behavior problems in one way or another. This experience brought him in contact for the first time with some of the "baser" elements of the youth of his day.

After a year's stay with the tutor, Samuel went on to study with the Reverend T. Hulme, who was motivated by high ideals in life and in education. He stimulated Samuel to think about the ethical bases of personal and social action, and he saw to it that Samuel was well prepared to enter Oxford.

In the fall of 1862, Samuel entered Wadham College, Oxford. Francis Barnett was not entirely happy about his son going to college, because he feared (in an exaggerated way) the evils of college living. Wadham College was chosen because of the conservative name it had achieved in politics as well as in morals. Samuel felt that he did not derive all that he might have from his college experience, primarily because there was no system of student guidance to direct his energies. He was certain, too, that he spent too much time with books and too little with people. "I made the mistake of using my time at Oxford to grind at books rather than to know men," he said later. Possibly his lack of social experiences led him later to stress such activities as being of prime importance in the development of personality.

Samuel took up rowing while at Oxford and was a substitute when the first-line men were incapacitated. His chief relaxation, however, was hiking. (Over the years, he would take innumerable trips on foot with his wife and friends throughout England and the Continent.) He seemed to be endowed with a "sixth sense" for direction, for he never got lost and sometimes took part in saving lost comrades.

Samuel was interested in religion at Oxford, but he disliked certain religious practices then prevalent, especially the undergraduate prayer meetings at which highly personal confessions were made publicly and where there was great stress placed upon emotions. His attention was on more practical matters, yet he never swerved from his choice of the ministry. He received his B.A. degree from Oxford in 1865 after three years of serious study, and he took second-class honors in law and history. His intellectual accomplishments were not meager, evidenced by the fact that he stayed on at Oxford for another year tutoring undergraduates. Then he accepted a position in Winchester as a master at the college. This postgraduate experience gave him some insight into the mechanics of schooling, which he would use later on many occasions.

With the money he had been able to save from teaching and some additional funds from his family, he set out in 1867 to visit America, a long-held goal. He visited New York, Boston, Philadelphia, Washington, Baltimore, Charleston, New Orleans, and other places, and since the Civil War had just ended, he came in contact with the bitterness of one region against the other, which characterized that period. His sympathies were with the North, although he did appreciate "the gentlemen's ways" of the Southern ex-slave owners. He also found in America the need for a radically different social philosophy, one that had as its aim the betterment of living conditions of the very poor. Samuel Barnett put the matter with his usual succinctness: "Born and nurtured in an atmosphere of Toryism, what I saw and heard there knocked all the Toryism out of me."

After he returned home, Samuel Barnett was ordained a deacon in the Established Church and assigned to work as a curate at St. Mary's church, London, under the charge of the Reverend W. H. Fremantle. A year later, he was ordained a priest of the Church of England. His career in the ministry had taken shape, and he preached his first sermon on February 9, 1867.

Barnett lived in a difficult time to preach the Gospel. The social conditions that surrounded him in London were disheartening to the young minister. Everywhere poverty was evident, bringing in its train the worst of human miseries. Disease was widely prevalent, and crime flourished without efficient prosecution (the police issued posters warning the populace against burglars). There were many groups or "societies" that were working for the relief of the needy: The Society for the Relief of Distress; The Strangers' Friend Society; The Society for the Suppression of Mendicity; The Society for Improving the Conditions of the Laboring Classes; and many others with similar purposes, but they were all more or less ineffective. In many instances they encouraged rather than hindered the very conditions that they sought to remedy. Thus, it was to a rather forlorn people that the Reverend Samuel Barnett, full of youthful enthusiasm, went to preach.

Barnett was not noted for outstanding or inspiring sermons. Like many ministers, he chose themes that interested himself, usually developing them on a high intellectual plane. He was scarcely able to speak to the common man of his time. Even his wife said that his sermons were "out of touch with life and 'difficult to follow.'" However, his failure to be a successful preacher belied his interest in people and in religion. His difficulty lay in the fact that he was so poorly able to communicate his real feelings and thoughts.

Barnett was a success in other aspects of his ministry. His efforts in teaching brought results. Of these, his fellow curate at St. Mary's, the Reverend A. S. W. Young, reported:

> He made a deep impression by his work in the school. The boys were his province; the girls mine. He might well have been content with giving Scripture lessons, but he must needs take up some other subject with the boys as well; and his history class became a noted feature. The teachers were all devoted to him and were always delighted to see him come in. His presence was an inspiration, and thrilled all the school with life and zeal. At his instance we held an amateur inspection of our own once a year, with the hearty goodwill of the teachers, who might have resented it, an examination to test the children's powers of thought and to bring out what was in their minds.
>
> The preparation of the boys for Confirmation fell to his share; and it was not limited to teaching them. It was a matter of close personal intercourse, and I often found one or two in his rooms.

With many of them he was the object of an abiding attachment, and I remember hearing from them that they had looked him up in Whitechapel, and what a pleasure it had been to both.[2]

He also worked with the men of the neighborhood in what today might be called a form of social-group work. Barnett established a club room for working men. The people who attended were very poor. No conditions for membership were laid down; the men simply came in the evenings to play dominoes and other games or to sit and chat with each other and with Barnett. Sometimes the conversation would become heated, and the members would call for comments by Barnett. At other times, he lectured on social themes to the men. Through this informal club, Barnett was able to understand the conditions that characterized that part of the city and gain first-hand knowledge of the people, their frustrations, and their aspirations.

Another of Barnett's interests was the Charity Organization Society being formed at this time under the direction of Octavia Hill. This organization was to take the place of most of the other formal efforts at charity. It became the standard in England and in the United States (through the initiating work of the Reverend Samuel Humphreys Gurteen of Buffalo) of the type of social welfare work that laid the foundations for modern social casework. One of Hill's first efforts, and one that Samuel Barnett supported, was organizing the existing helping services. In 1869, Hill brought together representatives of various relief-granting societies in London to share in joint planning. The meeting was a success. Members of different religious groups attended, and Hill was given the responsibility for the development of their mutual aims. The resulting Charity Organization Society coordinated the activities of the agencies, bringing each of them the benefits of mutual experience and planning. Barnett worked closely with Hill in the creation of the society.

On December 3, 1870, Samuel Barnett met his future wife, Henrietta O. Rowland, at a birthday party for Octavia Hill. Henrietta Rowland came from a wealthy family, and her interests were surprisingly similar to those of Hill. As a parish visitor to the poor for the Charity Organization Society, Rowland worked closely with Barnett for several years, helping him on several occasions on especially difficult problems. In February 1872, Samuel proposed marriage by letter. Henrietta was thoroughly surprised, or so she said. She openly disliked the clergy, and since he was twenty-seven and she was twenty at the time, she thought of him as a "kindly elderly gentleman." Perhaps his bald head and his shaggy beard helped create such an impression. Henrietta wrote back that she would like to wait for six months to see what developed before she gave her answer. The somewhat shy Barnett accepted her terms and waited patiently for the final day of reckoning. Fortunately for both, she decided to marry him, for they made an outstanding team.

In 1872, a charge near Oxford was offered to Barnett. In many ways, it was the sort of situation that he liked and for which he was suited. London, with its dense and downtrodden population, did not inherently attract him. He liked the rural life. But he felt that he should not make a decision that took only his own feelings into account. Therefore, he was susceptible to the suggestions of Hill and others that he remain in London where he was needed. Barnett and his wife (they were married in 1873) decided that they would like to have a charge in East London, the poorest part of the city.

It so happened about this time that St. Jude's, Whitechapel, fell vacant, and the bishop, knowing of the Barnetts' intentions, asked Barnett to accept it. In the bishop's letter is found the following frank comment on the vicissitudes of St. Jude's: "Do not hurry in your decision. It is the worst parish in my diocese, inhabited mainly by a criminal population, and one which has, I fear, been much corrupted by doles."

The Barnetts did not hurry in their decision. They visited the parish and found the views of the bishop confirmed. The church itself was in disuse. Part of it was crumbling, and the inside was dark, dirty, and cold. The living conditions of the neighborhood were much worse. The schools were shut and the beer-shops were full. The children were worn, ragged, and ill-mannered. According to Henrietta Barnett, "Vice and woe and lawlessness were written across their faces." Surely there was little in St. Jude's parish to attract a young man and his bride, except opportunity for service. After a brief vacation at Christmas in Bristol, the Barnetts returned to London to say their farewells at St. Mary's and to begin their new work at St. Jude's.

Samuel Barnett had thought that his main work was the direct preaching of religion, but the first Sunday there were only six parishioners in their pews at St. Jude's, and they were there essentially to get a handout for their faithfulness. Most of those who came to the church in the early days did so to receive financial help after the service or as payment for assistance already given. Barnett wanted his people to think of worship as a privilege unattached to material advantage. It was a long time, however, before they were capable of such an attitude.

The work at St. Jude's was discouraging indeed, but the newlyweds were filled with boundless and indefatigable courage. They accepted the people as they were and sought to introduce them to various advantages. As the people saw what the Barnetts intended, they responded. In time, some success was achieved, and by the end of the first year, the new parson was able to report the following on attendances and activities:

> The congregation has risen to about thirty in the mornings, and fifty to one hundred in the evenings; . . . a children's service has been started, and . . . a mixed choir is under training; . . . the schools have been opened for boys and girls together of whom 142 are on the register; . . . adult classes have been started in French, German, Latin, arithmetic, composition, and drawing which have attracted fifty students; . . . a mothers' meeting has been begun, a nurse and a mission-society initiated, a penny bank opened, a lending library organized, a pension scheme inaugurated, a flower show held, concerts and entertainments given, oratorios rendered in Church, lady visitors set to work, and last but not least, a system of relief for the poor thought out and established.[3]

The Barnetts deemed their activities at St. Jude's to be thoroughly religious. They were not interested in social improvement simply in and for itself. As Barnett put it, "The end we have in view is that every one may know God as a Father." Always, he felt that he was decreasing sin rather than human suffering. The success of the first year, moreover, was not considered by the Barnetts as being spectacular or even accept-

able. They were disturbed that they had not been more successful. They visited other churches, as time permitted, to examine
their programs and to see what was lacking in their own. They
found nothing elsewhere that solved their problems, but they
also did not lose heart. "We must wait and watch," said Samuel,
"with open eyes for the coming of the Spirit which will guide us
to new ways."

His labors with the poor in his parish exemplify the experimental spirit that characterized Barnett. He was discontented
with the previous ways of handling the needs of the poor. He
thought the methods of the Charity Organization Society to be
the best available. Three principles stood out in his conception
of assistance to the poor: "The equal capacity of all to enjoy the
best, the superiority of quiet ways over those of striving and
crying, character as the one thing needful, are the truths on
which we take our stand." These principles worked out in his
relief efforts in the following way:

> I will tell you our plan. When someone comes begging, I myself see
> him, talk to him and send him to the Charity Organization Society,
> who investigate the case, not so much with a view of finding out
> the applicant's deserts as to show us, from his past life, the best
> means of helping him in the present. A committee, composed of
> Mr. Hicks, Mrs. Barnett, Mr. Rowland, Mr. Polyblank, and myself,
> meet on Friday evenings, before which the man is summoned to
> appear. Perhaps it proves to be the best plan to give him efficient
> assistance in the shape of a substantial gift, or a loan; perhaps the
> most hopeful way of helping him will be by a stern refusal. In
> neither case does our watchful care cease. When there has been no
> interference we have seen success attend our efforts—the family
> has commenced to save; the children sent to school; the girls to
> service; but when visitors, no less kind, but less wise, have come in
> with their doles of sixpences, or their promise of help, we have seen
> the chains of idleness, carelessness, and despair fall again around
> the family. . . . Money pauperises the people; time, given as a child
> of God to those who, if degraded, are still our brothers, will ennoble
> and strengthen them.[4]

Barnett did not concentrate only on the perplexing problem
of relief; he also saw the larger problem of social justice. He was

certain that the very existence of poverty required certain social revisions, and he called upon the upper classes to take a more intelligent and spiritual interest in the needs of the lower classes. In 1878, he stated the proposition as follows:

> I wish charitable people could become more sensible of the injustice done by unwise relief. It is often said, it is best to err on the side of giving; seeing what I see I am disposed to say it is best to err on the side of refusing. The damage to the body of the applicant is less real and more distant than the damage to his spirit. We cannot, however, expect to welcome a charity fitting the knowledge of the present day, till money gifts cease to be an insurance against the discontent of the poor, a propitiation for the enjoyment of luxuries, or a relief to the giver. Gifts must be the expression of real and intelligent interest. Far then from wishing to stand in the way of relief, I appeal for more relief. . . . If this East End is to be helped, it must be by those Christ-like enough to give their best to those that ask.[5]

Barnett's demands for justice were not one-sided. He required a high standard of morality from those who came to him for help and became indignant if an able-bodied man begged for money. On one occasion, his wife observed him throw a much bigger man out of their house. When she asked why, he said, "He lied as well as begged and deserved what he got." While Barnett had a high standard of morality for those in need, he sometimes did not apply it with the understanding of human behavior that has become available in more recent years through the advances of the human sciences. Occasionally, his high moral standards became instruments of injustice and misunderstanding.

The Barnetts attacked the social evils that surrounded them and their neighbors one by one and tried cooperatively to build a better community in a variety of ways. For example, the district was especially impoverished musically. Although neither of the Barnetts could carry a tune, they realized the meaning that music can have for people, so they helped organize various singing groups. When Handel's "Messiah" was sung for the first time in the parish in 1874, the people were incredulous, but gradually they learned to love good music and to perform it.

From the first, outstanding persons were invited to the parish to deliver lectures on popular subjects. During one winter (1879), there were lectures on Carlyle, Milton, Spinoza, Chaucer, John Brown, Savonarola, Wesley, Marcus Aurelius, Epictetus, and others. But the people of the parish were not very interested. Although the lectures continued, their effectiveness was seriously doubted by their sponsor on more than one occasion.

Mothers' meetings were also established, which brought together the women of the parish to discuss important subjects of the day. Out of these meetings came the Maternity Society, a benevolent association intended to help expectant mothers finance their maternity care and obtain information about caring for children.

Religion in its more formal aspects was not neglected in St. Jude's parish. Barnett organized a society of communicants; the object of this group was to study the value of Holy Communion. While the purpose of the group sounds somewhat stuffy today, there is reason to believe that Barnett organized the group around devotional ends that required considerable study and scholarship.

There were many opportunities for direct, personal help to people in the parish. Especially was there need for assistance to young girls. Henrietta Barnett became interested in this aspect of the church's program and founded the Metropolitan Association for Befriending Young Servants. As the work grew in volume and importance, she required additional help, most of whom were volunteers. The girls who were assisted by the association presented many of the problems that currently come before a children's aid society—neglect by parents, alcoholism at home, lack of constructive recreation, ill health, inadequate employment possibilities, and so on. Some of the girls could be helped without taking them from their own homes, but in some cases it was deemed best to remove a girl from her home. The girls were not placed in foster homes, as that term is used today, but worked as "young servants" in homes known to the association. This arrangement was not ideal, but it did represent one attempt to assist young girls who were in dire need. In 1889, the number of girls so placed was 2,350.

The plight of mentally deficient girls also impressed

Barnett. He realized quickly that the city environment was not suited to their well-being, and he worked hard to secure Harrow Cottage in the country as a home for these girls.

Not all girls in need could be accepted by the various facilities established by the Barnetts. There were many who had to look elsewhere. Barnett believed that some of them might emigrate to Australia to strive toward a normal life. In 1885, fourteen of the girls who were having special difficulty with their parents were helped by the parish (and the government) to set sail for Australia. In the years that followed, the population of Australia was increased by infants named for the Barnetts.

The way in which Samuel Barnett established special services for his neighbors bears consideration, for it shows that he was not prone to decide what theoretically could be of help and then to force it on his friends. Rather, he allowed his plans to grow out of the situations he confronted from day to day. The program of St. Jude's was somewhat lacking in a strong central administrative organization due to the fact that it grew piecemeal.

Good housing also became a principal concern of Barnett, who realized that many of the social and health problems of the area were caused by poor housing conditions. To him, the situation had three aspects: to get inadequate houses condemned by a medical officer; to induce the authorities to set upon the condemnation; and to find wealthy and philanthropic individuals or companies that would be willing to build suitable homes for the poor. The first was somewhat difficult; the second was much more so; the third was the hardest of all.

Through the sale of some of Mrs. Barnett's jewels, a large building was purchased, one that formerly had been used by prostitutes. Cleaned up and remodeled, it was opened to fifty families of the neighborhood. The Barnetts put no condition or test upon the applicants except that none should gain a livelihood by prostitution. This procedure illustrates the curious blending of moral and objective factors at work in the lives of the Barnetts. Through their efforts, several philanthropists became interested in the Whitechapel section of London and invested their money in slum clearance. This work took years to accomplish and was secured only through the expenditure of great creative energy.

Several visitors of note came to St. Jude's as its reputation spread. Princess Alice of Hesse toured the church and community in 1876. The Barnetts were pleased, for they realized that the princess could publicize the activities of the parish. Sir Richard Gross, then home secretary, also paid the Barnetts a visit. This was heralded as momentous since it amounted to a distinguished recognition on the part of the government itself of the growing work of Whitechapel.

Samuel Barnett spent some time in securing adequate play space for the children of the neighborhood. A small piece of land called New Court was turned into a garden and became one of the highlights of the community. He also secured the Quakers' Burial Ground as a place for public recreation.

Granting financial assistance to needy persons upon request was something Barnett did not like to do. He felt that it led to many injustices. For one thing, he believed that the source of human economic improvement lay within the individual. He urged all persons to try to improve themselves.

Barnett also argued against "outdoor relief" (assistance given to individuals and families who reside in their own homes rather than in an institution). He advocated that relief recipients be given assistance through institutions created for them. He argued that giving help to people who lived at home leads to excessive financial support, dries up the "fountains of charity," weakens human relations, and relaxes private initiative. In his words, "Out-relief is a sort of monster which destroys its own parent, the local rates from which it is drawn."

The work of the Barnetts and others at St. Jude's represents one of the most socially and religiously progressive movements that occurred in England at the time. Motivated by religion, they sought by every means that they could devise to show their concern for people. They believed that everything that exalted a person was beneficial and that everything that debased a person was evil. They were not rigidly bound by theological restrictions, but they permitted their conservative theology to become the source for unusual social ideas as to how men, women, and children might be helped. Theirs truly was a humanitarian conception of religion—religion as a way of life. The Barnetts' efforts were part of a more general attack on the social evils of the East End of London. Among others, William Booth, the founder of the Salvation Army, also worked in this neighborhood.

Samuel Barnett's work at St. Jude's entitles him to a large place in the development of social Christianity in the modern period; but he was better known for his founding of Toynbee Hall, the first settlement house. This work embodied the approach to human problems that he constructed so patiently at St. Jude's.

The Barnetts visited Oxford for the first time two years after their marriage. They conceived of the young men of Oxford as comprising an important source of manpower for the development of their plans for the most impoverished section of London. Henrietta Barnett later told how the associations and plans formed at Oxford were the basis for the creation of Toynbee Hall:

"If men, cultivated, young, thinking men, could only know of those things they would be altered," I used to say, with girlish faith in human goodness—a faith which years have not shaken; and in the spring of 1875 we went to Oxford, partly to tell about the poor, partly to enjoy "Eights Week" with a group of young friends. Our party was planned by Miss Toynbee, whom I had met when at school, and whose brother Arnold was then an undergraduate at Pembroke. Our days were filled by the hospitality with which Oxford still rejoices its guests; but in the evenings we used to drop quietly down the river with two or three earnest men, or sit long and late in our lodgings in Turl, and discuss the mighty problems of poverty and the people. How vividly my husband and I can recall each and all of the first group of "thinking men," so ready to take up enthusiasms in their boyish strength—Arnold Toynbee, Sidney Ball, W. H. Forbes, Arthur Hoare, Leonard Montefiore, Alfred Milner, Philip Gell, John Falk, G. E. Underhill, Ralph Whitehead, Lewis Nettleship! Some of these are still here and caring for the people, but others have passed behind the veil, where perhaps earth's sufferings are explicable.

We used to ask each undergraduate as he developed interest to come and stay in Whitechapel, and see for himself. And they came, some to spend a few weeks, some for the Long Vacation, while others, as they left the University and began their life's work, took lodgings in East London, and felt all the fascination of its strong pulse of life, hearing, as those who listen always may, the hushed, unceasing moans underlying the cry which ever heard by an unheeding public.[6]

The young men and women came to visit St. Jude's and were inspired by its accomplishments and possibilities. Some wanted to observe and ponder the question of poverty. Some came out of curiosity that there should be conditions so vile as to distort the common humanity of those who lived there. Others came to help. These fitted themselves into the existing activities of the church and lent themselves to the development of others. Barnett's teaching interest was heightened, for in the volunteers he had a core of intelligent young people that he might lead to strengthen the work he had begun.

The Barnetts continued their trips to Oxford, where their host was the reknowned Greek scholar, Benjamin Jowett. At this time at Oxford and elsewhere, there was a great social stirring over the injustice that characterized life for many of the poor in England and in other lands. The writings of Henry George (the American advocate of the single tax) and others sensitized many to the depth of social evil and of the complexity of the measures required for a solution. Many Oxford students turned to activities that would help make life more tolerable for the poor. A group of these students met in the rooms of a fellow student, Sidney Ball, to discuss ways they could be of help. According to a report of the meeting, they wanted to support an effort different from an out-and-out religious institution. They knew that Barnett had been experimenting with new methods of helping people and invited him to one of their meetings. This meeting was held in the rooms of another student, Cosmo Lang, who later became the archbishop of York. Later in life, Lang, recorded his remembrances of the meeting that gave birth to the settlement house movement:

> Our conscience felt the rebuke of the contrast between the wealth of inheritance and opportunity stored up in Oxford and the poverty of the life lived amid the mean streets and monotonous labour of East London. In a vague way we felt the claim of that poverty on our wealth. Could anything practical be done to meet it? The

answer to that question was important. If it had not come, the movement might have drifted into mere vague sentiment or academic talk. It came that November evening. The Vicar of St. Jude's Whitechapel, Mr. Barnett, then in the prime of his life, in his fortieth year, read a paper in which he sketched the plan of a "University Settlement in East London." "Something," he said, "must be done to share with the poor the best gifts." Let University men become the neighbours of the working poor, sharing their life, thinking out their problems, learning from them the lessons of patience, fellowship, self-sacrifice, and offering in response the help of their own education and friendship. "This," he said, "will alleviate the sorrow and misery born of class division and indifference. It will bring classes into relation; it will lead them to know and learn of one another, and those to whom it is given will give."

I well remember the effect of those words, or rather of his personality. There was no gush, no exaggeration, no claim to provide a solution of the social problem. There was simply the quiet and earnest appeal of an Oxford man busy in the service of the people to other Oxford men to "come and see," to learn the needs by sharing the life of that, to us, strange and dim outer world of East London.[7]

The following students pledged their aid on that day to the establishing of a university settlement: Bolton King, P. Lyttelton Gell, J. E. Kelsall, F. S. Marvin, J. A. Spender, and E. T. Cook.

The six men found other supporters, and the growing group incorporated themselves, raised some money, and began to plan the opening of the settlement. The manner in which the settlement finally came to be known as Toynbee Hall was explained by Mrs. Barnett:

The 10th of March, 1884, was a Sunday, and Balliol Chapel was filled with a splendid body of men who had come in loving memory of Arnold Toynbee, on the anniversary of his death. Mr. Jowett had asked my husband to preach to them, and they listened intently, separating almost silently at the chapel porch, filled by the aspiration to copy Arnold in caring much, if not doing much, for those who had fallen by the way or were "vacant of our glorious gains." . . .

As I sat on that Sunday afternoon in the chapel, one of the few women among the crowd of strong-brained, clean-living men, the thought flashed to me, "Let us call the Settlement Toynbee Hall." To Mr. Bolton King, the honorary secretary of the committee, had come the same idea, and it finding favour with the committee, our new Settlement received its name before a brick was laid or the plans concluded.

On the first day of July, 1884, the workmen began to pull down the old Industrial School, and to adapt such of it as was possible for the new uses; and on Christmas Eve, 1884, the first settlers, Mr. H. D. Leigh of Corpus, and Mr. C. H. Grinling of Hertford, slept in Toynbee Hall, quickly followed by thirteen residents, some of whom had been living in the neighbourhood of Whitechapel.[8]

Arnold Toynbee (the uncle of historian Arnold Toynbee) was one of those young men who was interested in the movement from its beginning. He had come to the Barnetts at St. Jude's to spend his summer vacations. He spent himself without stint in helping those residing in the neighborhood of Whitechapel, though he was frail physically, and the neighborhood life was hard on him. He and the Barnetts took several vacations together in order to escape the oppressiveness of conditions in London. Three years after his first contact at Whitechapel, he married, and four years later, at the age of thirty-one, he died. Everyone judged Toynbee to be a man of great promise. He was a thorough intellectual, who faced the current social and economic issues with considerable force. At the time of his death, he vigorously opposed the views of Henry George. He spent his energies on some of the knottiest problems of the time. It was no wonder, then, that there was general agreement on a name for the new settlement. Toynbee Hall was dedicated to the type of spirit Arnold Toynbee had shown in his all-too-short life.

Samuel Barnett believed in the democratic administration of the settlement. Toynbee Hall began with thirteen residents, persons who lived in the hall and led the activities of the settlement. Barnett and the residents comprised what was called the Grand Committee. Meeting frequently, it made decisions about almost every aspect of the life of the hall. The residents were asked not to seek for uniformity in ideas or actions, but rather to try to cultivate their differences within the bounds of human limitations and social desirability. They could room by

themselves or with their friends. They ate together and discussed common problems with each other individually and with
the whole group.

The residents also met with Barnett at least once a week. He
was their practical and spiritual adviser. He believed in his
co-workers, and they were impressed by the strength of his mind
and character. Barnett constantly asked for "positive ideas." To
these he always brought the cool light of reason, asking that
every proposal be "practical." He was usually able, despite his
critical acumen, to find some positive element in a proposal. On
his wall he had placed a legend that summarized his spirit: "Fear
not to sow because of the birds." He was a valiant sower,
scattering his ideas over the wide stretches of the city of
London.

Barnett introduced at Toynbee Hall the ideas that had been
in practice at St. Jude's. They enabled many to gain a new
understanding of the role of organized religion in society. But
the church's sponsorship was a handicap in some ways. The
activities that Barnett and his co-workers initiated were valid in
themselves—without any support from the church. Moreover,
they were not always received in a positive way by those who
disdained the church. The work of Toynbee Hall in maintaining
and improving community relations also was more acceptable
to some since it was based more or less upon the acceptance of
the entire community.

Barnett believed that the poor in his district needed education. He felt that his neighbors could not better themselves
unless they knew more about themselves, their world, and ways
they could earn a steady income. He also realized that any
program of social improvement should be based on popular
education. He had applied this principle at St. Jude's from the
very first. There, he helped organize classes in literature, drawing, French, German, bookkeeping, singing, violin, shorthand,
carpentering, Latin, arithmetic, and physiology. Similar classes
were started at Toynbee Hall. Some were taught by the residents, but volunteer teachers also were used.

Hundreds of men and women, young and old, benefitted
from these classes. As the numbers of persons attracted to them
increased, new courses were added. The number and variety of
courses grew in time until they paralleled some adult education

programs in our major cities of today. These courses later were related to the London School Board and became the model for centers throughout London and elsewhere.

There was some cost connected with the giving of the courses, and Toynbee Hall did not have sufficient financial backing to bear the entire expense. In 1888, therefore, students were invited to fix their own fees for the courses. It was agreed that one shilling would be charged for registration, but beyond that each student decided how much he or she could afford to pay. This measure not only increased the income of the hall, but encouraged the students to take their work more seriously. They also felt that they were not being given charity.

In 1885, in line with Sir Edmund Currie's ideas and the London School Board's support, Toynbee Hall became the center for a teacher-training project. The board perceived that the hall and its educational program could be used to develop young teachers. Barnett also was interested in training teachers in other places, notably in universities. He drew to him a number of people, most of whom were leaders in British education, to form a Teachers' University Association, which had as its purpose the increase in number and quality of teachers.

Barnett was instrumental in forming the Toynbee societies, which organized young men and women for the study of various topics. All were formed as independent groups; they met their own expenses and followed their own procedures. Some groups were quite small, but others attracted dozens of people at a time. The list of such societies indicates their breadth of interest: Adam Smith Club; Antiquarian Society; Art Students' Club; Athletic Association; Camera Club; Chess Club; Economic Club; Education Reform League; Elizabethian Literary Society; Ethical Society; Football Club; Guild of Compassion; Leonardo Sketching Club; Life-saving Club; Limehouse and Popular Students' Union; London Pupil-Teachers' Debating Society; Library Readers' Union; Literary Association; Literary and Discussion Society; Natural History Society; Nursing Society; Old Students' Association; Orchestral Society; Philosophical Society; Popular Musical Union; Sanitary Aid Society; Scientific Reading Society; Shakespeare Society; Student's Union; St. John Ambulance Brigade; Swimming Club; Teachers' University Association; Workmen's Travelling Club.[9]

From the earliest days in Whitechapel, Barnett wanted to build a library that could be used by those with no other access to books. As early as 1876, his parish library was a success. It had over six hundred volumes; about one hundred books were exchanged weekly, showing that the library met a real need in the community. In time, as the library came under the auspices of Toynbee Hall, it expanded. In 1888, there were 3,878 volumes; in 1889, 4,353; in 1892, 5,803; and in 1900, 7,449. Most of these books were gifts, as there were no funds for buying books. Samuel Barnett was hopeful that in time the hall's library might be supported by the city government. The Free Public Libraries Act was before Parliament and was passed in the local election by a vote of four to one. One of its conditions was the voluntary raising of funds to erect a building to house the books that public money would provide. It fell to Barnett to raise enough money to meet the terms of the act. He worked hard on this project, and his efforts were well rewarded when, in addition to other gifts, J. Passmore Edwards provided $30,000. The project was assured.

The architectural planning of the library building was also a responsibility Barnett shared. One of the interesting features of the building was its adjoining natural history museum. For the section of London in which it was housed, this constituted a real triumph of scholarly interest over practical demands. In time, the museum demonstrated that it was not only worthwhile from an academic viewpoint, but also a success with the neighborhood people. But the building and the museum were not Barnett's only concern. He realized that the chief asset of a library, aside from its books, was its staff, and he promoted the professional training of librarians. Throughout his life, he encouraged the use of trained personnel by libraries. His views on this subject, as well as others connected with libraries, influenced the official board of the public libraries system in London, on which he served for many years.

The work at Toynbee Hall inspired other projects of a similar nature. Three years after the founding of the hall, a residential house for students, called Wadham House, was opened. According to Barnett, it had three chief purposes: it would enable each resident to pursue some line of study, to make a positive adjustment to the community of the other residents, and to do something every week, no matter how small, to help "the ignorant, the sad, or the sinning." Eighteen men took up residence. They came to know the conditions of that part of London and learned how to apply their minds to the problems they found.

Barnett assisted through the years in the establishment of a number of other and more formally religious settlements: Caius, 1887; St. Hilda's, for women, 1889; Mansfield House, 1890; Bermondsey Settlement, 1891; Canning Town, 1892; Browning Hall, 1895; Cambridge House, 1896; and Passmore Edwards, 1896. In 1887, Jane Addams of Chicago visited Toynbee Hall, and in 1889 she returned to learn more about the hall. Soon after, she founded the famed Hull House in Chicago, which in some ways led the settlement house movement throughout the world in the quality and variety of its ideas and activities. In 1891, when the Barnetts traveled to America, they stayed with Addams in Hull House. Henrietta Barnett opened the art exhibition of Hull House on that occasion, and Samuel Barnett gave an address on the place of the settlement house in society.

The settlement house movement grew more rapidly in the United States than in England. In 1913, only forty-six settlements were reported in England, while about four hundred were in existence in the United States. In America, the term settlement house was applied to some organizations that could not meet the original terms of Toynbee Hall; but even so, there were more bona fide settlements in the United States than in England. In England, as early as 1896, the Barnetts organized a Union of Settlements to coordinate and enrich their programs. In the United States, the National Federation of Settlements and Neighborhood Centers is the corresponding organization.

One of the basic tenets of the early settlement house movement was that no one should receive a salary for his work. This principle has not been followed in recent years because of a change in the motivation for leadership. Originally, no one connected with a settlement house received pay. The Barnetts adhered to this rule. The salary that Samuel Barnett received as warden of Toynbee Hall was turned over to the hall to help meet its expenses. The fact that no one received financial payment for services enabled the settlements to provide a relatively extensive program without the drain of the most costly of organizational expenses, that of staff.

Settlements were largely founded by men, although women soon became equally important to their operation. The participation of women in social service work has a long history, but it received a boost of no small value in the settlement house movement. The work of Henrietta Barnett, for example, cannot rightly be separated from that of her husband in the growth of Toynbee Hall. Within the hall were other women who devoted themselves to the work as she did.

The development of Toynbee Hall and the attack on the social problems surrounding it benefitted from the interest Barnett had in social research. Barnett realized that it was necessary to build his programs on a solid foundation of facts as well as on the strong motive of charity. One of the first efforts to understand the conditions that the hall was seeking to meet was undertaken by Charles Booth. His book *Life and Labour of the People of London* (in nine volumes) is a classic in social research. It constitutes one of the first efforts at a scientific appraisal of the social conditions of a depressed area.

One of the results of Booth's work was the establishment of the Arnold Toynbee Trust, which allowed the continuation of such research as had been pioneered by Booth and the publication of the findings. Some of the books made possible by the trust indicate by their titles the types of problems that were to be found in East London: *Inquiry into the Unemployed*, by A. V. Woodsworth and Viscount FitzHarris; *The Jew in London*, by H. S. Lewis and C. Russell; *Problems of Unemployment in the London Building Trades*, by N. B. Dearle; *The Lord on Police Court Today and Tomorrow*, by Hugh R. P. Gamon; and *Studies of Boy Life in Our Cities*, edited by E. J. Urwick.

The poor in the Whitechapel neighborhood often needed legal advice. On many occasions, they had legal cases for which they were unable to gain redress without help. The Barnetts informally aided many by providing the services of their lawyer friends. But the amount of such need was greater than could be handled by unorganized means. So, in 1889, a Tenants' Defense Committee was formed, which acted as arbiter of the problems of the poor. It acted in effect as a court. Samuel Barnett served as chairman, and the committee consisted of a lawyer, a resident, and an associate. The aggrieved parties could bring their problem before the committee and ask for advice but had to agree beforehand to the decision given by the committee. In time (1914), laws were passed that provided for legal assistance before the Royal Courts of Justice.

Labor disputes were almost as common in East London as personal problems requiring legal help. The founder of Toynbee Hall always affirmed his interest in the existence and strengthening of labor unions. He saw in them a means of protecting the poor, who often were penalized personally and as a group because of their lack of organization. In some of the major strikes, Barnett had a responsible share in bringing about equitable solutions.

The possibilities of adult education were also readily grasped by Barnett. From the time that he left Oxford as a student, he felt that the university should hold a more vital place in the development of the intellectual resources of the nation. He sought at least two developments: the reform of the financial and educational practices in the universities (mainly Oxford and Cambridge) and the extension of adult education facilities to include persons who could not afford to attend one of the universities. On the first point, he investigated Oxford and found that there was a wide disparity in the money spent for various activities by the member colleges. One college, for example, spent about $6,000 for servants for 118 undergraduates; another spent $2,000 for 70 students. One provided chapel services for its students for about $750 a year, while others spent as much as $5,000. He accused the university of providing large amounts of money for scholarships to only one class of the nation's people. He strongly believed that poverty should be no bar to securing a higher education.

In regard to his second point, Barnett believed that much of the money saved from extravagant and erroneous spending by the universities could be utilized in the development of university extension courses that would reach the masses of people who could benefit from them. In Toynbee Hall there was an actual demonstration of the possibilities of such education, and he constantly referred to it as a model.

Carrying out his plan for adult education was not easy. The

universities did not respond to his suggestions and criticisms. They believed that they were successful in the type of program they offered, and they should not change it. So Barnett turned to some sympathetic leaders in English education and urged with them the appointment of a royal commission to investigate the universities and to evaluate the possibility of extending higher education. At first, the efforts of this reformist group were not heeded; but, when they gained sufficient strength, Parliament had to listen. Under this pressure, Oxford came forth with a plan to investigate itself. Lord Curzon, chancellor of the university, appointed a committee that studied the issues raised by Barnett. The effect of its work was to confirm in the main the points that he had made. Lord Curzon's book, *University Reform*, published in 1909, shows that the agitation instigated by Barnett brought rich fruits. The university also took steps to extend its intellectual leadership by bringing its resources to persons who were unable to come to it. Barnett's work in creating new facilities for nonuniversity people was felt beyond Oxford. In many cities workers' groups and bands of private citizens formulated plans; the resulting schools have been called "peoples' universities." Barnett's contribution on this score would in itself entitle him to a place in the history of the British people.

In the winter of 1889, Henrietta Barnett contracted pneumonia, and when she had recovered sufficiently, the Barnetts decided to take a long trip. They embarked on a sea voyage to India by way of the Mediterranean and the Suez Canal. The Barnetts remained four months in India, visiting various cultural centers from one end of that immense land to the other. In the spring, they continued on to China, Japan, Canada, and the United States. They spent ten weeks in America, staying part of the time at Hull House in Chicago. Arriving home, the Barnetts felt refreshed and informed as they never had before and plunged into their work with new zeal and energy.

Art was continually cherished and encouraged at Toynbee Hall. Classes were set up to aid those who were interested, and exhibitions were held from time to time to show the community what had been accomplished. In time, Barnett felt that something more formal and effective was needed in Whitechapel to bring home the importance of art as an extension of the meaning of human experience. He strongly urged the erection of a gallery that would have several kinds of exhibitions, including modern pictures, objects illustrative of trades or periods from the national museums, and work done by local children or by the pupils of the technical schools of the neighborhood. It wasn't easy to convince donors of the wisdom of the project, so a committee was formed to help Barnett raise the money. Architectural plans for the gallery were drawn up, and a site was selected. On March 12, 1901, over 200,000 people attended the first exhibition; it was a great success. In the years that followed, thousands of people came to the gallery to view the collections assembled there, and artists who otherwise might have been overlooked had an opportunity to bring their works to a wide public.

After some twenty years at St. Jude's and Toynbee Hall, Barnett received an offer of the canonry at Bristol. He accepted for many reasons. The Barnetts were not in good health. In their twenty years at Whitechapel, they had poured out their energies in a way that would certainly have downed a couple with less vitality. Another reason undoubtedly was that the move was an advancement for Barnett, for the canonry at Bristol was an important post. It well might have been the start of an even more responsible career. The Barnetts also were interested in Bristol because it was Samuel Barnett's early home, and throughout his life he kept a particular attachment for that city.

As the canon of Bristol, Samuel Barnett continued many of the interests he had developed in Whitechapel. His sermons reflected his background; they aimed to show the plight of the poor and the resources of the Christian faith for their problems. For example, Barnett delivered six lectures on the topic "Christ and Workmen's Problems," which reveal in their titles the nature of Barnett's theological and social thinking: Christ in Relation to Wages and Work; Christ in Relation to Short Hours; Christ in Relation to the Educational Ladder; Christ in Relation to Women's Position; Christ in Relation to the Sick and Old; and Christ in Relation to the Unemployed. These lectures and similar activities did not always please those in positions of power in the English church, but they struck a responsive chord in the hearts of the people who heard him.

Barnett held the canonry at Bristol for thirteen years. In that time, he engaged in surveying the conditions that affected the welfare of the people, organized and planned means of improving living conditions, and promoted the ideals of social Christianity that inspired him in all his work. In his later years, Barnett broke with the charity organization movement, of which he had been one of the principal founders and leaders, because he believed the movement was no longer a progressive, adaptive organization that was willing to modify its program and principles to meet changing circumstances. He pointed out, in 1895, that the organization that was supposed to eliminate the overlapping of social welfare agencies in London had itself become administratively top-heavy and fragmentized. At that time there were forty district committees and bodies of workers who were responsible for the administration of relief for the poor. This state of affairs tended to defeat the very aims that had brought the movement into existence.

Barnett also felt that the leadership of the movement "idolized" certain solutions to poverty without taking into account their practicality. Thus, the movement's leaders spoke about "independence of state relief," but Barnett now saw that it was not possible for the problem of poverty to be solved on a basis of voluntary initiative. He believed that circumstances had changed in the twenty years of his experience with the society, and that private enterprise alone could not solve widespread unemployment. In other words, he was much more willing to include state participation and responsibility in social welfare work matters than were the leaders of the Charity Organization Society.

Barnett also attacked other stereotyped slogans that were offered by the society. "Savings" had been such a slogan, and the society stressed the importance of the poor saving as much money as they could in times of prosperity so that they could maintain their economic stability in times of economic depression. The leaders of the society (and originally Barnett, too) believed that accumulated savings on the part of the poor provided one of the best means of vitiating the work of the society. But in later life Barnett saw clearly that the argument was spotty; it was not possible for the poor to save for they were the last to benefit in times of prosperity and the first to suffer from retrenchment. As they "prospered," they also faced the debts that they had accumulated during periods of unemployment. And as they secured larger incomes, they needed to supply themselves and their families with necessities that had been denied them previously.

Barnett advocated an extension of government benefits for the unemployed and impoverished and called for improved methods of distributing public money to the poor. He also saw that changes would have to be made in the general social structure of England to abolish the condition of citizens who seemed perpetually to be dependent upon the charity of the rich or the government.

He implemented his intentions in various ways. Among other things, he became, the chairman of the Poor Law Board for Whitechapel, and through his agitation, the Poor Law Commission was appointed in 1905. He was asked to serve on this commission, but declined because of the pressure of other duties. When the Pensions Act, passed in 1908, granting universally a pension to persons at the age of sixty-five, he rejoiced to see another successful realization of his views. But his desire to see "automatic relief" had to wait a while longer before becoming fact. "Automatic relief" meant a version of what is now known in England and elsewhere as the welfare state. Benefits were to be supplied automatically, that is, without the qualification of need or any other attribute. Barnett advocated as "automatic relief" free breakfasts to all children at elementary schools, free medical care, national registry offices free alike to employers and employed, free art galleries, libraries, and swimming facilities, "free fresh air," free, that is, from pollution, cheap if not free transit, and universal pensions. His advocacy of a small "national authority" to be responsible for the welfare of the people of England has not to this date been achieved in just the terms that he laid down. Today, there are at least four national ministries holding welfare responsibility in England.

In his later years, Barnett divided his time between his duties at Bristol and at Whitechapel. Both of these concerns added greatly to the physical strain which at times confined him to bed. When in June of 1906 he was offered the position of canon of Westminster Abbey, he felt he should accept for many of the same reasons he had left Whitechapel for Bristol. The offer of the post was one of the highest recognitions possible from his church for a lifetime of service to the poor. Although in poor health, he accepted and was installed, and it was during his stay at Westminster that the coronation of George V was held. Oxford granted Barnett a Doctor of Civil Laws degree, an honor that he cherished above all others, for Oxford held a special place in his feelings, and in 1913 he was appointed as sub-dean of the Abbey, another distinction that brought him great satisfaction.

Toynbee Hall continued to prosper. During the Second World War, parts of the hall were severely damaged, but this damage was repaired and new facilities were joined to the old. New responsibilities also were assumed through the years. The Council of Citizens of East London established its headquarters at Toynbee Hall, and many East End organizations met there. Toynbee Art and Theater clubs were established, along with an extensive program for the elderly residents of the surrounding area. Today, experimentation in programs also goes on. Professional social work projects assist unmarried mothers who wish to keep their children, and the hall is seeking to apply new methods to meet the problems of those who are "down and out." Some young adults also receive counseling while they live in the hall.

A Barnett Fellowship was created in 1923 with funds jointly raised in England and the United States "with the object of establishing habitual communication between members of Oxford and Cambridge and other British and North American universities and members of the wage-earning class in any industrial community, and also of encouraging general interest in industrial and economic subjects and in social service." The funds are administered by a board of trustees, with headquarters at Toynbee Hall.

On June 17, 1913, Samuel Barnett succumbed to a long illness, but to the end, he continued to hold out hope for the future. "Do you believe in immortality?" he was asked by his wife during his last days.

"I can imagine life on no other basis," was his response.

His funeral service was conducted by his request, not in the Abbey, but in St. Jude's—a fitting place for a man who had given so much to enrich the life of that part of London. In time, a tablet was placed on a wall of the Abbey to commemorate the work of the man who truly loved God and his fellow men. Prominent on the tablet are these words:

> Believing that we are all members one of another he labored unceasingly to unite men in the service of God and by his counsel and example inspired many to seek for themselves and for the nation the things that are eternal.

Chapter Four
William Booth
(1827–1912)

Asked a few months before his death, if he would put into a sentence the secret as he saw it, of all the blessings which had attended him during his seventy years of service, The General replied: "Well, if I am to put it into one sentence, I would say that I made up my mind that God Almighty should have all there was of William Booth."[1]

In October 1965, the one-hundredth anniversary of the founding of the Salvation Army was celebrated around the world. In London, envoys of seventy countries in which the Army serves gathered for ceremonies in Royal Albert Hall. Queen Elizabeth was in attendance, as were the Anglican archbishop of Canterbury and the Roman Catholic primate. They all gathered to honor a Christian group who, for decades, had been dismissed as "tub-thumpers" and "tambourine-tossers." In the United States, celebrations were nationwide. New York City, for example, held a parade on Broadway, and a dedication service took place in the Episcopal Cathedral of St. John the Divine.

William Booth, founder of the Salvation Army, was born on April 10, 1827, in Nottingham, England. His parents met in the small town of Ashby-de-la-Zouch, where his father, Samuel Booth, a widower, was availing himself of the waters as a remedy for chronic rheumatism. His mother, Mary Moss, was the daughter of a well-to-do farmer. Throughout most of his life, Samuel Booth claimed to be a man of more substantial means than he actually was. His efforts to assume a position in middle-class English society were a failure, and yet he was persuasive. He was able to convince many that he had greater wealth than he actually had. Samuel Booth worked at a number of trades, but he usually called himself a nailer, although it is not certain whether he was a carpenter or a manufacturer of nails. He also liked to think of himself as an architect and builder and there is evidence that he designed some homes and built them, although he was far from successful in these ventures.

Mary Booth was a patient, helpful woman. She stood by her husband through thick and thin, assisting him with his schemes. When he was sick, as he was for a large part of his life, she nursed him. She accepted much of his pretense of wealth and selflessly cared for him and their children through economic deprivation. She was responsible, no doubt, for the sensitive, ameliorative spirit of her offspring. William Booth, speaking of the doctrine of human depravity, declared that he accepted it in general, but felt that his mother was "an exception to the rule."

Five children were born to Samuel and Mary Booth—three

girls and two boys. William was the third child. Not much is known about the education of the children, only that Ann was sent to "the best ladies' school of Nottingham," and William was sent "to a good school kept by Mr. Biddulph . . . the select academy of Nottingham." Mr. Biddulph was a Methodist minister, who, in addition to his ministerial duties, maintained a small but efficient school for young men. William remained in this school from his sixth to his thirteenth year, when he was forced to leave and find work so that he could help support the family.

Samuel Booth, always money-minded, succeeded in apprenticing William to a Unitarian pawnbroker in town. William was not anxious to be a pawnbroker, but his father urged him to try it, explaining that, after all, money is the most important part of life and there is no better place to learn its importance than in a pawnbroker's shop. William was idealistic and did not agree with his father, and his experiences in the business did not help him appreciate money more. As a pawnbroker's assistant, he came to know the misery of economic want in even closer detail than in his own home. Before long, he realized that there was no simple solution to the problem of poverty and that individual effort or wishing did not matter. But a job was a job, and the family was sorely in need of the small income that he could bring to it.

Within five months after William took the pawnbroker's job, his father died, and this event threw the financial burdens of the household on him all the more. The family was forced to move into an even poorer section of Nottingham, where Mary made a meager living by selling toys, tape, needles, cotton, and other small wares.

William early was an attendant at the Broad Street Wesleyan chapel in Nottingham; however, he did not undergo any marked religious conversion. On the other hand, he did lead a moral life. He was distressed because of small acts he committed; one in particular he felt held him back from the Kingdom of Heaven. Whatever the act was, it was taken by his companions to be an unselfish gesture that was rewarded with a silver pencil case; but the youthful William concluded that he had deceived his friends and was unworthy of the case. He felt he had managed "to make a profit out of my companions." The incident played on his conscience, and it appeared to him to be the blackest of sins. He sought forgiveness from one of those he had "wronged" and was relieved finally that he had achieved a "state of grace." In later life, he said: "I remember, as if it were but yesterday . . . the instant rolling away from my heart of the guilty burden, the peace that came in its place, and the going forth to serve my God and my generation from that hour."[2]

This experience "in the open street" became the chief basis of William's later activities. When it occurred, working in the pawnshop, which he hated anyway, became more onerous. The new life led him to a reading of the Bible and especially of the New Testament letters of Timothy. He found many "militaristic" passages in these letters that appealed to him and that called him to an increasingly active participation in religious affairs. The Unitarian owner of the pawnshop under whom he worked became more objectionable to William, who thought that his employer was a deceiver of true Christians and destined for hell. The contrast between his Methodist experience and the cold intellectualism of his Unitarian master accentuated the conservatism of his spiritual outlook. He also looked upon those who used the shop as being sons and daughters of God, persons in definite need of salvation. The pawnbroker's shop was too small to hold the expansive spirit of William Booth.

From the moment of his conversion, William Booth never doubted that he should become a preacher of the Gospel. Through his friendship for Will Samson, a local preacher, he was asked to help with a preaching mission, and William Booth gave his first sermon when he was only seventeen in a cottage in Nottingham to men and women assembled to hear the Good News. According to one old woman, the sermon "was very gentle and tender." From this occasion, Booth learned that he was an able, if untrained, speaker, and people encouraged him to think of a full-time career in the ministry.

Booth's success as a local preacher encouraged him to plan for the active ministry, but he realized that he would not be able to accomplish his full mission without some training. By the time he was nineteen, his apprenticeship at the pawnbroker's shop ended, and he had to look for other employment, but he did not wish to continue as a pawnbroker. He wanted to preach. But how could he bridge his lack of preparation? He got some support in his problem from the Reverend Samuel Dunn, minister of the Wesleyan chapel in Nottingham. Dunn wanted William to attend one of the Wesleyan schools, but this suggestion was refused. William's official reason was ill health, which probably figured to some degree in the situation, but it probably was not the main cause. William was committed first to the economic needs of his fatherless family. One of his sisters, Ann, had helped the family somewhat by marrying Francis Brown, a hatter, and moving to London. But there was still considerable financial need in the family.

William was unemployed for twelve months. At the end of this time, he went to London with a few coins in his pocket and zeal for things of the spirit in his heart. He had thought that he might live with his sister Ann and her husband, but when he heard that his brother-in-law was a convinced agnostic and that he drank excessively, he refused to live with them. When his money gave out, he worked in a pawnbroker's shop, this time in Walworth, a poor suburb of south London. His new employer was a member of the Established Church, but he did not permit his religion to affect his practical life. William was required to work long, hard days, but he was free for an hour or two, one night a week, though he had to be home by ten o'clock. And his Sundays were free.

William managed to maintain his evangelistic activities, and in time he came to the notice of Edward Harris Rabbits, a wealthy boot manufacturer, who was seeking someone to develop a freer type of religious expression than that allowed by the Methodists. Rabbits and Booth, separately and without knowing each other, had broken with the formal controls of Methodism. Both felt that the theological and polity disputes of the Methodist churchmen were intolerable and unnecessary in the face of the great need for personal salvation. They were more interested in saving souls than in establishing a perfect church organization.

Rabbits proposed to Booth that he quit being an assistant to a pawnbroker and take up full-time preaching. Booth replied that he could not live on air. When he was asked how much it would take to subsist as a full-time preacher, Booth suggested that twelve shillings a week would keep him in bread and cheese. "Nonsense," said Rabbits, "you cannot live on less than twenty

shillings a week, I am sure."[3] Twenty shillings a week it was!
This proposal and its acceptance were made in June 1851, and
shortly thereafter Booth left his employment and set up rooms
for himself.

At about the same time, Booth met and fell in love with
Catherine Mumford, who later became his wife. She, too, had
left the fellowship of the Methodists and had come to hear
Booth preach under the auspices of Rabbits. She was well versed
in theological matters and judged Booth to be a man of unusual
fire and energy. She was immediately attracted to him and told
Rabbits so. William and Catherine first met over tea in the
home of Rabbits, where William recited for the assembled
company "The Grog-seller's Dream," a particularly vehement
poem which struck the sympathies of the prohibitionist Catherine but not of all those present. They met on various occasions,
and William regularly escorted her home after meetings. The
more they talked about religion and life, the more they realized
that they had an unusually close communion of interests—in
short, they found themselves in love. On a Sunday evening, May
5, 1852, they became formally engaged, but there was no
immediate prospect of their marrying.

A rift gradually developed between Booth and Rabbits. Even
though Rabbits was paying Booth's full salary, Booth insisted
that he should be the supreme interpreter of the religious life to
the little band of reformed Methodists that had gathered around
them. Rabbits, on the other hand, believed that he should have
the major say in determining the policies of the group. There
was no solution to the dilemma, and William resigned.

Booth gave up his connection with the reformed Methodists
despite the fact that he had no other prospect of an income.
Catherine encouraged him to make the break, believing that she
should encourage her future husband's decisions, and suggested
that he might like to join the Congregationalists at the
Stockwell New Chapel, the Reverend David Thomas presiding.
After consulting with Dr. Thomas, Booth was sent to an
outstanding Congregational clergyman, the Reverend John
Campbell, for counsel. Campbell encouraged Booth to consider
the Congregational church as his spiritual home and to prepare
for its ministry by going to college. Booth reminded the famous
man that he did not accept the limited conception of salvation

preached by the Congregationalists, but this did not seem to matter to Campbell. On the advice of the Reverend Campbell, Booth visited Dr. James William Massie, head of the Home Missionary Society of the Congregational Union. Massie undid the bolstering of Campbell by telling Booth that it would take at least five years to become eligible for the Congregational ministry. Impatient Booth could not wait that long to bring his message of light and life to the poor of London. He felt God had called him, and he could not neglect his call even for education. The Reverend Campbell intervened and finally persuaded Massie that young Booth should be examined immediately for entry into the school conducted by the Reverend John Frost. All agreed that the time could be shortened in the case of William Booth.

William did not last long in the Reverend Frost's school. Calvinism, the sectarian bickerings, and the somber intellectualism that pervaded the school's atmosphere did not please him. He wanted above all things simply to be a Christian and to "save souls." So he quit the school, much to the dismay of his Congregationalist helpers.

Although his life looked bleak at this point, an opportunity soon came to him to preach at a number of churches near Spaulding, a small town in the south of Lincolnshire. After bidding his future wife farewell, he set out for Spaulding. The people there wanted him to marry right away and set up housekeeping, but he wisely thought that he should wait until he saw how permanent his connection would be. The work was hard. He traveled by horseback many hundreds of miles each week in the presentation of the Gospel. But in his letters to Catherine, Booth indicates that almost everywhere he met with striking success, winning many new converts to his own brand of Christianity.

Booth's life at Spaulding was pleasant enough, but he encountered two difficulties that finally forced him to break his connection there. For one thing, he was still haunted by the idea that he needed more education. An entry in his diary points out this need: "Monday:—Visited the British Museum. Walked up and down there praying that God would enable me to acquire knowledge to increase my power of usefulness."[4] The second reason for leaving was his desire that he and his congregation join the New Connexion branch of Methodism (against which they previously had revolted). His congregation was opposed to this move and urged Booth to stay as their pastor, but in the end he left, and the congregation remained independent.

When William came into the New Connexion, it was arranged that he should study theology and preaching in the home-school of Dr. William Cooke. Catherine again supported him in this decision, and he entered with high expectations, but the old conflict between the evangelist and the scholar came again to the fore. When studying, Booth wanted to be an evangelist; when he was simply an evangelist, he longed also to be a scholar. Fortunately, Cooke was able to discern this conflict in the young man and use it to prepare him in ways that were of service to Booth later. Cooke tried to give him books that might strengthen his evangelistic interests, and he also arranged for preaching assignments in London, where the school was located, so that William could have a practical outlet for his energies.

Eventually, Booth was offered the position of superintendent of a London district of Methodist churches. This was an honor, indeed, and a vote of confidence from Dr. Cooke. Booth felt inadequate for this job and asked that he be appointed as an assistant to an older man, and this was done. Rabbits, who had gotten over his earlier estrangement and had followed Booth back into the fold of the New Connexion, came forward again to assume the salary of his protegé. In addition to his new duties, Booth was invited to conduct religious services in various places and became widely known in London as a preacher of great power.

In this period, William Booth entered into one of the few conflicts he ever had with Catherine. Dr. David Thomas had preached a sermon in London in which he declared that women were the "weaker" sex, for, according to the Adam and Eve story, women were historically more susceptible to sinning than men. Catherine Mumford, who always upheld the rights of women, was deeply disturbed by this sermon and wrote about it to her fiancé. At first, William took the side of Dr. Thomas, and this led to some sharp comments from Catherine. One of her comments reveals the manner in which she could both appeal to a high standard and criticize it at the same time: "Jesus Christ's principle was to put women on the same platform as men, although I am sorry to say His Apostles did not always act up to it."

The dispute, however, did not continue for long. Booth was agreeable to the claim of equality for women and wrote saying that he had changed his mind. This incident was momentous in the later founding of the Salvation Army; from the very first, the Army stood for equal treatment and responsibility for men and women.

William Booth and Catherine Mumford were in agreement on one point from the very beginning of their relationship. Both believed that revivalism should not incite a flagrant emotionalism. This conviction was generally contrary to the conceptions of religionists of the time. In fact, many sincere religious leaders measured the degree of spiritual fidelity by the intensity of the emotional expression of the believer. William and Catherine felt that emotion was too insecure a bond between persons and their religion. They wanted converts, but on thoughtful grounds. They also took steps, even before the founding of the Salvation Army, to make certain that new converts would be given every aid in translating their conversion experience into practical day-by-day service and devotion.

Catherine and William were married on June 16, 1855, at Stockwell New Chapel in London by Dr. Thomas. Catherine's father and William's sister were present at the ceremony. The large, rough-appearing groom must have contrasted sharply with his small wife as they stood for the minister's blessing. As soon as the wedding was completed, they began a week-long honeymoon at Ryde on the Isle of Wight. After the honeymoon, they went directly to the island of Guernsey, where they were scheduled to lead a religious revival.

The ten years following their marriage were taken up with their growing family and conducting revivals. Catherine did not go on some of the trips because of poor health, so when William went from Guernsey to Jersey and then to the city of York on the mainland, Catherine did not accompany him. At home, Catherine had an additional problem: her mother continuously needed money. Some of the money collected by William on his evangelistic tours had to be spent to maintain the impoverished Mrs. Mumford.

On March 8, 1856, the Booths' first child was born, a son, named William Bramwell Booth. (His middle name honored a

Methodist minister much admired by the parents, even though he supported bizarre religious practices, such as taking to a tree to pray.) A busy home life and the responsibility of hyperactive revivalism took their toll. Booth suffered for many years from digestive disorders and at times he felt despondent, which contrasted with his temperament during revivals. These conditions worked together to plague Booth and to irritate his family.

In 1856, William Booth revisited his birthtown of Nottingham while on an evangelistic mission. The fame of the young preacher of twenty-seven had reached Nottingham before him, and the whole town turned out to hear the words of faith that he expounded. The town officials greeted him, and he renewed old acquaintances. Booth noted that over seven hundred persons signed a register of conversion, showing that his religious influence upon his home town was not small.

At various times, Catherine and William Bramwell accompanied Booth on his trips. Though traveling conditions were rough, Catherine felt she should be with her husband. Finally, in 1857, she reluctantly made up her mind to leave her son with his grandparents in London while she helped her husband with his missionary work. It was not easy for her to make this decision, but she felt that it served the religious ends to which she and her husband were devoted.

This course of living was changed abruptly by a decision of the Methodist New Connexion that sponsored Booth's travels. Certain local clergy were jealous of Booth's success and his travels from town to town and wanted him to be located in a stable charge. So, at the Methodist conference held that year in the town of Nottingham, it was decided by a close vote that Booth and his family should be appointed to the "low smokey town" of Brighouse. To Brighouse the Booth family moved in the summer of 1857, and soon after, a second son, Ballington, was born, named for a friend of Catherine's mother.

At Brighouse, Catherine Booth began to speak before women's groups on the subject of temperance. This preaching activity was the fulfillment of a conviction she had expressed much earlier regarding the rights of women. While she was only somewhat sure of women's rights politically, she was absolutely certain of them religiously.

By the time the next conference appeared on the calendar,

the Booths felt they had had enough of Brighouse, and they petitioned to be permitted to renew their evangelistic tours. William had a difficult time getting along with the superintendent of the church at Brighouse, and he deeply wanted to return to his prior work, but the conference was unwilling to grant his request. It was decided that he should remain in a church for another year, after which, at the next conference, he would be unanimously (but reluctantly) allowed to become an evangelist again. He accepted this decision, and consented to become the minister of a small congregation at Gateshead, whose minister had declared himself an infidel and run off. So, to Gateshead they went, and there, in September 1858, the Booth's third child, Catherine, was born.

Catherine Booth increased her involvement in public affairs during her stay in Gateshead. Instead of being simply the wife of the minister, she was, in effect, co-minister. When her husband conducted worship services and delivered the sermons, Catherine would offer the prayers or take part in other ways. During this time, she learned the social implications and possibilities of religion. She began to visit parishioners in their homes and often found them living in conditions contrary to her conception of the good life. She found that she had opportunities for semi-evangelistic "social work." These openings extended beyond the membership at the church to all of the downtrodden of the community. In one of her letters to her mother, she says, "I have commenced my operations amongst the drunkards." This statement can be taken as a text for the later work of many Army workers.

At the end of the year, William Booth planned to go before the conference to ask again for his old job, but the congregation at Gateshead requested that he remain with them for at least another year to consolidate the gains made. Catherine also felt that he might remain for another year. The conference was apathetic about its promise to him, and, in the end, he was almost forced to return to Gateshead.

The next year can be measured by outward success for the Booths; but, inwardly, William suffered greatly, because he was denied his ambition of being a traveling minister. By the time the next conference came, he was so ill that he was unable to attend. He was forced to go to a hospital at Matlock for treatment, so complete was his breakdown. Fortunately, despite William's absence and the additional burden of children afflicted with whooping cough, Catherine Booth was able to assume his responsibilities in the church. William's recovery was slow, but when he was well again, he was as determined as ever to re-enter the "roving" missionary field.

When the spring conference of 1861 was near, William wrote a long letter to the retiring president of the conference, the Reverend James Stacey, saying that he would like to be reconsidered for his chosen work. This time, even the people in Gateshead sent a petition to the conference supporting his request, and Joseph Love, a prominent leader in the local church, agreed to bear a large part of the expense of making William Booth an evangelist. There seemed to be no significant reason why he should not be appointed as an evangelist at large.

The conference did not make it easy for Booth. His proponents were essentially weak in their arguments, even though such men as Love and Rabbits spoke in his favor. Those who opposed him were more effective. The conference members did not favor Booth's evangelistic type of religious strategy, because they felt it often did more harm than good. Many stood for a less spectacular development of local parishes by local ministers. A great deal could be said for their arguments, but William Booth did not accept such a mundane appraisal of his potentialities. He felt that he and his wife were divinely ordained to undertake evangelistic work and no human conference could stand in the way of a supernatural mandate.

After lengthy debates, the conference finally decided that Booth should take a church but could arrange with the local officials for time off to conduct his campaigns—a grand compromise. The decision disappointed both Mr. and Mrs. Booth, and they were hardly able to restrain themselves from leaving the New Connexion then and there. But, with patience that grew in time, William accepted an appointment as superintendent minister of the Newcastle Circuit, one of the most important appointments that the conference could offer. In this position, he had considerable freedom in choosing his own activities, and he was able to devote almost as much time as he wished to evangelistic work.

Calls to preach from churches within the Connexion were

not so plentiful, for many ministers disliked Booth and his insistence on being a traveling evangelist. His work as superintendent suffered markedly. Dr. Henry Crofts, president of the conference, wrote Booth a letter in which he scolded him for his failure to live up to the agreements of the previous conference. Booth replied on July 18, 1861, that he intended to keep trying to be an evangelist and that only after he failed would he let go his aspiration. His break with the New Connexion came in July 1861, only a few months after the conference had appointed him to Newcastle. At the age of thirty-two, Booth began a new career that ultimately led to the formation of the Salvation Army.

After the break, the Booth family went to Nottingham to visit William's mother, and from there, they went to the home of Catherine's parents in London. Soon afterwards, William was invited to conduct a revival at Cornwall. No promise of payment was made, not even of expenses; but Booth, eager for his new vocation, plunged ahead. The services at Cornwall were a huge success. Some came many miles to hear the preacher whose passion for the Gospel instilled in them the conviction of sin and the hope of salvation. William primarily stressed the theological aspects of the Gospel, but Catherine was concerned with its social implications. Together they constituted a sincere and effective team, both for religion and for social service.

The Booths stayed in Cornwall for about eighteen months. They had not expected to be there that long, but their success was so unusual that they were compelled to remain. Booth estimated that during this period he initiated some seven thousand persons into the Christian faith. This, in itself, was a remarkable accomplishment. At the end of their stay in Cornwall, the Booths were invited to conduct evangelistic meetings in Redruth, and then they traveled to other towns and cities, bringing their own brand of nonsectarian Christianity to the people.

From the time of their stay in Cornwall, the Booths were regularly denied the use of church buildings. Church groups of various kinds spoke negatively of the work they were doing and refused to allow them to use their buildings, so they used nonreligious buildings wherever they went. Booth claimed later that the use of nonreligious buildings actually stimulated their success insofar as there were many persons who would not go to a church because of prejudices against traditional religion. Thus, a principle was established that carried over into the operations of even the present-day Salvation Army.

In the four years following their break with the New Connexion, the Booths experienced outstanding success as itinerant preachers in the English countryside. Some of their old physical and psychological difficulties seemed to pass away. The strain of continuous evangelism, however, proved too much. In 1865, William collapsed from fatigue; he had an ulcerated throat and a sprained ankle, and he suffered from acute anxiety. While he recuperated in Smedley's Hydropathic Hospital, Catherine struggled with the problems of family and church work. Weakened by caring for five children with a sixth on its way, she did not have the strength to continue the work of their earlier years. But rest gave both William and Catherine new energy and helped them to overcome most of their depression. In time, they were well enough to continue their religious labors. Even so, Catherine felt that they needed a more stable existence, if only to maintain their health, and William could hardly disagree.

Without a doubt, health was one of the principal reasons why the Booths finally settled in London. This decision affected their later life greatly and is indirectly responsible for the founding of the Salvation Army. Arriving in London, they were faced with the problem of subsistence. William believed in taking his message to the people, even if it meant preaching in the street. Catherine, on the other hand, felt that a more conservative solution to their problem, the taking of a local pastorate, was best. William won out this time, and he went from church to church in London to preach. His written works also brought some financial return, especially a hymnal he compiled. Soon the family income was the equivalent of $1,500 to $2,000 a year, as much as the best-paid minister of the New Connexion was making.

After a time, William Booth was asked by Mr. Morgan and Mr. Chase, who published a weekly paper called *The Revival*, to preach a revivalist series in Whitechapel, in the East End of London, where Samuel Barnett also worked. Their idea was to increase the Kingdom of God through the Booths' services and at the same time to swell the subscription list of their publication. Morgan had a difficult time accepting the idea of Catherine

Booth, mother of seven children, preaching in a "man's pulpit," but after some persuasion, he gave in. The length of Booth's preaching mission was originally to be six weeks, but it lasted much longer. The services began in an old tent set up on the Quaker Burial Ground. When the tent collapsed in a storm, William resorted to the open street when the weather was good and hired halls when it was bad.

At the start, it was decided that Catherine Booth would begin a preaching mission in the West End, the wealthy section of London. There is no indication whether this mission succeeded, since it is not mentioned in the records of the lives of the Booths beyond the statement that a concerted campaign was planned not only for the very poor, but for the rich as well. Seemingly, in the long run, the Booths had enough to do in bringing salvation to the poor.

During the meetings held in Whitechapel, Booth founded the independent Christian Revival Association, which had the primary purpose of the evangelical preaching of the Gospel to the poor. Much later, when looking back on the first night's work in Whitechapel, General Booth said, "That night, the Salvation Army was born."

At this time Booth concluded that he would no longer work in conjunction with sponsors, whether churches or individuals. This was a momentous decision, for it cut him off from the sources of help he had painstakingly established, and it also urged him forward to the type of program that later characterized the Army. On his own he began preaching on an empty and forsaken lot called Mile End Waste. He had no equipment save his Bible, and he found in a short time that it was practically impossible for a man shouting on a vacant lot in a depressed part of London to attract much attention. From this experience, he realized that he needed a hall, so he hired a dance hall for his purposes. This plan did not work out, because the hall was used during the best hours for its designed purpose, and few people wanted to stay around until the dances were concluded and chairs were placed on the dance floor to hear the zealous preacher.

In desperation, Booth sent a letter to Samuel Morley, a wealthy textile manufacturer, who helped many such projects in his lifetime. Booth asked to have an interview with the wealthy and influential man. After he explained his dilemma, Morley responded with a sizeable check, and Booth was able to feel secure in his work for some time to come. He looked about for better quarters, finding them in an unused chapel in Shoreditch, another section of the East End. He chose the title East London Revival Society to advertise his efforts.

The mission in Whitechapel flourished, despite some handicaps. (For one, Catherine had to go to the country for her health.) But it gained new importance when Henry Reed, a wealthy, retired Tasmanian sheep farmer, took an interest in the project. Reed decided that the work should have the financial support of the Evangelization Society of London, which had a special concern for such activities. After sending a visitor to Booth's meetings, the society agreed to pay the rent for larger quarters. Several locations were tried, each meeting with increased public response, until Booth settled in the Effingham Theatre, at that time an old and unused building.

As the work expanded, Booth saw the need for establishing new, subsidiary preaching stations in the East End. By 1868, he announced in an annual report that there were thirteen such stations with accommodations for about eight thousand people. He also established a council of ten influential philanthropists to help him with the planning of the growing activities. (While he was constantly accused of misusing the Army funds for his personal use, from 1868 on, his accounts were audited and available to the public.) The preaching stations, as well as the central headquarters, dispensed various social services in addition to their basic religious function. Evening classes for adults, day schools for the poor children of the district, reading rooms for leisured people, and soup kitchens for the hungry were all started. The organization also distributed small sums of money to the poor and brought whatever nonmaterial help it could to the needy. In the same year, a religious magazine was published, *East London Evangelist*, the forerunner of the Army's famed *War Cry*.

As the mission grew, its leaders saw the need for increased space for their headquarters and meetings. The Effingham Theatre was remodeled for theatrical performances, but the Booths were permitted to rent it on Sunday afternoons. Some, however, felt that it was incongruous for an avowedly religious group to pay rent to a secular and profit-making organization. They advocated, as did Booth, buying the People's Market, a large building that had failed in its use for business. John McAll, the owner, was a member of Booth's council. Then, on the last day of September 1868, Booth received an urgent telegraph from Reed asking to see him as soon as possible. When Booth arrived at Reed's estate, he was told that he could be the recipient of new headquarters as a gift from Reed, who knew of a plot of ground in the East End that he could purchase for $15,000 to $20,000. He also intended to spend up to $35,000 on a suitable building. The offer took Booth by complete surprise, and he thought that his oft-repeated prayers had been abundantly answered. But he was wrong. Reed said he wished Booth to have complete charge of the new quarters, except that he would also like to have services there occasionally under his private auspices. William had decided earlier that he did not want to share authority with anyone; and he certainly did not want to share quarters, not even with his benefactor. He asked Reed for the chance to think the proposition over before he gave his answer, but he did not have to think long, for when he returned home, he found a letter from Reed that said he had changed his mind. (This change of mind did not bring a break in the relations between the two men. Shortly afterwards, Reed entertained fifteen hundred of Booth's followers on his estate, a compliment to the esteem in which Reed held Booth.)

In October 1869, Booth, with the consent of his council members, agreed to purchase the People's Market for the sum of $6,500, a much smaller amount than had been proposed earlier. Although the Market brought great advantages, it also completely drained the treasury of the society. For a time, the Booths' indebtedness amounted to about $5,000. The Market, however, represented a notable organizational triumph for William Booth, who sought just such a place for his expanding ideas and activities. The name of the society at this time was changed to the East End Mission.

Booth solved his financial problems in a number of ways. For one, the soup kitchens he had established earlier gave him an idea for raising money. He called his conception "Food-for-the-Millions Shops." For a five-year period, he owned and operated five of these shops throughout London. In them, Londoners could buy hot soup day and night, and in addition, inexpensive meals were provided. The actual management of the shops was given over to Bramwell Booth. In time the shops lost their effectiveness as a money-raising device (as they increasingly failed to meet social needs), and William closed them as quickly as he opened them.

William Booth's ability to make decisions without regard for tradition was one of his strong points. The Food-for-the-Millions Shops represents just one example. The People's Market is another. Booth used the Market for twelve years, but when he decided that it had served its purpose, he got rid of it without sentiment.

During this period, the Booths were in constant ill health. After the birth of their eighth child, Catherine Booth never really regained her strength and led for the most part the life of an invalid. William also was ill periodically. At one time, he was away from his work for three months, although he managed somehow to keep his organization intact and flourishing. During his illnesses, he had an opportunity to write for his magazine, and in 1872, he published the influential *How To Reach The Masses With The Gospel* with the long subtitle, *Containing A Description Of The Means And Instrumentalities Employed In The East Of London And Elsewhere, Together With Some Of The Results Which Have Followed In The Remarkable Conversion Of Numbers Of The Common People, Including Infidels, Thieves, Drunkards, Etc.* This work had a wide circulation, attracting many of the religious leaders of the day to his activities. One young man who read the book was George Railton. With his father's urging, Railton joined Booth's movement, and in time, he became Booth's secretary and one of the chief leaders in the subsequent expansion of the Mission and Army. Others, including the members of Railton's family, rapidly became Booth's disciples.

Booth conducted many of the religious services in the Market, and his appeal brought hundreds of people into his movement. The main feature of the services was the preaching, and on this score Booth was most effective. He was able to inspire his hearers with the glories of salvation. The "straight Gospel" was his forte; not even singing interfered with that. Booth once summed up his dislike for choirs (which had been suggested to him as a means of improving the services) as being infested with three devils: the quarreling devil; the dressing devil (an interest in clothing); and the courting devil (male-female relations). The last, in his estimation, was the most powerful.

As the number of Mission stations increased, certain issues came to the fore. One was that of leadership. Each station required a person in charge who was responsible to Booth, and a collection of youthful leaders were willing to work in these subordinate positions. The successful growth of the work in this period is due to the fact that Booth, who often was incapacitated by ill health, was able to find enough efficient persons to keep the movement expanding.

Station personnel were called together in annual conferences to share experiences and to gain new directives for the following year. For six or seven years, these conferences were concerned about matters of organizational procedure. Some workers felt that a simple democracy should hold sway; others felt that a more military type of organization would be better. In January 1877, a small delegation led by Bramwell Booth and George Railton asked William Booth to create a benevolent dictatorship over the Mission. In part, they said, "We did not give ourselves to form a little Church as an appendix of Methodism. We gave ourselves to *you.*" While the conference members were certainly not unanimous on this proposal, all did accept it in time. More and more, William Booth took over the supreme leadership of the Mission (which had a new name—the Christian Mission). The conferences assumed lesser importance, even though they were still used as a means of bringing the entire group together. It was William Booth who made the rules and regulations, appointed and fired evangelists, and directed the general activities of the movement.

The term "Salvation Army" was not in use at this time, and the exact occasion on which it was introduced to the Mission is not known. There was, however, an extended use of military words in describing the operations of the Mission leaders. In 1877, a poster in Whitby advertised the coming of evangelist Elijah Cadman of the Army with the headline "War! War! In Whitby." The same poster spoke of Cadman as "Captain Cadman." The use of the name "Hallelujah Army" was widespread, and one issue of the Mission magazine spoke of Booth as the "General of the Hallelujah Army." Of a meeting, it was reported: "On Monday the victory was won and the devil defeated." This warlike terminology proved to be successful and was increasingly used. Even a special "Congress of War" was called in 1878 to further the aims of the movement, and in the same year, William Booth was openly called the "General." By 1879, the Mission had officially changed its name to the Salvation Army. This decision came about naturally in the development of the organization, and it was made, as might have been expected, by William Booth.

The militancy of the Salvation Army, notwithstanding its earlier titles, gave impetus to its terminology. But the time in which the Army was born also featured military language and events; 1865, for example, was the year in which the Reverend Sabine Baring-Gould wrote "Onward, Christian Soldiers." It also was the year of the American Civil War and the Russo-Turkish War.

The Army grew by leaps and bounds, but it met with serious problems in its expansion. For one thing, many people earnestly disliked it and its leader. As the movement gained strength, its existence became a subject of controversy in England. Many clergymen were troubled because it threatened their own activities, and even the national government had to take the Army into account. There is a report that Queen Victoria was angry because, she said, she recognized only one army in her realm with one resulting hierarchy of military leadership. But this sort of antagonism only helped the Salvation Army, for it brought it to the attention of even more people. The stress upon military features appealed to many as calling for the highest kind of moral, peacetime courage.

As the Army grew, it encountered defections from its own orthodoxy. Not all of the local evangelistic leaders within the fold were content to bow before the dictates of General Booth, but these did not last long. Booth saw to that. He could as quickly expel a heretic as he could sign his name. Some groups within the organization split from it on theological as well as general management grounds. Although a rather wide allowance was made for theological differences, many could not agree with the religious tenets of the Army, and others criticized the way in which the Army was run and went off to found their own organizations. But these schisms did not harm the movement in the long run; they only seemed to make it stronger.

The Army's rituals appealed to many: its colors were blue, red, and yellow; its watchwords, strung across banners, were "Blood and Fire." The uniform also set each member apart from the general community and made him feel that he was a cog in an efficient machine attacking evil. The titles used by the officers readily indicated rank, and the symbols of the Army received a significant response from a large number of persons.

While the ritual of the Army appealed to many, it was not in keeping with the usual sacramental ritual of traditional churches. Booth was aware that his movement made no use of the Christian sacraments, but he did not wish it to. He was convinced that there were only two essentials of the religious life: First, the individual needed to be converted. According to the religious philosophy of Booth, every person is born a sinner and is unredeemed until he or she experiences salvation. It was the mission of the Army to bring such salvation to the attention of the person. Second, there was the need for a consecrated life. The fruit of conversion was righteousness, not sacraments. In fact, Booth believed that no element in a church's program or in that of the Army should divert the energies of the believer from his primary task of living a pure and helpful Christian life. It was for this reason that he could not agree to include the traditional sacraments in his Army.

The Army grew rapidly. In an 1879 issue of the *War Cry*, the general reported that there were 120 stations scattered through England and about $20,000 in the Army's treasury. With the Army so well established in England, Booth and his compatriots turned their attention to other lands. James Jermy had migrated to Canada in 1872 and from there had gone to the United States. In Cleveland, he came upon a small group of devout people who worshipped in what they called the Christian Chapel. They responded to Jermy when he told them of the Christian Mission in England. Expressing a desire to be affiliated with the Mission, they wrote to Booth asking for advice, calling themselves the "Christian Mission in America." He immediately wrote them, thanking them for their interest. As the work in Cleveland expanded, a second station was founded there, and in time a third was established. But Jermy returned to England shortly afterwards, and the growth of the movement in America all but ceased with his leaving.

Then, in October 1878, two of the Army's soldiers, Amos and Ann Shirley, arrived in Philadelphia with their daughter. Amos found employment in a silk factory, but he soon felt that he should devote all of his time to the work of the Army. The Shirleys found a meeting place in an old chair factory, and soon their enthusiasm for the Army caught the attention of other Philadelphians. The *Philadelphia News* sent a reporter to their meetings, and the subsequent news stories attracted even more people. The Shirleys sent word of their work to Booth, who was impressed by its importance and gave it a featured place in the *War Cry*. Soon after, he dispatched Railton to Philadelphia, and he sailed for America with an assisting delegation in February 1880.

Eight men and seven women made up the party that was to bring the Army's program to America. Booth did not intend that they would become the officers of the new stations to be established in the United States, and before the group boarded the boat, there was a meeting at which the purpose of the trip was established. The officers of the U.S. Missions should come from the United States, and those sent from England were to be only instigators of an indigenous American movement.

When Railton and his group arrived in Philadelphia and established official Salvation Army headquarters for America in that city, the movement began to receive even more publicity and support than it had earlier. After Philadelphia was partially "conquered," Railton set out for other cities. New York would not allow him to hold open-air meetings, so he moved on to St. Louis, where he felt that he would be well received. He made some headway there, but in general his efforts were frustrated by both the city's political and religious leaders. It was in St. Louis that he published the first American issue of the *War Cry* (January 1881).

Railton's work lasted about a year and was terminated by a cable from Booth with the brief message "Come home." Railton did not relish being away from his beloved England, yet he wished to continue his efforts to win America to Salvationism. But Booth felt that he needed Railton in England and that now the American effort should stand on its own, financially and otherwise. The recall of Railton did not spell the end of the development of an American Salvation Army; instead, leaders emerged from the ranks and the movement began to grow. Today, the Salvation Army in the United States is an extensive and effective organization, served by over four thousand officers and cadets. It features over twelve hundred centers of work, more than six thousand service units, and maintains many services: 173 mobile canteens, 11 USO units, 55 camps, 37 hospitals and maternity homes, 29 children's homes, settlements, and day nurseries, 125 men's social service centers, and other activities. The Army seeks to serve the young, the aged, families, the hungry, the sick, the troubled, and others. Funds for the support of the Army's activities come from voluntary contributions, supplemented by fees and membership contributions.

In August 1880, Booth received an honor that must have given him tremendous satisfaction: he was asked to address the Wesleyan Conference, a group that had once rejected him. For them he outlined the eight basic principles that guided the Army:

> First, we go to the common people;
> Second, we get at the people by adapting our measures because there is a bitter prejudice amongst the lower classes against churches and chapels;
> Third, we set the converts to work;
> Fourth, and then we employ women;
> Fifth, we do not guarantee any salaries;
> Sixth, and success on the part of our Officers is a part of their going on;
> Seventh, we succeed through dint of hardwork; and lastly, the success of our work is not in our methods . . . but it is in the spiritual life which the Lord has been pleased to give us.[5]

When Railton returned and gave his report on the possibilities of expanding the work in other countries, Booth began to think seriously about extending the Army in new lands, for he had requests from several countries for more active assistance. He decided in 1881 to send his daughter Catherine as the official representative of the Army in the "waging of war" in France. Her record there was typical of those doing similar work in other countries. The poor listened and were helped; the organized churches and the government not only were critical of her efforts, but did many things to hinder her progress. In the end, however, the Army was able to secure a strong foothold in the spiritual and social life of France.

The Army at home in England was growing so rapidly that new headquarters were required. In 1881, the London Orphan Asylum, situated in Lower Clapton on over two acres of land, was offered to the Army at one-fifth its original cost. Having been constructed to house six hundred children, it possessed many features that could be used by the Army. By 1882, $100,000 had been raised for the purchase and remodeling of the buildings now called Congress Hall.

The expansion of the Army outside of England continued through the period of growth at home. Through the efforts of Frederick Tucker, who retired from his position as a judge in India to become a Salvationist, the movement was firmly established in India and the Far East. The work in Australia, begun through the efforts of volunteers in that land, was promoted by Booth until the Army held a significant place on that continent. In December 1882, a small band of Army personnel landed in Sweden, and in the same year, "forces were landed" in Switzerland. In every place where the movement "landed," it found resistance. Sometimes this resistance was brutal, but everywhere the Army advanced.

Its success was copied by other attempts to establish "armies." The list is long and included the Hallelujah Army, Holiness Army, Christian Army, and Blue Ribbon Army. Some of these had a minor effect on the life of the era, but mostly they failed. Their very existence, however, can be taken as a sign of the virility and promise of the Salvation Army.

In 1882, the Church of England approached Booth with the proposal that the Army become an adjunct of the church. This was a difficult idea for the leaders of the Church of England to accept and to foster, but it was even harder for Booth to consider the plan impartially. In the end, Booth decided that he did not want to relate the Army to any church, although he did wish to work with all. The Church of England, as a result, created the Church Army, which has proven successful as a social and religious force.

Success inevitably brought internal problems. Rivalry developed among the officers, though Booth did everything he could to keep strife at a minimum, and some Salvationists failed to live up to the high standards Booth promulgated. An adjunct to the internal problems of the organization was the problem of marriage among the Salvationists. At first, few of the Salvationists married; in time, many did. So impressed was Booth by the prospect of his workers marrying that he issued "Articles of Marriage," to which marrying workers had to give assent. Officers were then, as they are now, forbidden to marry outside the Army. Engagement rings were thought to be unnecessary. Women officers—as a means of discouraging husband hunters— were not allowed to marry until they had served two years in the ranks. Booth sent an order to local units regarding engaged couples: "Put a few hundred miles between them. That'll show whether they are in earnest."[6]

The Salvation Army grew not only because it preached a "military" interpretation of the Gospel but also because it was deeply rooted in social welfare service. Its social welfare work is as famous as its purely religious activities, and in the minds of Salvationists and others, there is no reason to separate the two. As in our own time, the Army has always had nonsectarian support, morally and financially, from many people who recognize the value of its social service program.

The practice of social work by the Army is as old as its history, but its advancement as a major activity came in 1888. Booth was returning home late one night to headquarters, and as he walked, he saw a number of men sleeping on a bridge. He could not erase from his mind the thought of these unfortunate men, and as he discussed their plight with his son Bramwell, he said simply, "Bramwell, do something."

William's desire to remedy the conditions of the poor was interrupted by the final sickness and death of his wife. Because of Catherine's personal strength and appeal, she held a prominent place in the growth of the Army. At almost every turn, she was called upon for advice, and her suggestions were found to be wise and practical. Her death, on October 4, 1890, deprived the movement of a devoted leader and the general of his most valuable associate.

In his sorrow, William Booth turned to writing his influential book, *In Darkest England and the Way Out* (1890). In it he suggests several remedies for poverty, the chief one being his system of "colonies." He sought to establish three types of colonies: a city colony, a farm colony, and an over-seas colony. A person unable to support himself in the city would be sent to an urban shelter (the city colony), where his immediate needs would be met; then he would be sent to the farm colony, where he would be built up physically and trained vocationally so that he ultimately could go to an overseas colony (to be established in Canada, Australia, South Africa, and elsewhere). Booth called this a plan for "social selection and salvation." Many approved the plan as a feasible means of alleviating poverty and its attendant conditions, while others vehemently criticized it as eminently impractical. In the latter group was found an effective molder of public opinion, Thomas Henry Huxley. The plan received considerable financial support despite its critics and accomplished some good, but it was not adequate by itself to meet the large-scale, socially entrenched problem of poverty in nineteenth century England. In the end it failed. Its spirit, however, expressed William Booth's willingness to attempt grand schemes for the benefit of the poverty stricken populace.

Toward the end of his life, Booth allowed his control over the Army to become less autocratic. The main power within the organization gradually shifted to his son Bramwell, who became chief-of-staff. Booth himself was willing to maintain the office of a functionary, while Bramwell ran the Army, and the elder Booth spent more and more time preaching to international audiences in South Africa, China, Canada, Australia, and elsewhere.

Bramwell apparently wished to assume the autocratic position in the Army that his father had held, but his brothers and sisters rebelled at his domination. William's son Herbert was the commandant of the forces in England, but he could not get along with Bramwell and asked his father to appoint him to a foreign command; he was subsequently sent to Canada. In 1896,

Commander and Mrs. Ballington Booth (another son and his wife) resigned their commissions in the United States largely because of friction with Bramwell. In March 1896, they founded a similar organization called the Volunteers of America with Ballington its first general. This organization found greater success than did most of the other imitators of the Salvation Army. In time, daughter Catherine and her husband also broke with the Army and went their own way, and Herbert, who finally became the commander of Australia, ultimately severed his ties with his father's organization, too. The family empire was in disarray.

These defections from the movement affected William deeply and seriously threatened the prestige of the Army. But Booth resolutely turned his back on the decisions that his children made and continued to stand firmly for the Army he had founded and loved. He did not need family consolation, for he was received everywhere as a hero in the moral realm. In 1903, he visited the White House and President Theodore Roosevelt. On several occasions he was invited to open the U.S. Senate with a prayer. In 1904, he was received by King Edward and Queen Alexandra of England and praised for the contributions he had made to the betterment of English life. The City of London presented him with an honor called the "Freedom of the City," as did his hometown of Nottingham, and Oxford University conferred upon him a Doctor of Civil Laws degree. In 1906, the king and queen of Denmark received him in an hour-and-a-quarter audience. These are but a few of the honors accorded him. Everyone wished to do him honor; he accepted whenever possible in the name of the Army.

In the spring of 1912, Booth suffered serious physical setbacks. His health failed; he became blind. Work was now impossible, and he had to remain confined to his room. On October 20, 1912, he died. Many proposed that Booth be buried in Westminster Abbey, but the dean objected, so Abney Park Cemetery became Booth's final resting place. Before burial, some sixty-five thousand people filed by his bier to pay their respects to the man who made the Salvation Army possible.

Among those present at the Booth funeral service were officers of the Army from all over the world, as well as reformed thieves, tramps, and prostitutes who had been influenced by the life of the Army's founder. Far to the rear of the hall, almost unrecognized, was Queen Mary. One of those present uttered a most fitting epitaph for William Booth: "He cared for the likes of us."[7]

Chapter Five

Dorothea Dix
(1802–1887)

Shall I not say to you, dear friend, that my uniform success and influence are evidence to my mind that I am called by Providence to the vocation to which life, talents, and fortune have been surrendered these many years. I cannot say, "Behold now, this great Babylon which I have builded," but "Lo! O, Lord, the work which Thou gavest thy servant, she does it, and God in his benignity blesses and advances the cause by the instrument He had fitted for the labor."[1]

Dorothea Lynde Dix is one of the most famous women in American history. Teacher, writer, social reformer, religious poet, nurse, friend to the poor—these and other roles were pressed into a busy life of thoughtful concern for the welfare of others. Dix did not herself have an easy and secure life; frail of body, she strove constantly to maintain sufficient strength and stability to be of help to others.

Dorothea Dix was born on April 4, 1802, in the little town of Hampden, Maine, six miles from Bangor. Her father, Joseph, married against his parents' wishes and had been, in effect, banished to this forlorn, wild spot, far from the comforts he had known in urbane Boston. Elijah Dix, Dorothea's paternal grandfather, was an example of a self-made man. Interested in medicine, but not financially able to attend a medical school, Elijah apprenticed himself to Dr. John Green, in Worcester. In time, he became a physician, and entered a medical and business partnership with Dr. Sylvester Gardner. Through this cooperative arrangement, Dr. Dix became successful, even wealthy, for both doctors were interested in making money from real estate transactions and were clever in their buying and selling. Dr. Dix also developed trading interests in the West Indies, and by 1795, he was living in Boston in a mansion called "Orange Court," where he practiced medicine and took care of his many business activities.

Joseph Dix, Dorothea's father, was one of seven sons brought up at Orange Court. Born in 1778, he was frail and moody. Throughout his life, he suffered from feelings of inferiority, although he sought to achieve the highest goal that a Dix at that time knew—to be a physician like his father. Because of his vocational interest, he was sent to Harvard College.

At the end of his first year of school, he married Mary Bigelow, a woman "from the wrong side of the tracks." Elijah sent the couple to Hampden, Maine, to oversee his land holdings. Hampden was a bleak, unattractive place, offering sparse living conditions to its one hundred fifty inhabitants. This was the setting, physical and familial, in which Dorothea Dix, who was to become so remarkably sensitive to the needs of others, was born.

Joseph Dix worked the land for a time, but the work was too difficult. Capitalizing on his partial education at Harvard and his religious conversion by an itinerant Methodist clergyman, Joseph Dix decided to enter the ministry. He packed his belongings, blessed his family, and began his journeying to spread the Gospel. Joseph was fairly successful in his new calling, perhaps in part because he had more education than some of the other preachers in that part of the country. But despite his modest success, he was not able to send much money home to his family.

Mary Dix, eighteen years older than Joseph, was fretful and sick. Joseph's parents, secure in Orange Court, looked upon their son and his wife as suffering "the miserable and loveless home which their son's own weakness and folly had created," but they were fond of their frail and socially deprived granddaughter. When Dorothea visited Orange Court, her grandfather found time to play with her and to shower her with the affection she found lacking in her own home. She responded eagerly when she received an invitation to the large brick house in the comfortable suburb of Boston. The walks and talks with Elijah in his garden filled with flowers created in Dorothea a love for nature that was to remain with her throughout her life. In later years, Dix loved to recall her many trips with her grandfather in his carriage as he called on the sick and on his business acquaintances. One day, as they were riding leisurely along Milk Street, they got to talking about horses.

"See," said Elijah, "these two horses of mine are well cared for. They do not pant after pulling our carriage about the city. They receive the best of care at Orange Court. But, not all horses are so well kept. See that horse over there? He's frothing at the mouth. A horse will do that on a hot summer's day if he doesn't get a drink now and then." Dorothea did not forget this incident. In adult life, she had a large watering fountain for horses erected on that spot in Milk Street.[2]

Her grandmother also left a deep impression upon Dorothea. The neatness with which she kept the house, the beauty of its furnishings, and her standards of perfection contrasted with Dorothea's home in far-off Hampden.

When Dorothea was seven years old, Elijah died, leaving Dorothea's grandmother alone in her large home. She developed a longing for companionship, especially for that of her beloved grandchild. Conditions at home were crowded, so in 1814 the suggestion that Dorothea live with her grandmother permanently was accepted. The arrangements were mutually satisfactory. Joseph and Mary did not seem to regret Dorothea's going, because they had a large, demanding family. Dorothea had few regrets, for she saw in Orange Court the opening of a new life.

One of the first tasks that Mrs. Dix assumed for Dorothea was that of her "training." Dorothea did not have the best manners, for life in Hampden did not encourage the social graces. Sometimes, under the pressure of her strict but well-intentioned grandmother, Dorothea felt that the changes called for in her personal habits were far too great. But, in time, she learned.

Her schooling was another matter. In Hampden, Dorothea had not attended school and was able to read only the Bible and her father's religious tracts. In Orange Court she was an eager and attentive pupil, and her quick mind was attracted to many subjects. Very early, she thought she would like to be a teacher, but this idea was not entirely acceptable to Mrs. Dix, who, in line with the common opinion of the day, considered marriage the only proper career for a woman.

Dorothea's desire to teach, however, was not quenched by her grandmother's attitude, so she spent several years with her Aunt Sarah in Worcester for further education. There she found many friends of her own age and was influenced by her second cousin, Edward D. Bangs, fourteen years her senior. While in Worcester, Dorothea got the idea to organize a private school in which she would be a teacher.

In 1821, when her grandmother was seventy-three and she herself was only nineteen, Dorothea Dix opened her school in Orange Court. It may seem strange that a young woman should be given the responsibility for the education of children, but such was the situation in early nineteenth century Boston. Public schools in the city would not accept students until they had learned to read. It was this preliminary training that the private schools were mainly called upon to give.

For Dorothea Dix, teaching was a passion. In a letter written to a friend during the 1820s, she said: "To me the avocation of a teacher has something elevating and exciting. While surrounded by the young, one may always be doing good. How delightful to feel that even the humblest efforts to advance the feeble in their path of toil will be like a seed sown in good ground."[3]

Dix was not content to teach only those children who were able to pay for their instruction. As soon as her school was well under way, she turned her attention to those less fortunate in the community. In a room over the carriage house, which was back of the stable on the Dix property, Dorothea opened another school for those who could not pay for their education.

The life of the novice crusader was filled with many responsibilities. Running two schools, reading avidly, attending to church duties, and maintaining her home life and other concerns would seem to have been enough for any person. But Dix still had time for friends, especially Ann Heath, who lived in a large white house on the top of a hill that overlooked what is now known as Reservoir Park, Brookline. Dorothea once wrote Ann: "I always leave your house with regret and feel that there I might always be happy." Among the poems Dorothea wrote to and about her friend is the following:

> Though many are to me both good and kind
> And grateful still my heart shall ever be;
> Yet thou art to me a more congenial mind
> More than a sister's love binds thee to me.[4]

Throughout her life, Dix was never too busy to write or call on Ann. Both had come under the influence of Unitarian idealism and were attracted to its demands for constant moral and intellectual improvement, and their early friendship grew and ripened into an intellectual and spiritual relationship.

In this period, Dix turned to writing in addition to her numerous other activities. For a time, she was drawn to a project of a textbook, or encyclopedia, for children, which she called *Conversations on Common Things*. It was published in 1824, and favorable reviews noted that Dix had covered over three hundred subjects, many requiring detailed research. By 1869, the book had gone through sixty editions.

In time, her many duties and interests became too exhausting and she suffered a physical and mental collapse. Her doctor prescribed a long rest, possibly for as much as three years. This was a hard prescription to take for one who had been so active and whose plans outstripped her energies, but she knew that there was no other course for her.

Dix did not rest completely, however. With the schools closed and her health partially regained, she turned to writing. She had a number of writing projects in mind; one, which she completed in 1825, was called *Hymns for Children*. Intensely interested in religious matters, she felt that her compilation of hymns for children would increase the range of materials available to schools and families. Many of the hymns published in the book were Dix's own creations; only nine of the two hundred can be traced with certainty to other authors. She also published poems in the *Christian Register*, a Unitarian journal, and she wrote a small book of devotional pieces entitled *Evening Hours* (1825).

In 1827, the Reverend William Ellery Channing, a famed Unitarian clergyman who embodied for Dix an ideal form of Christianity, invited her to "Oakland," his summer home on Narragansett Bay, as tutor for his children. From her close contact with Channing at Oakland, she gained inspiration that guided her in later years.

The next few years were busy again with writing. Ten short stories, which appeared during 1827–1828, were later published as *American Moral Tales for Young Persons*. *Meditations for Private Hours* was published in 1828. In 1829, she wrote two books—*Garland of Flora* and *Pearl of Affection's Gift*. While *American Moral Tales* was filled with the sentimentality characteristic of that time, it expressed the deeply held moral and religious convictions of the author.

In 1831, Dix was ready to open another school, a combination day and boarding school. It was relatively easy for her to get students, as her reputation had spread throughout New England. Soon the school was founded and Dix was once again a teacher. With characteristic zeal, she plunged into the tasks of the school. Dix's pupils were expected always to be decorous in their personal relations in and beyond the classroom. On one occasion, a young boy was listening to Dix. Some phrase caught his fancy and he laughed out loud.

"What was it that caused you to laugh at my instruction?" the peeved Miss Dix asked.

"I don't remember," said the boy.

"For that you may stand in the cloakroom for two hours every day for a week," replied Dix. "We cannot have such levity in our education."[5]

Most students came to love her despite such severity, and to depend upon her, not only for her formal wisdom but also for her personal counsel.

In 1836, after five years of successful operation, the school was temporarily closed when Dix suffered a second physical collapse. Her physician, Dr. H. S. Hayward, believed she would recover, but that she probably would never again be able to work. Forced to endure complete rest, she made arrangements for the continuance of her school under the supervision of George Barrell Emerson, the principal of a well-known girls school in Boston.

Dr. Hayward believed that Dix should not remain in Boston, a center of intellectual and cultural activity. He urged, as a complete change, a trip to Europe. The property that her grandfather had left her provided an annuity that made the trip possible, and, on April 22, 1836, in the company of long-time friends, Mr. and Mrs. Frank Schroder and Mr. and Mrs. Ferrar, she set sail from New York for England. Here, through the kind offices of the Reverend Channing, Dix was received at "Greenbank," the home of William Rathbone, a prominent merchant and Unitarian. Dix stayed with the Rathbones for about eighteen months.

While in England, Dix received news that her mother had died at Fitzwilliam, New Hampshire, at the age of seventy-six. Sometime later, she received word that her grandmother, too, had died, at the age of ninety-one. On her return to Boston shortly afterwards, she felt deeply the loneliness that marked the passing of her devoted grandparent. "I feel the event," she wrote, "as having divided the only link save the yet closer one of fraternal bonds which bind me to kindred." It seemed impossible to think of teaching again, for twice it had brought her to physical collapse. But what else could she do? To what could a young woman of thirty-six turn her hand in view of her scant physical resources? A contact with the East Cambridge jail answered her questioning in an unexpected manner.

In 1841, she heard that a student at the Harvard Divinity School, John T. G. Nichols, needed someone to take his place as a Sunday School teacher to women in the East Cambridge jail. The women offenders were unresponsive to the religious claims of the young divinity student, and he felt that more progress might be made by a female teacher. Nichols visited Dix and laid the problem before her. Many years later, he wrote, "On hearing my account, Miss Dix said after some deliberation, 'I will take them myself.' I protested her physical incapacity as she was feeble in health. 'I shall be there next Sunday,' was her answer."[6] She kept her word.

After she conducted the services for the women that Sunday, Dix went through the jail and talked with the prisoners. To her surprise, she found among them some who were seriously mentally ill. She was struck by the fact that the quarters for the insane prisoners were not heated and had none of the advantages granted to the sane prisoners. The jailer suggested that the insane did not really feel the cold as did the sane. On leaving the jail, Dix could not erase from her mind the picture of the unfortunate prisoners and especially of the condition of the mentally ill. Repeatedly, she asked that improvements be made, but to no avail. She was not content to let the matter rest and decided to take the case before the East Cambridge court, which was then in session. She also invited prominent Bostonians to visit the jail to confirm the conditions. Among these were R. C. Waterson, George Emerson, Charles Sumner, and Samuel Gridley Howe. As a result, Howe wrote a letter to a newspaper in which he exposed the situation; but many people did not believe him, and many of those who did excused the conditions on the grounds that the insane deserved no better. But others, notably Sumner, protested the public unconcern. Dix had stirred up a hornets' nest. She had found her career.

Her continued contact with the mentally ill prisoners of the Cambridge jail led Dix to wonder what the treatment of these social misfits was elsewhere, especially in her own state of Massachusetts. As she extended her experience, she was convinced that a broad survey was needed to expose the inhuman treatment of the mentally ill. She talked over the possibility of such a survey with Howe and Sumner of the Boston Prison Discipline Society. They pointed out that the task would take months to accomplish and was fraught with real danger. But Channing, now old and sickly, thought that the findings would be helpful if someone would bring them together for the benefit of the state legislature. Encouragement from Channing was all she needed. Dix began her state-wide journeys that culminated in the document known as the Massachusetts Memorial. (A "memorial" is a written statement of facts presented to a legislative body as a petition or a remonstrance.) Dix investigated all sorts of institutions, agencies, private dwellings, and jails. Wherever there were mentally ill persons, she went to study, to ask questions, to record. Weeks passed into months, and still she seemed to have only scratched the surface of the problem. The conditions she found were shocking. In two years of travel about the state she discovered the worst and the best means of treating the insane.

Dix's memorial presented not only a general and moving appeal for legislative action, but also concrete data. The cases were numerous and shocking. One, concerning an inmate of the almshouse at Danvers, shows the general tenor of her report:

> There she stood, clinging to, or beating upon, the bars of her caged apartment, the contracted size of which afforded space only for increasing accumulation of filth,—a *foul* spectacle; there she stood, with naked arms and dishevelled hair; the unwashed frame invested with fragments of unclean garments; the air so extremely offensive, though ventilation was afforded on all sides save one, that it was not possible to remain beyond a few moments without retreating for recovery to the outward air. Irritation of body, produced by utter filth and exposure, incited her to the horrid process of tearing off her skin by inches; her face, neck and person were thus disfigured to hideousness. She held up a fragment just rent off. To my exclamation of horror, the mistress replied, "Oh, we can't help it. Half the skin is off sometimes. We can do nothing with her; and it makes no difference what she eats, for she consumes her own filth as readily as the food which is brought to her."[7]

Wherever she went, the story was the same; only the details differed. Dix tried to point out the need to improve conditions to the keepers of the mentally ill, but often she was rebuffed as being too impractical and sentimental. Finally she returned to Boston. There was more to be seen, but she had seen enough to convince any open-minded person or group. At the home of Mrs. Channing (Dr. Channing had died in October 1842) she wrote the memorial that was intended to rouse the state legislators to the defense and protection of the mentally ill.

When she had finished her writing, working and reworking it many times, she waited until the legislature assembled in January 1843. Howe, also a leader in social welfare activities in Boston, had agreed to present the memorial to the legislature, and when the time came, he presented it well, but the response was disheartening. No one anticipated that there would be such an openly negative response to Dix's sincere and documented statement. Her memorial was termed an insult by many in and out of the legislature, who found that it named names and fixed responsibility exactly. The overseers of the poor at Danvers issued a counter-memorial. Others felt that the conditions described were so palpably tragic that they simply could not be true. Some, however, knowing Dix's integrity, came to her support and added their conviction to her own.

After a time, people were more willing to look at the evidence Dix had assembled. Certain leaders in the life of Boston stood by her faithfully—a fact that helped her cause with the public. The legislative committee to whom the memorial was referred began to take it seriously and advanced a plan for new facilities to be established to care for the mentally ill. Two hundred additional persons, for example, were to be cared for by new buildings at Worcester. Once accepted by the committee, with the support of backers in the legislature and the community, the idea of creating new facilities became a reality. The passage of new and far-sighted legislation marked the end of a long struggle.

Now the needs of persons in other states became a rallying cry to Dix. She knew something about conditions elsewhere, for, in her travels, she had made investigations, and she continued reading the available literature on the subject.

One year after the memorial to the Massachusetts legislature had accomplished its purpose, Dix presented a memorial to the legislature of New York State. Her demands always exceeded what she received. In New York, she asked for four to six new hospitals but had to be content with an appropriation for an extension to the hospital at Utica.

Dix also worked for the relief of the mentally ill in Rhode Island, where responsibility for the care of the insane was given to the localities. They gave the problem minimal attention, establishing relatively few adequate facilities to meet the need. She surveyed the state systematically, and found that the conditions that she exposed in East Cambridge were to be found almost universally.

One case, that of Abraham Simmons, drew wide attention because of its tragic aspects. Simmons was confined in a stone-roofed, stone-floored cell, seven feet square. There were two doors to the cell, but both were double-locked, cutting off light and ventilation. On the day that Dix visited Simmons, his cell was coated with frost. Simmons had two blankets, but one was soaking wet and the other was frozen stiff. Simmons, tied to the floor by an ox chain, stood chattering and shivering in a corner.

"How long has he been here?" asked Dix.

"About three years," answered the woman who was in charge. "My husband and I are glad that he is kept out here in the field, so we can't hear his screams through the night. Sometimes he wakes us up. That gave us the idea of the thick walls."

"May I go in to visit with him?" asked Dix.

"Heavens no," was the woman's reply. "He will surely kill you. I haven't been in the cage since he was brought here."

Despite the woman's warning, Dix climbed into the cell and spoke to the old man. She talked about his possible release and of his friends and relatives at home. By the subdued glow of the lantern, Dix noticed tears running down Simmons's rough face.

"My husband," continued the woman, when Dix emerged from the cell, "sometimes of a morning rakes out half a bushel of frost, and yet he never freezes."

And yet he never freezes. How these words struck Dix![8]

Such personal suffering as that of Simmons would probably have moved the state legislature in Rhode Island to initiate new and better services for the insane, but there were private sources of relief, too. Nicholas Brown, a merchant and founder of Brown University, was convinced that the state should establish proper facilities to care for the mentally ill. To that end he established a fund of $30,000 toward building or endowing such a project. In

1844, the year after Brown died, the state legislature issued the charter of the Rhode Island Asylum for the Insane. The provisions of the charter appropriately permitted the name of the institution to be changed to that of any patron who might substantially contribute to the project. Brown's contribution was a start, but much more was needed in view of the fact that the legislature was willing to grant only an institutional charter without any commitment of supporting funds.

Dix was interested in bringing the idea of the asylum into reality, but she needed money to add to Brown's starting contribution. When she inquired about persons who might be willing to aid in the financing of the institution, the name of Cyrus Butler, a bachelor who ultimately left an estate of $4 million, was suggested. She did not know Butler but secured an appointment with him through the good offices of the Reverend Edward Hall. She came immediately to the point of her visit, a practice appreciated by the busy Butler. Dix told about Simmons and the others she knew personally, and she related what other states had begun to think and do.

"What do you want me to do?" Butler asked abruptly.

The business-like Dix answered: "I want you to give $50,000 toward the asylum which will be called Butler Asylum."

"I will give $40,000 on the condition that a like sum be raised within the next six months," was his reply.[9]

Following the interview, Dix did two things. First, she appeared before the legislature to again press home the needs of the mentally ill. In response, the legislature appointed a committee to investigate mental health conditions throughout the state with a view to correction. Second, she began her appeal to various people, even to the citizens of the state, that the required money stipulated by Butler be raised. In a relatively short time, the money was oversubscribed. Dix and others were elated by the success. The facilities so sorely needed were guaranteed to Rhode Island's helpless mentally ill.

Turning from Rhode Island, Dix went on to other states. In Vermont and New Hampshire, she found excellent means of caring for the mentally ill. Such, however, were not characteristic of New Jersey and Pennsylvania—New Jersey had virtually no provisions for the mentally ill. Again she began her work by systematically surveying the state, visiting all sorts of persons, institutions, and organizations. In her memorial to the New Jersey legislature in 1845, she wrote of the responsibilities of the state towards the mentally ill, and she indicated, through a liberal sampling of biblical quotations and first-hand facts, that the legislature was not living up to either the requirements of justice or the reality of the times. Speaking to the legislators, Dix did not ask for charity: "I do not come to quicken your generous impulses and move you to emotion by showing the existence of terrible abuses, revealing scenes of almost incredible suffering. I come to ask justice of the legislature of New Jersey, for those who, in the providence of God, are incapable of pleading their own cause, and of claiming redress for their grievances."[10]

A committee representing both branches of the state legislature was established to consider Dix's proposals, and a month later, the committee reported with enthusiasm in favor of her plan. Not everyone, however, agreed with her. Some legislators believed that any adequate program to care for the insane would increase taxes, and they were committed to a reduction of taxes. With her usual determination, Dix visited the legislators to see who was on her side and who might be brought to see her views. She was a clever political lobbyist who used every honorable means available to win legislators to her ends. In time, she received a letter from Senator Joseph S. Dodd, who had introduced and championed her cause in the legislature: "I am happy to announce to you the passage of the bill for the New Jersey Lunatic Asylum." Another victory had been achieved in the long struggle for the sane treatment of the mentally ill.

On February 3, 1845, Dix presented a memorial to the legislature of Pennsylvania. It, too, was the result of painstaking analysis of the mental health conditions existing in that state. She found that facilities existed, but everywhere they were inadequate, and patiently she gathered facts to support the claims of her memorial. By this time, her activities were receiving broad attention by the general public, as well as by those who sat in the legislative halls. In addition to reforming existing practices, Dix succeeded in getting the Pennsylvania legislature to establish the Pennsylvania State Lunatic Hospital in Harrisburg, the state capital.

It was inevitable that in her investigations Dix should come to recognize the need for reform in penal institutions of the various states. Returning from Pennsylvania in September 1845, she set about organizing the materials that she had collected on this problem. In several months time, the writing was finished. In her report she established three principles: a prison should have clearly defined social objectives which discipline seeks to achieve; moral and religious instruction are the backbone of personal reformation; and juvenile offenders should be harbored in "houses of refuge" so as not to be "contaminated" by older criminals. These three principles were elaborated and illustrated to show how they might modify the then current practices of penal institutions. She sent her manuscript to the printers, then left for Kentucky to resume her state-by-state campaign for the humane treatment of the mentally ill. This was the first of the many trips she took to various parts of the country during the next twenty-five years. After Kentucky came Ohio and Indiana, then a steamer trip to New Orleans. Wherever she went, she stopped to investigate local conditions. Even when the boat stopped for a few hours, she would hunt out institutions. From New Orleans she went to Georgia, then north, and after more investigating, she retraced her route.

In September 1846, while visiting Columbus, Ohio, she collapsed from exhaustion. Two months later, she wrote the following in a faltering hand to Ann Heath:

> My robe of life is travel-worn
> And dusty with the dusty way;
> It bears the mark of many a storm
> And marks of many a toilsome day
> The morning shower, the damp night dews
> Have lent their dark discoloring hues.[11]

But her health returned rapidly. She believed that hers was a God-given task and that she must carry out the divine mandate. In December of 1846, she was ready to travel again. In January, her memorial came before the legislature of Illinois, and in March, a hospital bill passed.

From state to state Dix traveled, spreading enthusiasm for humane treatment for the mentally ill. She based her intended reforms on the facts confronting anyone with eyes to see. Her personal determination and winsomeness were valuable assets in capturing the minds of legislators.

Dix helped the less fortunate in many other ways too—collecting books for prison libraries, helping those in institutions for the feeble-minded, and gathering clothes for the poor. The following incident illustrates her broad social concern. When visiting St. John's, Newfoundland, she learned that storms near Sable Island wrecked many fishing ships and that the ships lacked adequate rescue equipment. A disaster that occurred during one of her visits encouraged her to try to do something to remedy the situation. She wrote to friends in Philadelphia, Boston, New York, and elsewhere for money to purchase life-saving equipment, and a few months later, the brig *Eleanora*, carrying two surf boats, one lifeboat, two boat wagons, one life car, a mortar with firing ammunition, and coils of rope, set sail for Halifax. Unfortunately, the *Eleanora* itself was caught in a violent storm and wrecked. Still determined, Dix began again, and this time the equipment reached Sable Island.

Dix's various activities in aiding the states to establish better programs of care for the mentally ill did not entirely meet the problem. While the programs were beneficial, they needed to be supplemented by a national program that would make certain that all Americans in need of mental care would receive it. Dix recognized this need, and she believed that Congress should cede public lands for the purpose of aiding the mentally ill. Already 134 million acres had been granted to the states for various purposes. Over 100 million yet remained. In her view, 5 million acres might form the basis for a fund out of which the needy might be helped. This amount of land did not seem unreasonable in view of the vast reservoir of land still held by the government and of practices in the past. The government recognized its responsibility for the educational needs of the citizenry by granting land to the states for land-grant colleges and universities. Was it not reasonable, Dix's argument ran, that it held a similar responsibility toward other needy groups?

Senator John A. Dix (no relation to Dorothea Dix), an influential senator from New York, presented Dix's memorial to Congress on June 27, 1848. He reviewed her work in the states up to that time, recalling to the members the value of her activities and the nature of the evils she was attacking. A land grant was asked as a demonstration of the responsibility that the federal government felt for the less fortunate. It would be divided among the thirty states that made up the United States at that time in proportion to their population. The land, valued at a dollar an acre, would signify an investment of about $5 million on the part of the government. There were an estimated twenty-two thousand mentally ill persons at that time, according to Dix, of whom only about thirty-seven hundred were being cared for by public means. The rest were neglected. Using data gathered over years of detailed investigation, the memorial told a story of this neglect. Cases were cited in some detail to make the record more vivid. Five thousand copies of the memorial were printed to publicize the proposed legislation. Dix asked that she be allowed to select a committee of congressmen to deal with the problem. On the committee she placed members of the dominant party, who carried political "weight" in Congress and in the principal states.

After the bill was formulated, Dix was active in its support. Most of her time was spent in explaining individually to the members of Congress what the nature of her proposal was and what it would do for the mentally ill of the country, and she was given the use of a small alcove in the Capitol Library for this purpose.

Dix also was busy meeting with people individually and in groups to explain the legislation she was supporting. Most people felt that there would be little resistance to the passage of the bill. The obvious need seemed to call for clear action, and the proposed means to meet the condition were clear and desirable. Many outstanding persons and organizations added their support to Dix's appeal. For example, the Association of Medical Superintendents of American Institutions (formed in 1844) went on record in support of Dix's work. Dr. Luther V. Bell, superintendent of the McLean Hospital in Boston, wrote Dix a letter in which he said he felt certain that the bill would pass in Congress.

Days passed into weeks, and weeks into months, and still the bill was not acted on in Congress. Dix was told the time was not propitious. In fact, the political climate had changed considerably, and doubts were raised as to whether the legislation was even desirable. Part of the problem was that many groups in Congress were seeking public land for special purposes. This was a period of "land raids." The citizenry had become increasingly aware of this and with their awareness, resentful. Some felt that the bulk of the public lands should be sold to poor individuals for from $1.00 to $1.50 an acre. Dix's bill for the insane was deferred, presumably until the political winds would change, but change they did not. The winter of 1848–1849 wore on. Spring came, and still the bill was not brought to the floor of Congress.

In December 1849, newly elected congressmen faced the prospect of a new bill. Dix's plans had changed somewhat. Instead of requesting 5 million acres, she now proposed the ceding of 12,225,000 acres to benefit in addition to the insane, the blind, the deaf, and the dumb. Of this, 10 million acres would be used to help the mentally ill. John Pearce of Maryland introduced the memorial in the Senate, and John Fremont of California broached it to the House. A committee was appointed by Vice-president George M. Dallas to consider the petition. Not long after, the committee reported favorably on the memorial, and everyone felt that legislation would be passed almost immediately. Supporting the measure were countless churches, the staffs of mental institutions, social and professional leaders, politicians, and others whose influence was substantial. But in spite of all this backing, the bill was deferred until the first month of the following Congressional session. Dix was openly dismayed. The following December, she returned to Washington after a trip "to the interior of Pennsylvania." In February of 1851, her bill came up again before the Senate. There were some doubtful moments, but victory finally came when the bill was passed by a large majority—thirty-six to sixteen.

Not so with the House. Surely, she thought, there would be no trouble here, for previously the House had passed a similar bill. As time was running short, she tried to get House leaders to suspend their rules so that the Senate bill might be acted upon, but the leaders were unwilling. Weeks passed. Political bickering held up the bill's coming to the floor, and Congress adjourned without passing the bill.

During the summer months, when Congress was not in session, Dix toured the South with Fredrika Bremer, the Swedish novelist. Together they visited institutions that housed the mentally ill in the Carolinas, Georgia, Florida, and elsewhere. In

1852, Dix was back again in Washington with new demands on Congress. In addition to the land that she previously requested, she asked for one-hundred thousand dollars to establish a hospital for the relief of the mentally ill of the army and navy. This hospital (now known as St. Elizabeth's Hospital) was to be established in Washington, D.C. The hospital bill was accepted, and in August the money was appropriated. The land-grant bill also passed the House, but now the Senate delayed its action. Under the circumstances, Dix felt that some progress had been made, but that the political winds were not favorable for passage of the bill by the entire Congress, so she decided to wait until a new Congress was sworn in. For the eighteen months in the interim, she devoted her time to improving treatment of the mentally ill in Maryland, Canada, the Middle West, and the South.

When Congress assembled in 1854, the time seemed ripe for passage of the land bill. Four years had been spent getting to this point, and everything seemed to be in order. Who could doubt that this time the bill would be passed quickly in both houses. Some modifications were made to take changing conditions into account, and then the usual work was initiated to bring the bill before the public and the congressmen. Five thousand copies of the memorial were printed, and on March 9, 1854, the bill passed the Senate by a large majority. Shortly afterwards, the House also passed the bill. Only the signature of the president was needed.

President Franklin Pierce's veto was entirely unexpected. The president declared that, Congress, in his opinion, had the power to make provisions of an eleemosynary nature, that is, relating to charity, within the limits of the District of Columbia but nowhere else. The president did agree that Congress had the power to make grants for schools, colleges, railroads, and various projects of internal improvement, but, he argued, whenever Congress went beyond this line, it was transcending its powers and setting up unsafe precedents. "If Congress has power to make provision for indigent insane without the limits of this district," he said, "it has the same power to provide for the indigent who are not insane, and thus to transfer to the federal government the charge of all the poor in all the States."

The president also argued that, if Congress were to assume

such power, it would dry up the "fountains of charity" in the several states. The previous grants by the federal government, the president contended, were for "value received." The appropriation of public land for the mentally ill would not return any appreciable value to the government. The bill was returned for further consideration by Congress, and a vote was taken as to whether the bill should be passed over the president's veto, but sufficient support was lacking. Despite the able defenses of the bill made by Dix and others, the veto stood. The bill was lost. The work of six years had come to nothing.

Overwhelmed with disappointment, Dix felt the need to escape from the situation. She set sail for England in September 1854 and at Liverpool met her old friends, the Rathbones, and retired to Greenbank for a rest. She had promised herself that she would do nothing for a month, but before two weeks had passed, she was visiting various institutions and conferring with leaders of the "mental reform" movement in England. She also took part in discussions of religion at Greenbank, which helped her gain new perspectives on her recent defeat.

Dix was interested in Scotland and its treatment of the mentally ill and made a visit to that country. In spite of resistance from the officials concerned, she visited institutions. Many of the conditions she found in her own country prevailed in Scotland. The need for reform was apparent everywhere. The problem of how to accomplish it in Scotland baffled Dix for a time, until, after consulting with certain leaders, she concluded that a conference with the home secretary in London, Sir George Grey, would be the first step.

Soon she was in London presenting her case before the home secretary, a meeting arranged by Lord Shaftesbury. She asked for and got two commissions of inquiry: one dealt with conditions relating to the insane in the whole of Scotland; the other was concerned with the abuses in Mid-Lothian. The commissions were ultimately approved by Queen Victoria, and on April 9, 1855, the commissioners began their work, using in part the materials gathered by the indefatigable Dix. In time the commission's study led to legislative action.

Following her work in Scotland, Dix began a series of trips to various places, mainly in Europe, to encourage the rising public awareness of the needs of the mentally ill. France held her

interest for some time. There she came in contact with the most
advanced of the French thinkers dealing with these problems. In
January 1856, she visited Italy and was shocked to see the
problems that lay in the shadow of the Vatican. She asked for an
audience with the pope in order to explain the needs of the city.
Pius IX received her and sympathized with her distress over the
treatment of the mentally ill in Rome.

"And did thee really kneel down and kiss his hand?" asked a
Quaker friend, upon her return to the United States.

"Most certainly I did," she replied. "I revered him for his
saintliness." The pope promised to aid in the correction of the
ills she had brought to his attention.[12]

After Italy, tales of the treatment of the insane in Turkish
institutions stimulated Dix to further travel. She arrived in
Greece soon after the close of the Crimean War and was able to
see the problems in general health and welfare connected with
that war. The institutions of Constantinople were relatively
good, a pleasant discovery for Dix. Starting up again, she
journeyed to Budapest and Vienna to learn of their practices.
From there, she went to Russia, visiting Moscow and St.
Petersburg (now Leningrad). To complete her trip, she surveyed
conditions in Sweden, Belgium, and the Netherlands. The long
trip finished, she returned to England somewhat refreshed,
feeling challenged to apply her newfound knowledge to her own
country upon her return.

At the end of September 1856, Dix returned to the United
States, where she received congratulations on her work abroad.
Institutions asked her to visit, and organizations approached her
with their problems. She was needed in many places, for her
abilities had been tested in various ways. One of her letters to
Ann Heath tells how busy she was during this time:

> I arrived safely and without accident on Monday night. Tuesday
> spent at Ward's, Randall's and Blackwell's Islands, Wednesday up
> the Hudson to Sing Sing prison, on Thursday (today) High Bridge,
> to juvenile asylums and reformatories; tomorrow to Bloomingdale;
> Saturday, hospitals in the city, and Saturday evening to Trenton,
> New Jersey. Thus you see the progress of my doings. I now think I
> shall go to Philadelphia on Tuesday, on Wednesday make the
> purchases for the hospital in Harrisburg, a day's journey; see the
> patients Friday; return to Philadelphia Saturday, spend Sunday at

the hospital; Monday, almhouses; Tuesday, Trenton; Wednesday set out for Buffalo, Geneva, Canandaigua, etc., to explain anew the miseries of their almhouses so if you do not hear from me, please do not consider yourself forgotten nor even unbeloved.[13]

At age fifty-four, Dix was a perpetual traveler in the interests of reforming the care of the mentally ill. In the course of the years, she was able to view her work with a broader perspective. She also saw the need for improvements other than in the treatment of the mentally ill. Religion and a social philosophy derived from her religious outlook made her work more satisfying. She felt that, in the final analysis, she was in the hands of destiny.

The new hospital for the mentally ill of the armed forces in Washington became her headquarters. There she could work quietly while looking out over the Potomac. The dome of the Capitol reminded her of her victories and defeats. The hospital site had been chosen by Dix. When she first visited the estate on which the hospital was later built, she remarked: "This is the best site that could be found. I will be satisfied with no other." But Thomas Blagden, owner of the estate, loved his ancestral home and refused to sell it for less than $40,000. Congress had appropriated only $25,000. Dix persuaded Blagden of the suitability of a pastoral setting such as his estate for the treatment of the mentally ill, and Blagden, who had helped her gain new perspectives on her recent defeat, was genuinely motivated to help. He agreed to sell for the amount appropriated by Congress. On the night of his acceptance, he penned the following letter to Miss Dix:

Washington, D.C.
November 13, 1852

Dear Madam:

Since seeing you today, I have had no other opinion (and Mrs. B also) than that I must not stand between you and the beloved farm, regarding you as I do, as the instrument in the hands of God to secure this very spot for the unfortunate whose best earthly friend you are, and believing sincerely that the Almighty's blessing will not rest on, nor abide with, those who may place obstacles in your way.

With Mrs. Blagden's and my own most friendly regards.

Very respectfully,

Your obedient servant,
Thomas Blagden[14]

Dix did not spend all of her time in Washington. She went again to the states she had visited previously and won new advances in the care of the insane. Pennsylvania, for example, appropriated $55,000 for its institution at Media, and South Carolina appropriated $155,000 for its extension of institutional services to the mentally ill.

Wherever Dix went, she saw the approaching clouds of the Civil War. The problems of the South and the North were constantly in her mind, yet she did not become involved in discussions of the political issues that so tragically led to war. She was able to separate the problems of the insane from the larger political issues of the day. The South's generous acceptance of Dix indicates that she was able to meet individuals and groups on other than sectional terms.

In spite of her efforts to remain neutral, Dix could not avoid the effects of the war. On one of her trips, she heard of a plot to seize the city of Washington and to declare a de facto victory for the South. Dix went to Samuel Felton, president of the Philadelphia and Baltimore Railroad, and he was so impressed by the story that he hired detectives to investigate the plot and to gain access to its inner operations. It was found that the scheme also included a plan to stop Lincoln from getting to Washington to be inaugurated.

Dix's own state, Massachusetts, provided some of the first soldiers for the Union cause, and on April 19, 1861, the Sixth Massachusetts Regiment was instrumental in drawing Dix herself into service for the Union. The regiment was passing through Baltimore on its way to a train station when it was attacked by a mob. The fighting that followed was brief but fierce. Exaggerated accounts of the struggle soon reached Washington newspapers, and almost everyone in that city was shocked and dismayed by the thought that the dreaded war had begun. On hearing the news, Dix went to Baltimore to do what she could for the soldiers who were hurt, but by the time she arrived and located the scene of the skirmish, there was little for her to do.

She returned to Washington and went directly to the Department of War, where she offered to work under the surgeon-general in caring for wounded soldiers. On April 23, her services were officially accepted by Secretary of War Simon Cameron. As an unpaid worker, she was given the title "Superintendent of United States Army Nurses," the first commission of its kind ever issued.

Her first task was to ascertain the condition of the Medical Bureau. She found it sadly inadequate, with too few workers, shortages of bandages and other medical equipment, and a lack of spirit. Dix eagerly met these emergencies. Her work extended not only to the nurses employed by the Union, but to the volunteers in back-home communities who were rolling bandages, knitting clothes for the soldiers, and otherwise helping the war effort. For a time, Dix worked with the women who accompanied their husbands to the battlefields.

Nurse recruitment was also a major part of Dix's responsibility. Her standards for army nurses were especially severe; Dix said: "No woman under thirty need apply to serve in the government hospitals. All nurses are required to be plain-looking women. Their dresses must be brown or black, with no bows, no curls, no jewelry, and no hoop-skirts."[15]

The Washington house where Dix lived during the war was large and spacious. Here, at her own expense, she maintained two secretaries to deal with official correspondence. Newly recruited nurses were welcomed and could stay until their living arrangements were completed. Here, too, nurses and convalescent soldiers assembled for rest and refreshments.

Dix was unbending in maintaining high standards of conduct and efficiency. At times, her prejudices were obvious and unfortunate; for example, she would not hire Roman Catholic nurses on the grounds that she was opposed to any extension of Catholicism, and she did not hesitate to bring doctors to task officially for drunkenness. In many ways she sought to impose her own views and practices upon those over whom she had responsibility, which did not enhance her prestige with her fellow workers.

There had always been differences between the superintendent of nurses and the Medical Bureau, and they finally came to a head when the bureau was reorganized under the leadership of Dr. William A. Hammond. On October 29, 1863, the Secretary of War issued General Order 351, which relieved Dix of responsibility in the selection of nurses. She did not resign, for she had devoted three years to her work and wished to see it come to success whether under her control or another's. She continued in the office until the surrender of Lee at Appomattox.

Her next move was to return to her beloved New England. Somewhat later, Secretary Edwin Stanton asked her what she would like in recognition of her services to the cause of the Union, and she said, half in jest, "The flag of my country." Not thinking that the request would be so faithfully fulfilled, she was somewhat surprised when a box arrived containing a stand of the national colors together with a commending letter from the secretary. This gift was later bequeathed to Harvard University.

Once back again in New England, Dix renewed old acquaintanceships. Before long, she began to make plans. She wanted to undertake another extensive inspection trip of American institutions for the mentally ill as she had not been in contact with them much since the start of the war. But first, she wanted to aid the project of the newly established cemetery at Hampton, Virginia, near Fort Monroe. From her friends, she quietly gathered $8,000 to erect a monument at the cemetery in honor of the soldiers who had died in the war.

From 1867, for a period of fifteen years, Dix traveled throughout the country in her task of inspecting the conditions of the poor, the insane, and the criminal. At many places, she found results of her earlier labors; yet much remained to be done. With characteristic enthusiasm, she became once more the self-appointed advocate of the less fortunate, and she was able to accomplish significant social gains.

In 1870, her travels came to an abrupt halt when malaria brought her close to death. When she was well enough to travel, she was cautioned to take shorter trips and in general to cut down on her activities. In her later years, she was periodically ill, and the end came on the evening of July 18, 1887. Under her pillow was a copy of John Greenleaf Whittier's "At Last." She was buried in Mount Auburn Cemetery, near Boston. The burial service included the following scriptural quotation:

I was ahungered, and ye gave me meat: I was thirsty, and ye gave me drink: I was a stranger, and ye took me in:

Naked, and ye clothed me: I was sick, and ye visited me: I was in prison, and ye came unto me. (Matthew 25:35–36)

Chapter Six

Samuel Gridley Howe
(1801–1876)

Wouldst know him now? Behold him,
The Cadmus of the blind,
Giving the dumb lip language,
The idiot clay a mind.[1]

A friend once rebuked busy Samuel Howe for his lack of regular church attendance. The deeply religious Howe replied, "I pray! I pray with my hands and feet."

Unusually creative and active in the service of others, Howe left a trail of pioneering effort that many have followed. His life was his prayer. There were few aspects of charitable action that his genius did not touch, although he is chiefly remembered for his pioneer work with the blind in America.

Samuel Howe was born in Boston on November 10, 1801, the son of Joseph Neale and Patty Gridley Howe. Old patriotic New England stock was represented on both sides of his family. An uncle, Edward Howe, was one of the "Indians" at the Boston Tea Party; another uncle, Richard Gridley, helped fortify Bunker Hill the night before the fighting began. Not much is known of Howe's parents' lives, however, as it was not customary for New Englanders to write private journals—especially those who were not recognized literati. Joseph Howe was engaged in the manufacture of cordage—an important business in the days of the sailing vessel. He was so successful, in fact, that the family lived in more than modest circumstances for years. His father's economic status helped provide Samuel with a good formal education and later specialization.

At age eleven, Samuel was sent to the Boston Latin School, known at that time for the severity of its discipline as well as for its classical instruction. On one occasion the principal of the school announced that he was going to make Samuel cry and proceeded to beat the child's hand severely, but Samuel would not cry.

There were five other children in the Howe household—two boys and three girls. By the time the Howe children were old enough to attend college, their father had fallen on hard times. The business floundered, in part, due to the national government's failure to pay for a large quantity of rope it had ordered during the War of 1812. Joseph Howe decided that he could afford to send only one of his sons to college, so he gathered his three sons around him, opened the family Bible, and asked that each read a chapter. "The one who reads best," he explained, "shall go to college." Samuel decidedly was the best reader, and he was selected.

Samuel was seventeen when he began his studies at Brown University. Joseph Howe was an ardent Democrat, and Brown represented that political philosophy, while nearby Harvard was strongly Federalist. At Brown, Samuel did well in his studies, but few duties interfered with his practice of playing jokes on others. In later years, when calling on the retired president of Brown, he was to hear, "I declare, Howe, I'm afraid of you now. I'm afraid there will be a torpedo under my chair before I know it."

At the age of twenty Samuel was graduated from Brown and entered Harvard Medical School. With a new academic seriousness, he worked so hard at his studies that he took his degree in three years. Following graduation he faced the varied vocational world before him. He could turn to private practice in medicine, but also pressing upon his conscience at this time, as for others, was the Greek War of Independence. In an age of "the rights of men," almost everywhere the signal for self-determination had been given. The United States was not long over its own War of Independence, so enthusiasm for the idea of freedom ran high. Also, Lord Byron had dramatized in his poetry and his personal life the appeal of the Greek conflict. The glamour of the Greek war appealed mightily to Samuel, and he discussed it on many occasions. Once, when his sister Jennette overheard him talking about the subject, she rushed tearfully into his room and asked, "Why Samuel, you do not think seriously of going?" But Howe had made his decision and set sail for Greece in the winter of 1824–25. (Byron died at Missolonghi in April 1824. Some have said that he died in the arms of young Samuel Howe, but this is apocryphal. At any rate, Byron's helmet did come to Samuel, and he took great pride in it. Later, in 1926, it was taken to Athens where it was presented by one of Howe's daughters to the Greek government for display in the ethnological museum.)

The Greeks had suffered under the rule of the Turks for four hundred years. The uprising was led by Prince Alexander Ypsilanti, one of the Turk-appointed officers of the Greek regional government, with the blessing of the Greek Orthodox church. To further the cause of the Greek insurrectionists, Samuel Howe went to Greece as a physician. He related his early experiences there in a letter to Horace Mann, the famed American educator:

At first, there was an attempt to organize the army, and I attempted to create hospitals and to provide ambulances for the wounded. . . . The Turks advanced fiercely and rapidly up the Peloponnesus. I joined one of the small guerrilla bands that hung about the enemy, doing all the harm they could. I could be of little or no use as surgeon, and was expected to divide my attention between killing Turks, helping Greeks, and taking care of my bacon. . . .[2]

The new life of the young physician was hectic and physically demanding. His food consisted mostly of olives, stripped from trees on the rocky hills, and raw onions. Sometimes he managed to find wild figs. His bed was the stony ground with a goatskin for a blanket. But he was deeply inspired by the ideal of Greek independence, and this was sufficient to counteract the hardships.

In May 1825, Howe was transferred to the Greek fleet in the office of chief physician. He spent some time in Hydra with the British sailors stationed there, and then in the fall he accompanied the Greek expeditionary forces as they attempted to take the island of Crete. The following account from his journal tells of his personal dilemma and the plight of the people of Crete:

I know not what is to be done; there are not provisions enough in the place to last us a fortnight. And then for the hundreds of families who have taken refuge under the walls of the fortress, God! what must be their sufferings! As for myself, come what will, I am ready. I had half made up my mind to leave the place, but now that ill luck has come and danger thickens, it would be dishonorable; nor can I think of quitting my wounded, though the time for which I was engaged expired a week ago. . . .[3]

After the fall of Athens—a notable victory for the rebel forces—Howe turned his attention more and more to the problems of general relief for the civilian population not only of Athens but also of the whole of Greece. With funds provided by the Greek government and friends abroad, he spent considerable time in several communities, ministering to the needs of the people.

The first distribution of relief took place at Astros. Here he found about four hundred families living in "huts and holes." Some were so weak that they lay about in silent despair. All held life together by eating such herbs and grass as could be found. To these he distributed mainly clothing and flour. A hostile general sent a message to Howe requesting that Howe and the recipients of supplies acknowledge the general's political authority. Howe replied with a sturdy no. He would grant assistance on no grounds other than genuine need.

Following his experience at Astros, Howe moved on to other cities and towns. First came the needs of Nauplion, and a few days later he went to Leonidion, then to Lerna and Chavati. Everywhere there was tragic need. Supplies, meager to begin with, were fast running out. After careful consideration, Howe decided to leave Greece and return to America to urge his countrymen to raise the necessary funds for relief of the Greeks, and on November 13, 1827, he set sail for New York.

After visiting with his family for a few days, Howe sought to develop a plan to aid the people of Greece. Edward Everett, statesman and orator, urged him to begin a nationwide speaking campaign, but Howe thought that a written description of the recent events in Greece should be prepared first. He feared that without an understanding of recent Greek history, his appeal might fall on deaf ears. Thus Howe set his hand to writing a book, which he called *An Historical Sketch of the Greek Revolution*. To write a first-class account of the subject, more time would have been required than he had to give. But whatever the defects of Howe's book, it illustrated the intensity of his feelings on the Greek situation.

Next, Howe traveled to various cities—on Everett's suggestion—eventually covering most of the United States. Wherever he went, he spoke of Greek idealism and nationalism, appealing to the patriotic sympathies of Americans. Many who heard him were moved to contribute clothes, money, and other supplies. For Howe, finding support for the Greeks was a "sacred duty."

In November 1828, Howe landed on Aegina with a shipload of food and clothing. This island near Athens was filled with war refugees from all parts of the mainland. Several hundred of them were engaged in building an orphanage for the government. Their work was exhausting, but it was paid for in food. Many people, however, were not so fortunate as to find work, and for these, the prospect of starvation was imminent.

Howe tackled the problem of the unemployed and starving. He realized that his responsibility included more than the mere distribution of materials—in some way he wanted to help build an economy, even if temporary, to meet the continued needs of the people. He found that the port of Aegina was in sorry disrepair; it was "reduced to a state nearly resembling a marsh upon its border, preventing the boats from approaching the shore, and giving out an unpleasant and unwholesome odor." This was his opportunity. His plan included building a solid wall around the border of the port, reinforcing it with stones and earth, dredging the mud from the part within the wall, and covering the whole with stones.

In the middle of December 1828, one hundred men and two hundred women started work on the project. To choose these people was difficult, for there were many in need. Dividing the men and women into groups of twenty, he placed over each group a leader responsible to him. The pay was three pounds of Indian meal per man and two and one-half pounds per woman. The psychological lift the project granted was incalculable. In time, the number of workers was increased to six hundred.

Howe saw yet another way that ingenuity and supplies could be utilized to the best advantage. Some of the people asked for seed so that they could become self-supporting. The idea met with Howe's approval, but on one condition—that the people who accepted the seeds would turn over a third of their crops for the maintenance of a public school—a condition that was gladly accepted. With $100 worth of seeds, Howe succeeded in giving a large number of persons a start to economic self-dependence and provided in time $1,300 for the support of a local school. The good news quickly spread. Some Greeks left their distant homes and traveled to work for the foreign doctor. Howe offered hope to the ordinary Greek citizen, and it was readily accepted.

The living conditions of many of the people lay heavy on Howe's conscience. Needy boys were housed in a new government institution, but women and girls had no official shelter. Howe sent a letter to the president of Greece requesting that he be allowed, with government support, to build a women's shelter and hospital. After months of waiting, the effort was richly rewarded; the president said that he should build a model community. Selecting twenty-six families, Howe set out to establish his ideal community. First came homes for the people, then a school, and finally the other necessary buildings and equipment. For some of the needs of the community, such as agricultural equipment, Howe once again called on American friends, who were only too willing to help. In time, there remained only the minor problem of a name for the new village. Dr. Howe called it Washingtonia, although many Greeks preferred the more familiar name Hexamilia.

In 1830, while traveling from Corinth to Nauplion, Howe contracted a virulent form of swamp fever and barely escaped with his life. The physical marks of the disease were to remain with him for the rest of his life. Realizing that his health was seriously threatened and that his presence was not as needed in Greece now as it once had been, Howe turned his thoughts to the West and started home, traveling through Italy, Switzerland, England, Spain, and France before sailing for the United States. Arriving in Boston in 1831, Howe was confronted again with the problem of a career. He thought about devoting his time to a regular medical practice, but this prospect was not enough of a challenge after his strenuous years abroad. Offers of employment came to him, as he was deemed a valuable man for many types of work. The managership of a new daily newspaper in Philadelphia attracted him; the request that he take charge of a Negro colony in Liberia also held his attention. There were other tempting offers; but none seemed to be his life's work.

As in so many careers, circumstance was to make up Howe's mind for him. In 1829, the legislature of Massachusetts had passed an act establishing trustees for the New England Asylum for the Blind. But by 1831, the institution had not yet been built. One of the trustees, John D. Fisher, had journeyed abroad to observe European methods of dealing with the blind and was enthusiastic about establishing a first-class institution embodying recent knowledge and practice. The first and one of the largest problems that Fisher (and his colleagues on the board) faced was the selection of a man to direct the asylum. One day, so the story goes, Fisher and two fellow trustees were discussing the problem as they walked along the street. Fisher looked up to see Samuel Howe approaching and exclaimed, "The very man we are looking for!" While explaining his plan to Howe, Fisher and his colleagues sensed that they had found a man waiting for just such an opportunity. Howe knew immediately that he had met with a plan that would satisfy his vocational requirements.

Upon his acceptance, Howe set sail again for Europe to study first-hand the problems of the blind and to find teachers for his new institution. His quest was interrupted, however, by a letter from Lafayette requesting that Howe travel to Poland to help distribute 20,000 francs in relief supplies among political rebels who were also the heroes of a revolution—the Polish Revolution. Howe could not refuse. But before the work of helping the Polish rebels was complete, Howe received a peremptory letter from the standing Polish government demanding that he leave Poland *persona non grata*. There was nothing to do but leave.

Leaving Poland, Howe traveled to Berlin, where he ran into further difficulties. On the way to his hotel, he met a fellow visitor, Albert Brisbane. After exchanging greetings he retired for the night. A few hours later, he was aroused by three men who requested that he immediately appear before the German police. Howe asked if he might not put this off until the following morning, and his request was granted. As soon as they left, he stuffed his official papers in a plaster bust of the king of Prussia. In the morning he was arrested and imprisoned without trial.

After a month of confinement, Howe wrote to Dr. Fisher of his plight and he also corresponded with the American ambassador to France, William C. Rives. In the meantime Brisbane had returned to the hotel and asked for Howe. He was told that Howe had never been registered and that no one knew anything about him. Becoming suspicious, Brisbane also wrote to Ambassador Rives and made a requisition upon the German government on behalf of the unjustly detained American citizen.

At first there was some resistance to the idea that an American was so detained, and the German government refused to acknowledge Howe's presence. But after continued effort by a number of friends, Howe was summoned before the minister of police and told that he should leave the country promptly and quietly. Although he protested the lack of a fair trial and the chance to prove his innocence, Howe left the country immediately.

Years later Howe could only guess that the Germans, apparently by Polish direction, sought to punish him for his work in the Polish revolution. Howe, in time, received a gold medal from the Polish government in recognition of his American work with the blind, an act he assumed was a diplomatic apology. He noted that the medal was worth about as much as he had paid his jailer for food and other necessities while he languished in prison. Howe visited the same German hotel on a later visit, and carefully retrieved the papers he had hidden.

In the summer of 1832, Howe returned to Boston to begin in earnest his work as the head of the New England Asylum for the Blind.

Even before the building construction began, Howe and Dr. Fisher visited a family in Andover, where they found "two pretty little girls, one about six, the other about eight years old, tidily dressed. . . . It was a touching and interesting scene. . . . In a few days they were brought to Boston . . . as the first pupils. . . ." Six children in all quickly were found and taken into the Howe home.

The arrival of the six blind children called for certain adjustments on the part of both the Howe family and the young students. Apparently, however, there was no great protest from either side, and in fact, the family members helped out on many occasions. Howe acquainted himself with the problems of the children by going about the house blindfolded.

The first months of the asylum's existence were not easy, and Howe described the early difficulties in the *New England Magazine*. By January 1833, the trustees found that they had expended all their funds and were several hundred dollars in debt. In consequence, they arrived at a plan to "exhibit" the blind children before the state legislature to demonstrate the accomplishments of the first months and to appeal for money. The exhibition made "such a powerful impression as to induce the two houses to vote, almost by acclamation, the sum of $6,000 per annum to the Institution, on the condition that it should educate and support twenty poor blind from the State gratuitously." Other exhibitions were held in such cities as Salem and Boston: "The ladies of Salem first suggested the idea of a fair; and assisted by those of Marblehead and Newburyport, they got up a splendid fete, which resulted in a net profit of

$2,980." The ladies of Boston, not to be outdone, opened a bazaar on May 1, 1833, in Faneuil Hall, netting $11,400. By such means as well as private contributions, the work of the asylum progressed.

The next step was to find more suitable housing for the students. Colonel Thomas H. Perkins offered his own spacious house and gardens in Boston for the institution, provided that $50,000 be raised for its maintenance. The sum was large for the times, but it was soon collected, and the new institution moved to the big house on Pearl Street. By 1839, the name was changed to Perkins Institution, and in 1877, "and Massachusetts School for the Blind" was added. Today it is known as the Perkins School for the Blind.

The work of managing the institution was extremely demanding and severely taxed Howe's physical stamina. He found that he had to limit his interests if he was to continue to care for the many responsibilities of his office. Howe found that most of his work was true pioneering in that there were no American models and few suggestions to be found anywhere for the principles and techniques that he used at the school. In every situation, he had to analyze and imaginatively respond to the problems that arose with insistent regularity.

The results of Howe's work can be found in his yearly reports, which were circulated widely in the United States and Europe. While not all of his findings are in agreement with today's practices, Howe did discover ways of treating the blind that have since been found to be scientifically valid.

Despite the strenuous nature of his own program, Howe found time for activities outside the school. He was among the first to try to develop interest in the blind in other states; in one of his reports he mentions that he had spoken before seventeen state legislatures in the interest of the blind. Soon the practices begun in Boston were in use in many other areas.

One of the barriers to the education of the blind was the paucity of reading materials specifically made for them. The limited resources available included one volume in raised type containing summaries of certain English authors, the Gospel of John, and a theological work entitled *Christian Doctrines* by John Gail. Howe turned his efforts to remedying this situation.

Howe's first problem was to choose a kind of type that might be used in printing books for the blind. It was possible to use either a phonetic alphabet, a series of stenographic characters, or the common alphabet. After some deliberation, he chose the common alphabet, reducing the size of the type as much as possible. The next step was to secure funds, and this was not too difficult because of the appeal of the project. The money was collected, and the work began. In time, many books were made available to the blind, including *Paradise Lost, Paradise Regained, Hamlet, Julius Caesar, Pilgrim's Progress,* histories of the United States and England, selections from Byron, Pope, Baxter, and others, encyclopedias, atlases, and dictionaries.

Howe eventually decided that printing books for the blind was a proper activity for the federal government, so in the winter of 1836–1837, he traveled to Washington in hopes of convincing Congress to undertake this enterprise. Nothing came of this visit. In 1845, he revisited Washington for the same purpose, this time in the company of some of his students and representatives of other institutions for the blind. Again he failed. In 1879, however, Congress was finally moved to appropriate $250,000 for the printing of books with raised type.

Under the leadership of Howe's apprentice and successor, Michael Anagnos, the Howe Memorial Press was established to make more literature available to the blind. Today the press is still attached to the Perkins School. Blind persons are employed by the Howe Memorial Press, thus giving work to those who ultimately benefit from the product. The library of the Perkins Institution is one of the largest of its kind in the world, and its books are circulated to many thousands of "finger readers."

Howe's work with the deaf and dumb came into being in a roundabout way. In the spring of 1837, James Barrett, a student at Dartmouth College, visited the farmhouse of Daniel Bridgman, a selectman of the town of Hanover, New Hampshire. On this visit Barrett noticed a pretty little girl, Laura Bridgman, the selectman's daughter, who had been deaf and dumb as well as blind from a very early age. Barrett described the girl to Dr. Mussey, head of the Medical Department of the college. Mussey visited the child and was so touched that he wrote up the case for newspapers.

Howe read the story and immediately wanted to help Laura Bridgman if he could, so he set out at once for Hanover. Mrs.

Bridgman informed Howe that when she was two years old Laura had suffered an attack of a form of scarlet fever, which left her totally blind, deaf, and dumb. It was not until she was four years old that she was able to move about—so great was her weakness. Gradually she had become an active, intelligent child, with strong affections and dislikes.

With permission of the Bridgmans, Howe brought Laura to the Perkins Institution in October 1837. The former individuality of care could not be completely duplicated at the school. Laura felt the changes and for a period did not respond positively. There were many hours of weeping and homesickness and trying to meet the new regimen. After giving Laura a chance to adjust to the new environment, Howe began to teach her the alphabet. Howe's early efforts with Laura have been preserved in the Ninth Report of the institution:

> The first experiments were made by taking articles in common use, such as knives, forks, spoons, keys, etc., and pasting upon them labels with their names in raised letters. These she felt very carefully, and soon, of course, distinguished that the crooked lines *spoon* differed as much from the crooked lines *key*, as the spoon differed from the key in form.
>
> Then small detached labels, with the same words printed upon them, were put into her hands; and soon she observed that they were similar to the ones pasted on the articles. She showed her perception of this similarity by laying the label *key* upon the key, and the label *spoon* upon the spoon. She was here encouraged by the natural sign of approbation, patting on the head.
>
> The same process was then repeated with all the articles which she could handle; and she very easily learned to place the proper labels upon them. It was evident, however, that the only intellectual exercise was that of imitation and memory. . . .
>
> After a while, instead of labels, the individual letters were given to her on detached pieces of paper: they were arranged side by side, so as to spell *book, key*, etc.; then they were mixed up in a heap, and a sign was made for her to arrange them so as to express the words *book, key*, etc., and she did so . . . now the truth began to flash upon her—her intellect began to work—she perceived that here was a way by which she could herself make up a sign of anything that was in her own mind . . . and at once her countenance lighted up with a human expression: it was no longer a dog, a parrot—it was an immortal spirit, eagerly seizing upon a new link of union with other spirits! I could almost fix upon the moment

when this truth dawned upon her mind, and spread its light to her countenance. . . .

The result, thus far, is quickly related, and easily conceived; but not so was the process; for many weeks of apparently unprofitable labor were passed before it was effected.[4]

In time, through a variety of techniques, Laura began to read and to express herself. The course of this development was painstaking for teacher as well as for student. To her credit, Laura was always patiently responsive, eagerly seeking to achieve. Dr. Howe, on his part, devoted hours of his time and the deepest insight to provide a means of learning for Laura. Together they were an ideal teacher-student team.

For five years the learning process continued. Especially difficult was the development of religious values. On this point, Howe, a Unitarian, believed that he should do nothing to hinder the development of Laura's own mind and experience. He was opposed to the presentation of any theology as a means of indoctrinating Laura. Some objected to this procedure; they believed that her salvation depended on a certain type of religious instruction. Howe won out, at least for a time, but when he left Boston for a visit abroad, some of his subordinates took the opportunity to teach Laura the meaning of Protestant Christianity. This was entirely to Howe's regret. In one report (1841) Howe tells something of the religious quest of his pupil:

> During the past year she has shown very great inquisitiveness in relation to the origin of things. She knows that men made houses, furniture, etc., but of her own accord seems to infer that they did not make themselves, or natural objects. She therefore asks, "Who made dogs, horses and sheep?" She has got from books, and perhaps from other children the word *God,* but has formed no definite idea on the subject. . . .
>
> I am now occupied in devising various ways of giving her an idea of immaterial power by means of the attraction of magnets, the pushing of vegetation, etc., and intend attempting to convey to her some adequate idea of the Creator and Ruler of all things.[5]

The case of Laura Bridgman received world-wide attention, and letters came to Howe and his associates from many parts of the United States and England. Charles Dickens praised the excellent relationships maintained between teacher and student, and Thomas Carlyle wrote a long letter to Howe in which he expressed his admiration for the project. Americans also held great respect for the innovative doctor. Chief among these was Laura Bridgman herself, who throughout her life was quick to praise Howe's work.

The Perkins School is noted for its work with Helen Keller, which was done under the leadership of Howe's successor, Michael Anagnos. Anagnos chose Anne Sullivan, a graduate of the school, to work in Alabama with the two-year-old Helen Keller, who was blind and deaf. Sullivan had entered Perkins because she was nearly blind, but through a series of operations, she regained most of her sight. Sullivan used the techniques that Howe had created in his work with Laura Bridgman to teach language to Helen Keller. Keller and Sullivan spent the years 1889 to 1893 at Perkins as the guests of Anagnos.

The institution developed over the years until it was crowded with eager students. By 1839, efforts were made to secure increased facilities, and the Mount Washington House was decided on as its new home. This building had been a large, fashionable hotel catering to the wealthy in Boston. Some thought of it as the finest hotel in the country, but at this time it was old and shabby. Howe saw in the house a fine place to locate his school, and broached the subject to his board. The house was purchased, and the school was transferred, remaining there until 1912, when it moved to Watertown, Massachusetts.

Howe disliked the use of the word *asylum* in connection with the institution and preferred to think of the institution as a home for his friends. These people, he felt, were "above" the charity connoted by the term asylum. He believed that all persons are equal and are entitled to the treatment they need without regard for their social position or their need. On more than one occasion, Howe encountered difficulty because he wished to accept people at the institution on the basis of need, without regard to race, nationality, creed, or other dividing factor in social affairs. Some of those close to the institution felt at first that such a policy was wrong and impractical. There was even more protest from those not directly connected with the institution, but Howe stood firm, saying, "I should no more think of refusing to help one of my fellow-mortals on account of the color of his skin, than the color of his hair." He called upon his trustees to provide "every facility for educating all blind children, black, white, or red, who may apply to them." In this spirit, Howe was maintaining not only the principles of the Christian faith but also the demands that he felt were implicit in the federal Constitution.

Howe sought to provide individual attention for all of his students. To carry out this aim, he selected those teachers who were strongly interested in their students as well as capable in their subjects. He was fortunate during his term as head of the institution that by and large he succeeded in securing talented co-workers. They, like Howe, believed in individual attention for the children. The conditions under which the blind lived made such care not only desirable but necessary. Every student had a teaching master who helped him with his own unique needs and aspirations.

The Perkins Institution was not Howe's only interest. He had many friends, and it was said that every foreigner coming into Boston counted him as a personal friend. Poles looked upon him as a national helper; Greeks had undying admiration for the work that he had accomplished in their homeland. He was a friend who was ever willing to help. Howe's closest friends were Charles Sumner, Horace Mann, Theodore Parker, and Francis W. Bird. Sumner and Howe shared common ideological goals. He greatly admired the Unitarian preacher Parker, but disagreed with him on many points. Bird was his friend and counselor in later years. With Horace Mann, Howe battled against the forces of inhumanity and ignorance. Mann's feeling toward his friend was expressed many years later in an address to the students at Antioch College in Ohio, of which he was president:

He [Howe] is the best specimen extant of all that was noble and valiant in the old chevaliers; and in their day he would have been as terrible and as generous a warrior as Godfrey or Amadis de Gaul. He is a man capable of all moods of mind, from the stormiest to the gentlest; with a voice that could shout on a charge of cavalry, or lull a sick infant to sleep. When that ocean of feeling he carries in his breast is calm, the halcyon bird might there build her nest and brood her young; but when the tempest of a holy indignation rouses it, navies could not survive its fury. . . .[6]

Up to 1842, Howe lived in a wing of the institution with his unmarried sister, Jennette, as housekeeper and companion. Content as he was with this arrangement, circumstances changed. Henry W. Longfellow, a member of an informal club with Howe, and Sumner became interested in three sisters, Julia, Louisa, and Annie Ward. They were the daughters of Samuel Ward of New York, head of the banking firm of Prime, Ward, and King. In the summer of 1841, Julia accepted an invitation from Longfellow and Sumner to visit the institution and meet Laura Bridgman and Dr. Howe. She recorded how Sumner, looking from a window, said: "Oh, here comes Howe on his black horse!" In her eyes, however, she saw "a noble rider on a noble steed."

Thus began the acquaintance of Samuel Howe and Julia Ward. Their ages seemed to be against their creating a permanent affection that would lead to marriage, since Howe was forty at the time and Julia only twenty-two, but on almost every count they were in perfect harmony; both were humanitarians and both were scholarly. The friendship thus formed grew into love, and they were married in April 1843. In time, six children were born into the household. Of these, five grew to maturity.

The Howes toured Europe on their honeymoon, taking with them Julia's sister Annie. Howe's work with Laura Bridgman was widely respected in England, and wherever the Howes went, they were well received. Many wanted to hear him talk about his work with the blind so that they could learn how to improve their own practices. Dickens took him on tours of prisons, hospitals, and asylums, and Howe took copious notes, storing ideas for the day when he would resume his duties at the institution.

Following their visit to London, the Howes went to Wales, Scotland, and Ireland. Always interested in improving his institution, Howe kept himself alert to opportunities of learning. In a letter to Sumner from Dublin, Howe wrote, "I run now to see a deaf, dumb, and blind boy, seven miles out of town." In August of that year they crossed the Channel to Belgium and then visited Germany, Austria, and Italy. In Italy, Mann and Parker joined them. Now five, the party went on sight-seeing tours of the country and especially of Rome.

Soon after the birth of a daughter, Julia Romana, on March

22, 1844, Howe decided that he had been away from his work in Boston long enough. Gathering his family, he started home, stopping a short time in France, where methods of dealing with the blind and the deaf were advanced for that time. In England, the Howes met Florence Nightingale, then a young woman of twenty-four, and she invited them to her home in Hampshire. Howe encouraged Nightingale to assume her vocation of nursing, and throughout her career, the Howes showed keen interest in her work. At Howe's death in 1876, Nightingale wrote a letter to Julia Howe expressing the appreciation she had felt over the years for the encouragement she had been given.

In the fall of 1844, Howe and his family returned to Boston to take up again the work of the Perkins Institution. There were new responsibilities to be assumed. Dorothea Dix had been working hard to improve the conditions of the mentally ill, and what she found was to shock the people of Massachusetts into initiating a broad program for the relief of the insane. But she did not work alone. One of those on whom she depended was Samuel Howe, who was at the time a member of the state legislature. He introduced the memorial drawn up by Dix. When it was not received in a quick and warm fashion by the legislators, he conducted an investigation of the East Cambridge jail and published supporting evidence in the *Boston Daily Advertiser.* Some disregarded his findings, but most accepted his report and Dix's memorial.

Howe's interest in the deaf led him to study the problems they presented. At one time, he was convinced that the method of teaching the deaf should be one of articulation instead of sign language, accepted then as now. Dr. T. H. Gallaudet, founder and president of the American Asylum for Deaf-Mutes in Hartford, Connecticut, the first free school in America for the deaf, opposed him in his methods, believing that sign language was the only feasible method for teaching the deaf. The results of Howe's experiments with the articulation method were embodied in a small school at Chelmsford, near Boston.

Another of Howe's interests was the public schools. Along with Horace Mann, he believed that the schools needed vast improvement. The two held also to the idea that teachers should be specially trained in "normal schools." One trip Howe made to the western part of the United States convinced him that something had to be done to improve the quality of instruction in the schools. On his return, he joined forces with Mann and others to fight for such improvements. With Mann as the leader, a small group of citizens, organized as the Boston School Committee, analyzed the school system in Boston and brought various charges of inefficiency and neglect to the attention of the people.

Howe was an early advocate of prison reform in Massachusetts. Although he favored a mode of treatment which was not to win out in the long development of prisons in the United States (the so-called Philadelphia system, whereby prisoners were completely isolated), he did encourage various reforms that have lasted. The Prison Discipline Society (later called the Prisoner's Aid Society), which met in Howe's office, sought to alleviate some of the personal needs of convicts. It also helped discharged criminals find work and offered counseling for prisoners. Perhaps the fact that Howe had once been a prisoner himself helped him to appreciate the plight of prisoners, but whatever the source of his motivation, he strove for the betterment of prison conditions and the rehabilitation of criminals. In this work, as in his work with the blind and others, Howe believed that individual attention was the secret of successful rehabilitation. He wrote, "It is hard work to make straight a single crooked stick—harder yet a bundle of them, taken together."

Howe was also concerned with the plight of the mentally retarded. Very little had been done up to his time for the systematic care of such persons. Most retarded were cared for by their own families; others were placed in almshouses or poorhouses, which acted as catch-alls for persons who could not care for themselves. Howe studied the problems of the mentally retarded during his travels in Europe, where he visited many institutions, especially in France. He had first-hand knowledge of their problems, as he had taken several retarded children into his own school. Some responded positively, others poorly.

Two chief difficulties existed in trying to help the mentally retarded. One was the fact that no one was certain how much improvement they could make as a group. Most people viewed them not as individuals capable of personal improvement and of service to society, but as social misfits who permanently needed to be cared for as dependents. Howe realized that it was necessary to test this popular conception in his own experience before attempting reforms. He used his own cases in his later reports (as well as the cases of other workers throughout the state of Massachusetts) as an indication that the condition of the mentally retarded was far from hopeless. Howe concluded from his investigations that the mentally retarded were capable of certain constructive activities and that many also were able to take care of themselves financially. One of the conclusions of Howe's work is that while the mentally retarded person needs to be understood as an individual possessing particular limitations, he also has compensating potentialities that need to be stressed and developed.

The second problem was that little exact information existed on such matters as the numbers of mentally retarded in the state or the basis on which they were or were not receiving help. In the winter of 1845, Howe resolved to make an effort to remedy this situation. Under the sponsorship of Judge Horatio Byington, an order was introduced on January 22, 1846, in the House of Representatives of Massachusetts that called for the appointment of a committee "to consider the expediency of appointing commissioners to inquire into the condition of the idiots of the Commonwealth; to ascertain their number and whether anything can be done for their relief, and to report to the next General Court." Howe was one of the three commissioners appointed.

In the spring of 1846 the commissioners began their work, and before it was finished, two years had passed. They visited sixty-three towns and examined the condition of "five hundred and seventy-four human beings who were condemned to hopeless idiocy, who are considered and treated as idiots by their neighbors, and left to their own brutishness." The report that followed was a sad portrayal of the conditions the mentally retarded faced. The conclusion of the report, as penned by Chairman Howe, was: "There is not one of any age who may not be made more of a man and less of a brute by patience and kindness directed by energy and skill."

In addition to the formal report required of the committee, Howe wrote an article for the *Massachusetts Quarterly Review*, which proved to be sensational in its effects. In it he reiterated the descriptions embodied in the official report and the conclusions he had drawn. Some accepted the report and the popular article as examples of enlightened humaneness. Many, however, viewed the work of the committee as distorted and sentimental. One friend of the family said to Julia Howe that the doctor had written a report for idiots as well as concerning them!

The legislature received the report with reservations, but appropriated $2,500 per annum on an experimental basis to provide for the teaching and training of ten mentally retarded children. Howe was given the responsibility of carrying out the program. He found the children readily enough and selected James B. Richards as their teacher. Howe established the new unit in a wing of the Perkins Institution and personally directed the program. At the end of the first year his report included the following passage:

> They have all improved in personal appearance and habits, in general health, in vigor, and in activity of body. Almost all of them have improved in the understanding and the use of speech. But what is most important, they have made a start forward. They have begun to give their attention to things; to observe qualities, and to exercise thought. . . . It has been demonstrated that idiots are capable of improvement, and that they can be raised from a state of low degradation to a higher condition. . . .[7]

A year later, Howe was able to report even greater progress with the mentally retarded under his care:

> A great change has come over them. They have improved in health, strength, and activity of body. They are cleanly and decently in their habits. They dress themselves, and for the most part sit at table and feed themselves. They are gentle, docile, and obedient. . . . They have learned their letters, and some of them, who were speechless as brutes, can read easy sentences and short stories. . . .[8]

The success of the venture seemed to be established, but the development of work with the mentally retarded within an institution that was devoted to the care of the blind raised fundamental problems. Howe and his staff were greatly relieved when, in 1855, a site was chosen in South Boston, some distance from the Perkins Institution, for the erection of a school specifically for mentally retarded children. Samuel Howe remained involved with the School for Feebleminded and not only managed the affairs of the school, but traveled to other states to tell about the work of the school and the needs of the mentally retarded generally. As a result of Howe's visits and reports, several states established institutions similar to the school in Boston.

Until 1868, Howe received no salary or financial aid from either the institution or the school. As was the case of many other social welfare pioneers, his work was a personal contribution. In fact, Howe contributed financially to his projects. Howe also gave unstintingly of his time. He needed only four or five hours sleep a night, which enabled him to manage a wide variety of activities and responsibilities, but not to the neglect of his family. The life of his family in the institution was naturally hampered, however, by official responsibilities, so in 1845, Howe and his family moved to a six-acre estate in Washington Heights called "Green Peace." Here Dr. Howe was able to take up gardening and get some needed rest. In the large house, the family gathered frequently for recitals and performances by family members and to entertain friends.

Howe's opinion was generally respected in the area of public affairs. The slavery issue and his early response to it clearly shows this. There was no mistaking Howe's attitude on the ethics of slavery—he opposed it at every turn. From time to time he was called on to speak to large groups on the subject, and Howe did not hesitate, so great were his convictions. In 1846, when a New Orleans slave named Joe was kidnapped on a Boston Street to be returned to his former home, Howe was the organizer of a protest meeting at Faneuil Hall. John Quincy Adams was the presiding officer; Charles Sumner, Wendell Phillips, Theodore Parker, and Howe were the speakers. Howe's outspokenness has been preserved in the following excerpt of his speech on that occasion:

The "peculiar institution" which has so long been brooding over the country like an incubus, has at length spread abroad its murky wings, and has covered us with its benumbing shadow. It has silenced the pulpit; it has muffled the press; its influence is everywhere. . . . Let there be words of such potency spoken here this night as shall break the spell that is upon the community. Let us devise such means and measures as shall secure to every man who seeks refuge in our borders all the liberties and all the rights which the law allows him.[9]

As a result of the meeting, a Vigilance Committee of forty persons was formed to aid fugitive slaves in the region and to enlist popular support for "the cause of the Negro." In this work Howe took a prominent part, and in 1862 he was appointed a member of a national commission to study the possibility of emancipating the slaves. After Emancipation, Howe was made a member of the Freedmen's Inquiry Commission, the successor to the Vigilance Committee. It, in turn, was succeeded by the Freedmen's Bureau, in which Howe's activities were notable. Throughout his career Howe maintained an active and practical interest in the betterment of the conditions of Negroes.

One of Howe's early steps to help the antislavery movement was a decision to run for Congress. In the election, however, he was defeated. Some of his friends viewed this outcome as advantageous in that it enabled Howe to maintain and develop his various welfare activities, which he would have had to abandon if he had been elected. Howe's defeat did not keep him from working hard on several occasions to secure the election of his friends. In 1848, for example, on the death of Congressman John Quincy Adams, he exerted great effort to help Horace Mann take Adams' place, this time with success. In 1851, he labored to elect Charles Sumner to his seat in the Senate. Howe often dropped important personal matters to bring before the electorate his views on debated issues in public elections.

In 1851, Howe took on another responsibility. Louis Kossuth, a Hungarian patriot, arrived in the United States hoping to raise money to renew his struggle for democracy against the reign of the House of Hapsburg. Congress was sympathetic to Kossuth's proposals and provided a ship for this mission. When Kossuth arrived in Boston he was met by Howe, who sought to arouse Bostonians to support the revolutionary. Boston bedecked itself with slogans of welcome for the noted patriot, but did little more. In fact, Howe's campaign for Kossuth was a financial failure in Boston and elsewhere. After an unsuccessful national tour, Kossuth was forced to return to Hungary, a disappointed man.

Soon afterwards, another cause took the place of the fruitless efforts to aid Kossuth. Many of the slave-states of the South were sending settlers into Kansas with the hope of claiming it for the cause of slavery. The Northern states were engaged in the same pursuit with the goal of making Kansas a "free" state. Two companies of settlers went out from Massachusetts in 1854 to form the town of Lawrence. Under a Massachusetts charter, a New England Emigrant Aid Company was organized that had as its objectives "to supply information, cheaper transportation, and set up saw-mills and flour mills in the new territory." Thousands of people rallied to support a "free" Kansas. Howe worked hard on committees that were set up to support the Northern sentiment. He was the chairman of Boston's Faneuil Hall Committee and a member of the National Kansas Committee, which he had helped establish in Buffalo in 1856.

It occurred to Howe that he himself might transmit some of the aid that the groups had provided for Kansas. He set out in July 1856 in the company of Thaddeus Hyatt, chairman of the National Kansas Committee. He described the journey as being rough; of the passage through Iowa, he said: "I have traversed the whole length of the State of Iowa on Horseback or in a cart, sleeping in said cart or in the worst lodgings, among dirty men on the floor of dirty huts."

Throughout the summer, Howe worked in Kansas to help the emigrants achieve their objective. The opposition was determined, and strong feelings were stirred on both sides. But the primary purpose of the trip was accomplished in the end, and Howe returned to Boston in the early fall. Kansas remained in his memories; the idea of living there was so attractive that he bought several parcels of land in Kansas and contemplated moving there.

Several days after his return, President Lincoln called for volunteers to defend the Union, and Massachusetts responded with three regiments. Less than a week later, two boats laden with supplies for the troops left Boston for Washington. The governor of Massachusetts, responding to the offer of service tendered by Howe, asked him and Judge E. R. Hoar to follow the boats to check on the health conditions of the soldiers. So, at the age of sixty, Dr. Samuel Howe started out on another mission of mercy.

In Washington Howe cared for the troops from Massachusetts, but there were other problems that called for his attention. At the request of the Union commander-in-chief, General Winfield, Howe wrote a report on the living conditions of the soldiers in Washington. This report was remembered for the bluntness with which Howe described and condemned the poor conditions he found. Partly as a result of Howe's efforts, the Sanitary Commission was founded in June 1861. While accompanying her husband as he made rounds among the troops, Julia Howe wrote the lyrics of the "Battle Hymn of the Republic." Also in this period, Howe came in contact once again with Dorothea Dix, who was in Washington as superintendent of nurses.

Along with others, Howe realized that the war was only one step in the full emancipation of the Negro. He believed that constructive efforts were needed to prepare the public for the positive implications of Emancipation, so he called together some of the antislavery leaders. Out of this meeting developed the Emancipation League. *Commonwealth*, a journal that had been devoted to constructive thinking about the future of the Negro, but that had ceased publication, was revived as a part of the program of the league.

At the close of the war, Howe again returned to Boston and his work with the blind and the deaf. He envisaged changes in the organization of the institution; he wanted small, separate buildings instead of the large institutional structures of the past, so that there would be a greater intimacy among the children and the staff. He felt that the smaller buildings would encourage a family feeling in the residents. It was Howe's habit, when in Boston, to arrive at the institution at six o'clock in the morning to read the morning devotions to the assembled children. The service was always simple—a hymn, a Bible reading, and the Lord's Prayer. Practical Unitarianism was the keynote of Howe's life. His attitude toward religion is well summarized in his words: "My own views upon religion are that it should rather be an affair of the heart than of the head; of the feelings than of the intellect. I hold him to be a truer Christian who religiously feels and acts than him who religiously believes and thinks."[10]

Howe had a prominent role in the establishment of the first state public welfare department in the United States. In December 1862, Governor John Andrew of Massachusetts wrote to Howe asking him to "place on paper for my edification your views in reference to general and systematic improvement in our method of public charities." The correspondence that resulted helped formulate the Board of State Charities of Massachusetts. From the beginning, Howe held the highest hopes for public welfare systems, believing that they could accomplish much good.

Among Howe's avocational interests was the Saturday Club, to which he was elected during the first year of the Civil War. In the membership were some of the brightest names in the history of New England culture at the time: Sumner, Agassiz, Longfellow, Felton, Emerson, Holmes, Dwight, Andrew, and Whipple. The members of the club were not only reformers but possessed a breadth and depth of general learning as well.

In 1866, the people of Crete rebelled against Turkish rule and sought their independence, but the uprising was not successful. Howe, hearing the old call to Greek freedom, responded once again. After a meeting in his office, a committee was formed to support the Cretans. Public meetings were held in the Boston Music Hall, and some of the speakers who rallied to the cause of the Cretans were Oliver Wendell Holmes, Wendell Phillips, and Edward Everett Hale. The response of the people was generous.

The following year, Howe sailed for Greece with his wife and two daughters. The Turkish government had declared that Howe would suffer the death penalty if he were to land on Crete, but this did not deter him. He delivered his supplies and did what he could to help meet the pressing material needs of the people. On his return, Howe wrote a small book, *The Cretan Refugees and Their American Helpers*, in which he told of his efforts on behalf of the people of Crete. He also helped organize a fair to raise money for the cause, and a newspaper called *The Cretan* further publicized the issues. Though the cause was ultimately unsuccessful, Howe's efforts in Crete again emphasized his humanitarian values.

It was on the trip to Crete that Howe met an enterprising and capable Greek, Michael Anagnos. Because of the help that Anagnos gave to Howe in Greece, he was asked to return with the Howes to America. In time, he married Howe's daughter Julia and became Howe's secretary at the Perkins Institution. Upon Howe's death, Anagnos became head of the institution.

The last decade of Howe's life was characterized by ill health, yet he still managed to supervise the successful development of many of his projects. In January 1874, he fell seriously ill and was directed to leave New England for a warmer climate. He decided to go to Samana, in the Dominican Republic, where he had once worked as a member of a commission appointed by President Grant. By May, he felt well enough to return home. For several more years he was able to take part in various welfare activities, but on a reduced basis. He resigned the chairmanship of the State Board of Charities, but maintained active association with the Perkins Institution.

On January 4, 1876, while on the way to work, Howe suffered a stroke, and a few days later, he died. A great memorial service was held in Boston, and on the stage sat "the silent orator of the occasion," Laura Bridgman.

Today the Perkins School for the Blind, the first school founded in the United States for the education of blind children, still stands as a living monument to Samuel Gridley Howe. The institution is both a residential and a day school located in Watertown, Massachusetts, just west of Boston on the banks of the Charles River. It seeks to educate blind children so that they can take their place in adult society as competent and contributing members. In general, its curriculum is similar to that of the public schools, although it also has many features of a private boarding school. With more than three hundred blind students attending, the Perkins School continues the work pioneered by Howe.

Chapter Seven

Frederick Ozanam
(1813–1853)

Frederick Ozanam was not born to the purple, nor was he called to martyrdom, and yet in his short life . . . a brief space of forty years, he accomplished so much that Holy Scripture best describes it saying: "Few were his years, but in them he did the work of many." His life, diamond-like, had many facets, so many and each one so brilliant that you wonder if Ozanam should not be regarded as a genius —a kind of a "superman." In the space of a decade he was a lawyer, author, literateur, sociologist, religionist, economist, lecturer, professor, while dominating all his studies and his life was one consuming passion—his love of the poor.[1]

Frederick Ozanam, noted for his part in the founding of the Society of Saint Vincent de Paul, packed a large amount of social usefulness into his forty brief years. He was a creative leader who saw in the principles of the Roman Catholic church the requirements of social service.

Ozanam was born in Milan, Italy, on April 23, 1813. At that time, Milan was under the domination of the French. The Ozanam family lived there for three years after the birth of Frederick, until the city was taken by the Austrians, following the defeat of Napoleon. The fact that the Ozanams remained in Milan only so long as it was a French city shows the degree of French patriotic fervor held especially by Dr. Jean-Antoine Ozanam, Frederick's father.

Jean-Antoine enlisted in the French Army when he was about twenty years old. He knew the glories of French might, as well as the unpleasant aspects of the warrior's life. During the Napoleonic campaigns, Ozanam distinguished himself for bravery and devotion to his country. On several occasions his valor came to the attention of Napoleon himself, and he was given diplomatic assignments of a minor nature. In Napoleon's hour of defeat, young Jean-Antoine sympathized with him and shared his resentments. Captain Ozanam (the rank he finally achieved) was greatly impressed by the heroic figure of Napoleon, but he did not like the leader's failure to develop democratic principles in his political empire. Captain Ozanam admired power, but believed that it must have bounds, moral bounds, or else the whole structure of power would fall. His Roman Catholic background convinced him of this. It was probably this reason that prompted him to leave the army in 1798, at the age of twenty-five.

As soon as he was released from the army, Jean-Antoine went to Lyons to renew his friendship with Marie Nantas. She was nineteen at the time of their marriage in 1800, he was twenty-seven, but this difference did not matter. They were admirably suited to each other, as each was devoted to the interests of the other in practical ways. They decided to leave Lyons for Paris to begin a silk business (Marie's parents were in the silk trade, so it seemed a likely field of economic activity). In

Paris, the new couple succeeded both at business and at home. In time, they gained a good income from the business and raised a family.

Generosity undid the fortunes of the Ozanam family. Jean-Antoine loaned a great deal of money to a friend or relative (which is not known exactly), and the borrower went bankrupt and was unable to repay the money. The Ozanam family found that its means had been stripped away. Friends brought Jean-Antoine's plight to Napoleon's attention, and Napoleon offered Ozanam a position as captain in his special guards. Later, several other governmental positions were offered, but Ozanam decided against these positions. He had made up his mind regarding Napoleon, and he saw no reason to change it. He chose instead to go to Milan, a city in which he had made friends on one of his military missions. Because he had received a good education (he was graduated with honors from the Oratorian College in Lyons), he was able to find a job tutoring. This, however, was not enough to support his family adequately, and he realized that he would have to turn to something else.

Ozanam had wanted to be a physician. Now, he began the study of medicine in addition to his schedule of teaching. This required considerable study and physical effort. Too poor to buy a stage-coach passage to Pavia, where he was required to take examinations every three months, he walked the nineteen miles each way. At the end of two years, he was so well prepared that he was licensed to practice medicine.

It was during this period in Milan that Frederick was born, the fifth son of the Ozanams (two sons died in childhood). He was baptized Antoine-Frederic, but his friends and family called him Frederick. Baptism was postponed for about a month because a typhus epidemic was raging in the city, and Dr. Ozanam was exceedingly busy. He worked so hard for the welfare of the Milanese that he was decorated by the emperor's stepson, Prince Eugene Beauharnais. In May of 1813, Frederick was baptized in the Church of St. Charles Borromeo in Milan.

When Frederick was three, the Ozanam family settled in Lyons. It was difficult at first for Jean-Antoine to establish himself in his profession in the new city, but in time he was able to attract patients. Because he had published a paper in a scientific journal, he had a reputation beyond the borders of Milan.

Frederick's mother, Marie, gave her family great affection and help. Her own life had not been easy; she had experienced wars and epidemics, which made it possible for her to appreciate the troubles of others. While Jean-Antoine tended to be strong in the face of adversity, Marie knew from experience that it is necessary to depend on greater-than-human sources of strength, especially in times of crisis. Marie Ozanam bore fourteen children during her lifetime, but only four grew to maturity. Alphonse, who was older than Frederick, entered the priesthood and later wrote a biography of Frederick. Charles became a physician, and Elisa died when she was only nineteen.

Most of Frederick's early life centered in his home, where he found a rich life. The interests of his mother helped him to appreciate many activities. His father's love of learning and his patience in instruction helped Frederick form a deep and continuing feeling for scholarship. The companionship of his brothers and sister (he was seven when she died) made his family days complete.

The Ozanam home life stressed a vital and pious form of religion, exemplified by the lives of the parents. Jean-Antoine often prayed for his family, the world, and himself. He acted charitably by freely giving his medical services to the poor in Lyons.

Until he was nine, Frederick received his education at home. Then he became a student at the Royal College of Lyons, a member of the fifth class. The college trained in the classics, graduating students with the Bachelor of Arts degree. The college had a positive effect on Frederick. He wrote that, before college, "[I was] headstrong, passionate and disobedient. If I were punished, I revolted; I wrote letters of complaint to my mother; I was frightfully lazy." After he entered college, he changed, according to what he wrote years later. "There I gradually became better. The spirit of emulation conquered my laziness." There is no evidence that he was brilliant in his studies, but, on the other hand, no indication exists that he was less than average.

No matter what his formal school experience may have

shown, it is clear from his later development that Frederick Ozanam had a brilliant mind. The education he later achieved required outstanding intellect. His written contributions also show that his was an incisive and broad mentality. But in his earlier years, intellectual problems were not as important to him as his moral shortcomings. At times he was inclined to be morose and worried about his spiritual health. He was capable of great sympathy for the underdog or the oppressed, but he was also capable of being selfish and defensive. Seldom could he admit that he was wrong, and sometimes he was even willing to come to blows defending his opinions.

In 1829, Dr. Ozanam wrote in his family diary: "I desire to make Frederick a Barrister, or preferably, a member of the Magistracy or a Judge in the Royal Court of Justice." To Frederick, as with many sons, his father's choice was less attractive than another field—in this case, literature. He felt that a lawyer's life is taken up with small details, which lacked vital appeal. Dr. Ozanam supplied Frederick with two teachers, one for German, the other for drawing. It is impossible to say what his efforts were in drawing as no examples of his art have been preserved, but his interest in language was marked. He studied not only German but also English, Hebrew, and Sanskrit. These were in addition to the French and Italian of his youth and the Latin and Greek of his early schooling. With these tools for research, he read books from many fields. His feverish desire to know everything kept him busy almost all of his waking hours.

Frederick had no serious difficulties with his studies. His emotional life was different. At the time of his stay at the Royal College, he fell into a period of deep religious despair, which he finally resolved. He described this period as follows:

> In the midst of an age of scepticism, God gave me the grace to be born in the Faith. As a child I listened at the feet of a Christian father and a saintly mother. I had as my earliest teacher an intelligent sister, as pious as the angels whom she has gone to join. Later, the muffled din of an unbelieving world reached me. I experienced all the horror of doubt, which by day gnaws at the soul without ceasing, and by night hovers over our pillows wet with vain tears. Uncertainty as to my eternal destiny left me no rest. In despair I grasped at sacred dogma, only to find it crumbling in my

hands. Then it was that a priest who was also a philosopher came to my rescue. He dispelled the clouds and illumined the darkness of my thoughts. From then I believed with faith grounded on the rock. Touched by such a grace I promised God to consecrate my days to the service of truth. That restored peace to my soul. [2]

The "priest who was also a philosopher" was the Abbe Noiret, a teacher at the college. It was to the abbe that Frederick turned when he fell into despair. They walked together along the river bank and talked about the doubts that Frederick's mind entertained. The priest showed Frederick that there was no essential conflict between knowledge or science and Christianity. The meaning of faith rested upon a sound framework of understanding plus an additional insight into the ultimate mystery of all life. Drawing upon his knowledge of science, philosophy, theology, and the various disciplines, Abbe Noiret succeeded in demonstrating to Frederick's satisfaction that religious experience has a genuine validity in personal life and in institutional expressions. The influence of Abbe Noiret was decisive in formulating Frederick Ozanam's later activities.

Frederick did not spend all of his college period brooding over ultimate questions. There was time and energy for play. In one of his letters to his family, Frederick paints a picture of the gaiety that occurred at times during those preparatory years:

Sometimes there are memories. The amusing episode of college, and the first Communion, that touching scene whose minutest details are deeply graven on my heart. Then the initial delights of study, the uncertainties, the explorations, the healthy and stimulating philosophy of the Abbe Noiret, and, in the midst of all that, many friendships begun on the benches at school which still endure. And all the games we played, from Noah's Ark and the tin soldiers to our sentimental rambles and our serious parties at chess. Afterward, as background to the picture, life at home, your caresses and spoilings, your gentle words while I worked at the table beside you, consulting you about my themes when in the sixth and reading you my French discourses as a rhetorician; the counsels and, sometimes, the good-natured growls of Papa, my long walks with him and his stories which used to give me so much pleasure. . . .[3]

Frederick seldom had a chance to proclaim his faith in the teachings of Roman Catholic Christianity, nor was he pressured to deny it. But there was at least one instance when his moral bravery was evident. While he was working in the law offices of Monsieur Coulet after finishing college, he fell into the company of other workers who, at best, sneered at all religion. Frederick stood these conditions as long as he could, and then he exploded. He told them what he believed and how their actions violated his beliefs. He did not censure them so much as make plain the basis of his own life in his faith.

He soon got another chance to defend his beliefs when the doctrines of Saint-Simonism became rampant in his city. Saint-Simonism (derived from a socialist writer, Count Claude Henri de Saint-Simon) swept over urban France in the years following 1830. It met many of the emotional needs of the times. Preaching a despairing and disparaging message regarding the value of traditional religion, Saint-Simonism glorified the power of individuals. Its utopian elements were received like balm by the workers in France. They saw in Saint-Simonism a means of attaining a settled and abundant life for all people, especially for those who had notable material lacks. Many of the newspapers in Paris and other French cities supported Saint-Simonism.

To Ozanam, however, these new doctrines were the work of the devil: they deluded persons with legitimate needs into thinking that these needs could be quickly and almost miraculously met, and they misguided the intellectuals, who already were prone to overvalue the strengths of human reason. Most important of all, they misinterpreted the meaning of genuine religion and attacked the church, which was the hope of the oppressed. So Frederick sat down to write two articles for the *Precursor,* a liberal newspaper that was willing to print his comments. These articles received a great deal of attention from the readers. Ozanam's friends urged him to develop the two articles and publish them and the resulting hundred-page booklet brought the eighteen-year-old author fame as a writer and intellect. His views on the system of Saint-Simon are summarized in the following words taken from the book:

> It was announced as true in dogma, remote and holy in origin, fruitful and beneficent in its effects. But history proves it false,

conscience condemns it, common sense rejects it. Its primitive revelation is a fable, its novelty an illusion, its application immoral. Self-contradictory, it would be disastrous as well as impossible in its final development, it would impede human nature on its journey to perfection and civilization.[4]

This statement not only epitomized Ozanam's thinking but also revealed the excellence of his literary style. And yet, he apparently did not think too well of himself in this regard, for in the first article that he wrote for the *Percursor* he openly admitted his youth and his inexperience in intellectual matters. This seemed only to increase his popularity.

Several famous persons in French life noticed Frederick's writings and called attention to the quality of the efforts expended against Saint-Simonism. Among these were the imaginative priest, Felicite de Lamennais; politician and writer Francois Rene de Chateaubriand; and poet, historian, and statesman Alphonse Marie Louis de Lamartine. In the summer of 1831, Lamartine wrote to Ozanam about his booklet:

> I have just received and read with pleasure your work, which you have done me the honour to send me. When I consider your age, I am astonished and filled with admiration for your genius. Please accept my best wishes. I am proud to think that a thought of mine, merely expressed, should have inspired you to write such a beautiful critique. Believe rather that the thought was not mine but yours; mine has been but the spark that fired your soul. Your first effort guarantees one more combatant in the crusade of moral and religious philosophy against gross and material reaction. I, too, look forward to victory.[5]

As a result of this experience, Ozanam's defense of Roman Catholicism became even more intense. He realized, however, that the best defense was not based solely on emotion. He was quick to appreciate that the value of his case against Saint-Simonism lay in the fact that he had employed expert reasoning girded by an appealing literary style. Thus, he decided that he would devote his life to the maintenance of the Roman Catholic faith. He envisaged a tremendous writing project, which he assumed would take up the better part of his lifetime. He was not certain how many volumes the project would entail, but he vowed to bend every effort to its completion. He saw one of the values of this work to be a guide for the future of society. He felt it would enable persons to see, once and for all, the efficacy of the faith that possessed him and others of his time. This faith, becoming universal, would provide the moral goals toward which all society could move.

To carry out his plan, Ozanam felt that he would have to know a great deal about all of the disciplines known to man. He would first have to gain a mastery of at least a dozen languages, and then he would need to learn about all the religions of the world, as well as the accumulated nonreligious learning. This knowledge he wished to place in the setting of the physical sciences. Of these responsibilities and challenges, the youthful scholar said, "But it little avails to contemplate the road before me. I must put myself in the way for the hour has come, and if I wish to make a book at thirty-five, I must begin at eighteen." He was unable to predict that the work would take longer than he had years. At one point, he spoke of the project as being a kind of religious mission given by God, which he recognized as a "calling."

Frederick's father, with his usual persistency, was more interested in his son's law career. So Frederick found himself in Paris in the fall of 1831, matriculating in the University of Paris—in law. In addition to his courses in the School of Law, however, he enrolled in philosophy and history courses in the College of France.

Frederick had a difficult time adjusting to his new life away from home. His heart was not in his studies, and he was troubled because so many of the young people in Paris were not of his own religious faith. Many of the people with whom he associated in the classroom and in his lodgings were openly opposed to organized religion. He tried to fill his time reading a wide array of books relative to the subject he had chosen for his life work. As a part of that program, he translated Bergmann's book on the religion of Tibet and Mone's book on the mythology of Lapland. He renewed his study of Hebrew so that he could read the sources of his own religious tradition. But, despite all, he could not escape being lonely. Depression and despair were a part of almost every day. Once, in a letter to his mother, he said, "To confide in, I have but you, mother—and God. But these two are legion."

In December of 1831, he changed lodgings, and his state of mind improved considerably. His new landlord was a prominent scientist, Andre Marie Ampere. Frederick had written a letter to Ampere and called on him. Ampere asked the young student about his life in Paris and his troubles of adjustment. When he learned that Frederick was unhappy with his rooming arrangements, he led the youth to a large, attractive room overlooking a garden. He explained that the room had been occupied by his son, who at that time was in Germany. "Would it suit you?" he asked. Frederick was almost too embarrassed to accept. The insistent Ampere told him that he could have the room on the same terms he had with his previous landlord. In addition, he urged that Frederick consider himself a member of the family, eating and praying with Ampere's sister, daughter, and son. Frederick gladly moved in with the Ampere family.

Ampere made a great impression on the quick mind of Frederick Ozanam. It was under his influence that Frederick became even more convinced that there is no necessary conflict between science and religion, if each is viewed properly. When he saw the great man of science in deep prayer, he realized that religion had a powerful influence on Ampere's thinking.

As time passed, Frederick visited other well-known men in Paris. Some were personally known to him through the letters they had written him on the publication of his book opposing Saint-Simonism. In 1832, he visited Francois Rene de Chateaubriand, who had published a volume in 1802 called *The Genius of Christianity*. This work had carried his fame throughout the French- and English-speaking worlds.

For a time, Chateaubriand had disavowed the Roman Catholic faith, but gradually, in part as a result of his wide travels and hectic political and social experience, he began to see the value and beauty of the Christian religion. His book reflected the search of a man for the reality that is religious faith, and was popular in large part because it so accurately mirrored the experiences of many who were oppressed by lack of faith.

The moral development of Ozanam is expressed to some

degree by an incident that occurred on this visit to Chateaubri-
and. The famed author asked Frederick if he frequented the
theater. Ozanam said that his mother had advised him that the
theater was immoral and that he should never attend. Chateaubriand did not try to dissuade Ozanam from his resolve. In fact,
he told Frederick to remain true to it, since it was a part of his
relationship with his mother. Frederick kept this resolve until
he was twenty-seven, when, under the urgings of his friends, he
did attend a performance of Pierre Corneille's *Polyeucte*. He was
disappointed with the play and never again visited the theater.

In 1832, a cholera epidemic broke out in Paris, and a bloody
civil war enveloped Lyons. Frederick was torn between two
responsibilities. On the one hand, he wanted to be of help to
those around him, but his parents and loved ones were also
threatened. After some deliberation, he decided to stay in Paris.
Even the request of his father that he return home did not
change his mind. In Paris there was much to do, and Frederick
pitched in to serve his neighbors and friends. He felt some
anxiety about the possibility of falling victim to cholera, but he
survived the ordeal and attributed this to divine mercy.

When the disease had run its course, he returned to the more
ordinary activities of a busy student. Many demands were made
on his time, and he was eager to be of help wherever he could.
He felt a sense of unusual responsibility:

> Because God and education have endowed me with some breadth
> of ideas, some largeness of tolerance, they would make me a sort of
> leader of the Catholic youth of these parts. A number of young
> people, full of merit, give me an esteem of which I feel very
> unworthy, and men of ripe age make advances to me. I must be at
> the head of every movement and, when there is anything difficult
> to do, I must bear the burden of it. Impossible that there should be a
> reunion, a conference of law or literature, unless I preside at it. Five
> or six magazines or journals ask me for articles. In a word, a crowd
> of circumstances, independent of my will, besiege me, pursue me,
> and draw me out of the line I traced for myself. I do not tell you this
> as a boast. On the contrary, I feel my weakness so much, I who am
> not twenty-one years old, that compliments and praises rather
> humiliate me, and I almost feel a desire to laugh at my own
> importance.[6]

Throughout his career, Ozanam was a lay defender of the faith. When he later became a professor at the Sorbonne, he was noted for his able defenses of religion. But even while he was a student, he did not allow professorial challenges to the validity of the Roman Catholic conception of life to go unmet. Letronne, for example, one of the leading intellectual teachers at the Sorbonne, declared that the papacy was a "transitory institution, born under Charlemagne, dying today." Letronne was not alone in his critical estimate of Roman Catholicism. As these teachers attacked the dearly held tenets and practices of loyal Roman Catholics, clear-cut responses came from students. Ozanam joined several others in drawing up rebuttals to some of the more blatant comments of the professors. Usually the teachers would read the letters to the classes, thus making for a kind of formal reply to the points that they themselves made. It was not that Frederick wanted to show that Roman Catholicism was incompatible with reason (a view he abhorred), but he did wish to indicate that the highest reason and the highest religion were synonymous.

Perhaps the greatest victory for Ozanam and his followers occurred in connection with an attack made by Professor Theodore Jouffroy, who had said, among other things, that Christianity was "quite, quite passé." Ozanam sent him a reply, but the professor did not read it before the class. Two weeks passed. Frederick thought Jouffroy would never mention it, so he drew up a longer and more pointed summary of his position, gained fifteen signatures to it, and presented it to his teacher. Professor Jouffroy had to take notice of it. In order to save his position and reputation, he apologized profusely to the audience and declared that he had meant to offend no one. He gave his promise that, in the future, he would violate no one's religious sensitivity. Of course, there is no indication that Ozanam and his friends succeeded in changing the teacher's mind on the subject; however, Jouffroy did change his mind later in life and came to champion the Roman Catholic system of thought and action as being the final answer to life's problems.

In 1833, Ozanam took part in founding a sort of debating club that was called the Conference of History (sometimes the Conference of Literature) with headquarters in the Latin Quarter. Over the group presided Emmanual Joseph Bailly, a friendly, philosophic man. Bailly's residence was near the Sorbonne, and was a convenient place for young Catholic men to gather and to read and discuss topics of the day—a kind of Newman Club. The first members were active in recruiting some of the best students in the Sorbonne. Many from Lyons clustered about the conference, which was something like a "bull session." It gave the membership a means of expressing themselves on the social and intellectual problems of the time. And there were plenty of problems to be considered.

The chief challenges to the orthodoxy of the group lay in politics and philosophy (so far as they can be separated). Saint-Simonism was rampant in Paris and elsewhere in France, an intellectual fad of the time, and everyone looked forward to the coming socialist economy. The conference gave some study to the system and then sought, on the basis of Roman Catholic doctrine, to dispute it.

The second threatening force considered by the conference was the philosophical doctrines of Francois Marie Arouet de Voltaire and his followers. Voltaire's philosophy, seemingly opposed to much of the Roman Catholic tradition, had gained acceptance in intellectual circles in France at that time. Voltaire, no less than Saint-Simon, was seriously wrong in the eyes of the conference members. What fun they must have had waging verbal warfare against such formidable antagonists!

The debates, however, were unsatisfying to Ozanam for they failed to change matters. The challenge of one speaker at the conference stuck in his mind until he could not ignore it: "Christianity has been a force in the past for good, but what is it doing today?" He vowed to himself that he would find some kind of answer to that criticism. He found an answer in the Society of St. Vincent de Paul.

In a sense, the origins of the society date to a gift of firewood in Paris in 1833. Ozanam and his friend August Le Taillandier took some of their own firewood to the flat of a neighbor who couldn't buy fuel. It was a simple gift to someone in need. The response they received was heartwarming, and it opened their eyes to the possibilities of organized charity. They asked themselves, "What are we going to do to translate our faith into deeds?" Their answer came almost immediately: "Go to the poor." Paul Lamache, the last surviving member of the original band that founded the society, said, regarding this experience: "I can see the flame burning in Ozanam's eyes. I can hear his voice trembling a little with emotion as he explains to [Jules] Devaux and myself his project of a charitable association." Lamache said later: "He spoke of his plan to me in terms so warm and moving that only a man with no heart or faith in him could have failed to give it instant adherence."

It was logical that they should first talk with Bailly, who advised them to take the matter up with their parish priest, the Abbe Ollivier. This man had little understanding of the intensity of the flame that burned within them and of the practical need for such a movement as they proposed. He told them only to return to the teaching of the catechism. They were undaunted by this advice and turned again to their consuming passion.

The next step in giving the idea form was to organize a meeting of those who agreed with the idea of a new charitable association. Bailly suggested that they meet in the office of his newspaper, *The Catholic Tribune*, so, on an evening in May 1833, the little group came together. Among those known to have been present are the following: Emmanuel Joseph Bailly, in whose office the meeting took place and who became president of the first unit of the society, and later, for eleven years, the first president-general of the entire society; Jules Devaux, twenty-one years old and a student of medicine; Felix Clave, a Parisian law student; Paul Lamache, also a law student, in his second year; Francois Lallier, nineteen years old and a law student; Auguste Le Taillandier, the law student who went with Ozanam on his first mission of mercy; and, of course, Frederick Ozanam.

Bailly, being older than the others, was chosen as the first leader of the small group. He pointed out at the first meeting that they should not intend their charity only to meet material needs. He believed, and on this point there was general agreement, that the workers should consider the total needs of the person—social and spiritual, as well as material. This principle, enunciated at the first meeting of the society, became a cardinal rule of its organization and practice. (It is also a tenet that is being more and more confirmed by modern casework insights.) Another principle established early in the movement's history was that no member of the group was to benefit personally from the organization. This was in contrast with several other societies then in existence, which consisted of bands of young men who wished to help each other. The new association concentrated upon doing good for others outside the group.

It is not possible to say how the group chose its name. Its foundations rested on the Conference of History, but in time that name was changed to the Conference of Charity. Later, the name of St. Vincent de Paul was selected. It may have been suggested by Bailly, since the saint was specially revered in his family. There was ample reason, aside from the personal ties of the group, for the selection of St. Vincent as the representative symbol of the intention and work that the society had chosen for itself.

St. Vincent de Paul was born in 1581 to a humble peasant family in a Gascon village. During his nearly eighty years, he was a helper of the poor, an assister of the clergy, a father to orphans and foundlings, an emancipator of Christian slaves, a friend to galley slaves, a provider to whole provinces in wartime and famine, and the founder of seminaries for priests. He was an appropriate symbol for the new organization.

The new society met once a week in Bailly's office. Meetings began with an invocation and a reading, often on the life of St. Vincent de Paul. Following this brief religious service, reports were heard on the progress that members were making with their cases. Each member was assigned a family in need, but there were always two visitors who attended each family. After the reports on practical work were heard, a collection was taken, into which the young men poured a sizeable share of their regular income. Contributions from nonmembers came in time, but in the beginning, only the members provided the funds for the work they did.

The first family that became the responsibility of Frederick Ozanam consisted of a father, mother, and five children. The father was a heavy drinker who recklessly spent whatever money he could lay his hands on, including some earned by his wife. When he was drunk, he became violent and beat his wife and children. The mother was a patient woman who worked incessantly to help herself and her family.

Because there was no valid marriage contract, Frederick counseled the woman to leave her husband. Ozanam took up a collection so that she could return to Brittany with the two youngest children. Bailly agreed to hire two of the oldest boys in his printing establishment, while other work was found for the fifth son.

The success of the society is due in large part to the fact that the members were capable of a high degree of effective team-work. This is made plain in a comment of Paul Lamache, made in 1892, when he was eighty years old:

> To tell the truth, not one of us, not even Ozanam, who had certainly the greatest initiative and most ardent zeal, could be described as the founder of the Society of St. Vincent de Paul. We were influenced solely by the desire of finding for ourselves, for we were so weak, mutual support in the practice of doing good. After having fought with pen and speech in the Conference of History for the defense of religion, we felt the need of the support, strength, and consolation which are to be found in devoting ourselves to some little works for the sake of the love of Our Lord and Saviour Jesus Christ. It is then God and God alone Who has done all. That is exactly why we have every reason to hope that the Society of St. Vincent de Paul will live.[7]

At first, the little band thought that it should limit its membership to the charter members. Ozanam, however, was the first to object to this, for he felt that the spirit of giving was too appealing and too pervasive to be confined within the society. He also knew that the needs of the people of Paris far outstripped the meager resources of the group. At the earliest opportunity, he advocated adding new members. Francois Lallier brought a young poet, Gustave de la Noue, to the attention of the membership. After a brief debate on the policies of the organization, the poet was admitted. Another early admission to the society was Leon Le Provost, a man in his forties. He was immensely interested in literature and the humanities, and he was quick to notice the vast potential of the growing movement. In time, many new faces were found at the Tuesday evening meetings.

Once the group had begun its operations in earnest, they approached the local parish priest to tell him of their presence. Abbe Ollivier had left the parish, and in his place was Father

Faudet. Felix Clave carried the greeting of the group to the priest. Clave expected that the priest might feel they were competing with him, but Father Faudet did not. He accepted Clave's invitation to visit a meeting of the society, and was impressed with the deep piety and genuine sincerity of the men. He gave them his cooperation and blessing.

The society soon ran into difficulty. Most of its members were college students, and when vacation times came, they were tempted to return to their homes for a rest. They had given their money and time during the regular school year without any reward save that of increased personal and spiritual growth. Yet, they realized that the needs of the poor did not take vacations. This problem, like all others affecting the welfare of the early group, was discussed at length. Ozanam declared that the young men could not, in good conscience, leave the poor to their own devices. He argued that they had assumed obligations that they could not lightly throw off. Others agreed with him, and as a result, the principle was laid down that, so far as the poor were concerned, there would be no vacations. A member could take a vacation, but during his leave, his family in distress was allocated to another member.

Frederick took a vacation in 1833 to renew his family ties. No sooner was he home than his father took him and the rest of the family off to Italy. When Frederick returned to Paris to begin his third year in legal studies, he was still pondering the problem of what he wished to study. There was no doubt about what his father wanted him to do, but Frederick's heart was not in the law. He wrote his mother that she need not worry about his legal interests; he would complete them largely for the sake of his parents. He added that he wished for his "recreation" to "work in literary matters, which will adorn dry jurisprudence." His scholarly life is described in another letter to his mother: "Thus, in the evening with Virgil and Dante beside me, it pleases me to write occasionally my Italian impressions and to traverse again by myself the ground which I covered so delightfully with you. I shall not at all neglect my legal studies for that."

In addition to his school work, Frederick had growing responsibilities with the society. In the last months of 1833, there were twenty to twenty-five persons meeting regularly on

Tuesday evenings. Almost every week someone new was taken into the fellowship. The larger the membership, the heavier became the administrative responsibilities, and Ozanam assumed a considerable part of these obligations. He also carried his full share of work with the poor of the city.

Ozanam, along with Le Taillandier, Le Provost, and Lamache, became interested in the plight of criminals, believing that the society's responsibility for Christian charity extended to the so-called least of mankind. Near the Sorbonne was a prison that housed young criminals. Ozanam got permission from the prison authorities to visit the men and help them with their educational and spiritual problems. For two years, the team visited the delinquents, but then the prisoners were transferred to another institution at the other end of Paris.

Frederick and his friends were also interested in presenting Roman Catholic Christianity to a wider audience of Parisians under the auspices of the archbishop of Paris. It was Frederick's plan to have Father Lacordaire, a prominent and popular preacher of the time, present a series of lectures, believing that this would stimulate a renewal of religious interest. He and his friends approached the archbishop with this idea, carrying over two hundred signatures on a petition. The archbishop, however, did not agree with the plan and instead he selected seven of the regular clergy to give the lectures. The society accepted the archbishop's plan, but they knew full well that the seven could never equal Father Lacordaire's intellectual and oratorical power.

In the early days of the society a problem arose that almost wrecked the developing organization. Ozanam brought up the idea of sanctioning a new unit of the society for Nimes, under the direction of Leonce Curnier. This request was carefully considered by the other members, and they agreed. Then he suggested that the Parisian unit of the society, which had grown by the end of 1834 to a membership of one hundred, be divided into three parts. There was good reason for this, as the group had grown so large that it was hard to keep the close relationship between the members that was envisaged by the founders. And there was a problem of finding adequate space for the meetings. Ozanam's proposal was not accepted, and even his staunchest friends opposed the move. Perhaps the most able of those who opposed Ozanam was Paul de la Perriere, who was known for his oratorical ability. Under his emotional persuasion, the group was deeply divided, and no possibility for a compromise seemed possible. The meeting held on December 23, 1833, ended with no decision reached. Several more meetings were held, one on Christmas eve, but still the group was stalemated. By New Year's Day, there was still no conclusion, so the matter was turned over to the board of the society for decision. As the bells of the New Year rang out, the decision of the board was announced—the division of the original group would take place. Frederick Ozanam approached Perriere and embraced him, asking for his continued support and friendship, and the opposing groups within the society rallied to the cause for which the organization stood.

The decision was a momentous one for the future development of the society. The spirit of St. Vincent was to be offered to countless more men and women with social vision and to more persons who stood in need of help. Ozanam's suggestion freed the society from its provincialism and realized for it effective world-wide service.

In time, a number of new units came into existence within Paris and throughout the surrounding countryside. But, as the separate meetings were held, it was quickly realized that there was need also for general unity within the movement. The various branches decided to hold a monthly meeting in Paris under Bailly's leadership. In time, general conferences were established in other French cities, as the movement spread to ever-distant places.

> Here, at last, is the commencement of the written constitution for which we have so long wished. It has had to wait for a long time, for already some years have passed since our association came into being. But were we not bound to feel assured that God wishes that it should continue to live, before laying down the form in which it should do so?[8]

Thus begins the statement of rules that were to bind the society in the course of its later development. The constitution was commissioned by the various city conferences in France. Its

authors were Bailly and Lallier, although Lallier did the original
work on it. Its purpose was to create a form by which the
organization could be guided as it sought to accomplish its basic
aims. In regard to the multiplication of branches, the constitution stated:

> Having become numerous and being obliged to divide into sections
> —moreover many of us desiring to meet together in other towns,
> where they were to reside henceforth, the name of Conference has
> continued to be applied to each of these sections, all of which are
> comprised under the common denomination of the Society of St.
> Vincent de Paul.[9]

The basis of communion for the society was stated in the
now famous words: "Firstly, to maintain its members, by
mutual example and advice, in the practice of the Christian life;
secondly, to visit the poor at their dwellings, to bring them
succor in kind, to afford them also religious consolation." While
other objectives were listed, this was the essence of the society's
purpose.

The constitution also forbade giving to a conference the
name of any member. It was thought that there should be
principally two chief guides for the work—the life of St. Vincent
de Paul and the life of Jesus. From only these two was inspiration sought.

The maturity of the social insight achieved by the early
society is apparent in another regulation: "We should not
attempt to make them [the poor] receive it [charity] as from
authority and by command." This principle closely mirrors the
attitude of modern social caseworkers, who prefer to allow their
clients the determination of their own actions. The earliest
Vincentians saw the folly of trying to dictate the ways in which
others should live. Certainly, they believed, the giving of charity
should not be used as a whip to accomplish any purpose.

The constitution also spoke of the need for the members to
"love one another and for ever." This need was to be expressed
not only in the local groups but also "from nation to nation."
Perhaps the inclusion of this reference to the international scope
of the work was somewhat gratuitous at the time that it was

written, but before long it became a clear reality. Groups sprang up in many lands to meet the challenge of aiding the poor in the spirit of St. Vincent de Paul.

While the organization was growing, Ozanam was hard at work on his studies. In April 1836, he completed the work for his doctorate in law and received the degree with high honors. He had accomplished the goal that his parents had placed before him, but he was not satisfied. He still wished to study literature and especially to finish a doctorate in that subject. The problems of law seemed to be less momentous to him than the general problems of human culture. His spirit was not content with the narrow horizons of the professional lawyer.

He returned to Lyons to practice law and remained there for the next four years. But he did more than practice law. He visited religious shrines and gained encouragement from them, he continued his reading, preparing himself to write his great work, and he plunged into the work of the society. In Lyons there was no thriving group as in Paris, so Frederick helped form a local unit. Within the first year, twenty families were cared for by twenty Vincentians. In the following year, the group had doubled, as did the number of families.

The movement was disliked on several fronts, within the church and without, but the persistent goodwill of Ozanam and his friends finally won out. No amount of envy could thwart the vitality of this spiritual and social crusade. In time, the group in Lyons was subdivided. A club organized in one center featured a library, and in time an informal school was organized around the club and the library and many benefited from the instruction of the members.

In the spring of 1837, Ozanam returned to Paris to study literature. Soon after, he received notice that his beloved father had died, and upon Frederick's shoulders fell the responsibility of supporting the family, since his brothers were either away from home or too young. Reluctantly, but recognizing his duty, he returned to Lyons to resume his work in the courts. In addition to his legal activities, he took upon himself the responsibilities of tutoring three young men "who are too grand to sit at the desks of a school," for this brought some additional money to the family. During this period he continued to write, and one short study on church property was later expanded into an important work. Wherever he could advance the cause of his religion, he willingly gave of his writing talents, and he wrote regularly for the Society for the Propagation of the Faith.

By the end of 1839, Ozanam felt himself ready to take the doctorate in literature at Paris. He had thoroughly studied the works of Dante, and this investigation became the basis for the degree that was granted him, again with high honors. The entire faculty of the Sorbonne turned out to examine the young scholar, and all were deeply impressed with his ability to handle the Latin and French materials. Throughout his career, Ozanam was noted for his eloquent speech. Whether he was defending a thesis or speaking in open forum in the society, he always commanded attention.

In October 1839, with Frederick at her bedside, Marie Ozanam died. Soon after the death of his mother, Frederick was appointed a lecturer in law at the University of Lyons. In this capacity, he was able to apply more of his talents than he had in the practice of law. The scholarly life appealed to him. From various accounts, it is apparent that he was able to attract a wide following of students in his courses, while retaining the respect of his colleagues.

At about the same time, a vacancy occurred in the literature faculty at the Sorbonne. Examinations were announced for the position, and at first, Frederick thought that he could not successfully compete with others. He also believed that his Roman Catholicism might be held against him. Nevertheless, he felt he should try. The examinations consisted of two eight-hour theses, one in Latin and the other in French, three days of examinations in Greek, Latin, and French texts, and one full day of examination in German, English, Italian, and Spanish texts. Finally, each candidate chose a subject that he had to defend. Frederick's was "The History of the Latin and Greek Scholiasts." When the results were announced, the name of Frederick Ozanam stood at the head of the list. It was an occasion of celebration, but it also called for a decision. Should he sever his relations with the University of Lyons to take a temporary position at the Sorbonne?

Frederick discussed the matter with the rector of the University of Lyons, Mr. Soulacroix, who thought (with some natural bias) that Frederick should stay at Lyons. After consulting with friends and a long period of prayer, he decided to accept the position at the Sorbonne. This step in his career was more momentous than it seemed at the time.

Frederick was in love with Amelie, the daughter of the rector of the University of Lyons, and wished to marry her. He had met her one day when he visited the rector on university business and found her a "fair young girl" who was busy attending an invalid brother. "How sweet it would be to have a sister like that to love me," thought Frederick. From that time, he realized that he wished to meet with her and develop a friendship. These plans met with the approval of the rector as well as with Amelie. It was his attachment to Amelie that made Frederick's decision difficult.

After a short period in Paris, Frederick returned to Lyons, and on this visit, on June 23, 1841, he and Amelie were married. She was twenty-one years old; he was twenty-eight. A month was spent on a honeymoon in Naples, Sicily, and Rome, where they had an audience with Pope Gregory XVI. After Frederick presented the pope with a copy of his Dante thesis, the two talked about the general importance of religious literature. Frederick and his bride settled down in Paris, where Frederick was to take up his lectures.

Frederick threw himself into his work with great zeal. He realized that he had to prove himself to the students and to a hostile press. But he was a master and students thronged to hear him as he opened up for them the mysteries of historical literature.

Ozanam's presence at the Sorbonne was interpreted as something of a victory for religion. His willingness to defend his religion publicly was not appreciated by some of the faculty members at the Sorbonne. On more than one occasion Ozanam had to call upon his courage to stand in favor of the teachings of his church. When the question of his permanent appointment to the faculty came up, he felt that it was entirely possible that he would be rejected, even though he had proved himself capable of the work. He badly wanted the appointment, but he said, "I shall sacrifice nothing, neither my duty to the State through imprudence, nor my duty as a Christian through cowardice." In spite of his fears, in 1844 he was accepted unanimously by the faculty. Two years later, he was made a chevalier of the Legion of

Honor in recognition of his outstanding contribution to the cause of teaching.

But so great were the demands on him and so heavy was the schedule that he set for himself that, from time to time, he had to take leave from the Sorbonne in order to repair his health. He usually traveled, gathering materials that he thought he would be able to use in his book in defense of religion, and Amelie and his young daughter, Marie, accompanied him. His first leave lasted eight months. When he returned to the Sorbonne, he fell into his old schedule. His lectures consumed much of his time, but his writing and the work of the society were not neglected. In two years' time, he was advised by his physician to take another leave, this time in the mountains. For a time he did rest, but being restless by nature, he soon began his travels again. In the succeeding years, he spent less and less time in Paris and spent his energies in the various projects connected with the society and his researches.

Ozanam said on one occasion, "My knowledge of history forces me to the conclusion that democracy is the natural final stage of the development of political progress, and that God leads the world thither." This belief was translated into all of his dealings. He considered each person to be of supreme worth. He believed this not only because he accepted the Christian tradition that makes such belief possible, but also because he was convinced that the very goal of democracy made such practice desirable and necessary. He favored the Roman Catholic church, and yet he believed that the church should be separated from the state for the benefit of both. Possibly, he derived this conception from his investigations of Dante, who held to something of the same view in De Monarchia. Because he held this belief, Ozanam was not fully accepted by some Roman Catholics. They felt that he was too liberal in his religious and social interpretations. But this did not disturb Ozanam, for he believed that his long fight for truth simply could not be misunderstood. Seldom did he take time out to reprove his friends from within the church who criticized him.

Ozanam also believed in the efficacy of books, but he was not willing to accept the view that all truth derives from reading. For him, there was validity in practical experience that exceeded and corrected the value of "truth" as found in the writings of various authors. On one occasion he said, "Knowledge of social well-being and of reform is to be learned . . . in climbing the stairs of the poor man's garret, sitting by his bedside, feeling the same cold that pierces him, sharing the secret of his lonely heart and troubled mind." This conclusion stood in opposition to that held by some utopians who believed that social progress depended not so much on love of one's fellow man in practical ways as in the triumph of theoretical reason. But Ozanam had climbed too many stairs leading into the garrets of the poor. He believed that the ultimate social forces are feeling and action for one's fellow men. On these points he allowed no exception. He held this conviction not only as a personal philosophy, but also as a practical program of action.

These beliefs were tested during the Civil War in France, at the end of February 1848. The displeasure of the working groups in Paris combined with the rising discontent of the middle classes (who despised the excesses of the aristocrats) to break loose in a bloody but rather brief revolution. Barricades were erected in the streets, and each side tried to force its will on the city. Frederick took his place behind a barricade as a member of the National Guard. By June, thousands of Frenchmen had been slain.

Some sections of Paris were more dangerous than others, and it happened that the location where Ozanam served was rather peaceful. There were some alarms and excursions, but it was not necessary for him to fire on anyone. He was thankful for two things: that he did not have to shoot at anyone, because he greatly feared killing another person, and that he was spared for his own family. He said, "I am free to admit that it is a terrible moment when a man bids what he believes to be his last farewell to his wife and child." Many were not so fortunate, and among those who lost their lives was the archbishop of Paris, who, in the interest of stopping the battle, had walked down the center of the street as a missionary of peace. A shot rang out, and the archbishop fell to the ground. No one knows who fired the shot or which side it represented, but even this heroic gesture was not potent enough to halt the strife.

During the summer, however, the uprising ceased, and then began the tasks of healing the wounds and caring for the destitute. The Vincentians took a prominent part in the work of reconstruction. At a meeting of the society held in a church hall in August 1848, Ozanam called upon the members to recognize the profound meaning of the lives that had been given in the struggle and to take steps to help those who continued to suffer both physically and socially. Special funds were raised to care for the injured and destitute. The National Assembly also contributed funds to the society that it might act as an agent of the government, and several groups within the city gave money and supplies.

The work of reconstruction continued through the winter. In the spring of 1849, a cholera epidemic spread through Paris, and Ozanam called the society together in a special meeting to ask for volunteers to meet the emergency. Forty men responded. After the epidemic was conquered, the problem of the orphans left in its wake needed a solution. Ozanam was instrumental in getting the help of the new archbishop of Paris to place orphans in homes and institutions throughout France.

The society gained strength through the years and faced its work with increasing ability in social administration, and in other countries of the world, branches of the society were established. The old antagonisms to the movement were largely dissipated through continuous examples of self-giving. New members were found to take the new responsibilities that came to the society. There seemed no end to the needs of people and the willingness of some to meet these needs.

The society operated on a nonsectarian basis. This principle was imbedded in the organization from its inception and was due, to a large extent, to the spirit of Frederick Ozanam. Once, when the movement was still in its infancy, Ozanam reported to a local meeting that he had been given money by a Protestant minister, who wished to have a part in helping the needy. Someone suggested that most of the money be given to poor Catholic families, while only a small amount should go to aid Protestants. Ozanam replied, "Gentlemen, if this suggestion is followed, if we do not bear in mind that our society is to help the poor irrespective of belief, then I will at once take this money back to the donor and tell him that we are not worthy of his confidence."

In the fall of 1849, Ozanam resumed his work at the Sorbonne, but as the academic year progressed, he found he could not meet all his lectures, due to his failing health. In February of 1849, he wrote: "My health is almost altogether gone: that is why I pray and ask my friends to pray, that it may please Heaven to deliver me. So many prayers cannot remain unanswered." He barely managed to finish the year with a minimal teaching schedule. His illness was finally diagnosed as pleurisy. In the summer he asked for another leave, and on this trip he visited southern France, where a cure for his pleurisy seemed possible. His brother Charles, a physician, tried to help Frederick regain his health, but although some improvement was made, there was no final cure. He could not return to teaching the following fall.

On his travels Ozanam met many people in connection with the work of the society. In fact, his poor health made it possible for him to be a semi-official delegate-at-large to the various branches of the society. He also thought much about his boyhood dream of writing a major work on the defense of religion. Wherever he went, he collected data that he thought he might be able to use in his writing.

Ozanam's final days were spent in the seaside village of Antignano in Italy, where he never lost hope of recovering. His attitude may be summarized in one brief sentence: "I shall be cured this autumn." In August of 1853, his brother Charles was summoned from Paris to attend the dying man.

While he appreciated the natural splendors of his village by the sea, Frederick Ozanam longed to see his beloved France once more. On the last day of August, he was carried to a ship that was sailing for France. It landed at Marseilles, and he was pleased to see his own country and the towering cathedral of Notre Dame again. He said, "God will do with me what he wills." In the evening of September 8, 1853, he gained strength long enough to say, "My God, my God, have pity on me." Soon afterwards, he died.

Many of those who had opposed Ozanam during his lifetime joined in acknowledging the worth of this man, who died at the age of forty. His example became a source of inspiration to thousands who saw in his spirit the central meaning of Christianity and humanitarianism. The recognition of his worth was universal. Steps toward his beatification by the Roman Catholic Church were begun in 1925.

Two years after Frederick Ozanam's death, the movement he founded had grown to such proportions that there were more than one hundred units in Italy, Germany, Belgium, Spain, Great Britain, Ireland, and the Netherlands, and there were branches in many other countries, also: one in Greece; one in Turkey; three in Asia; seventeen in Africa; and seventy-two in the Americas. While Ozanam was still alive, the first conference in the United States was established in St. Louis in 1845, and Milwaukee founded its conference in 1849. France led all the other nations in membership; over thirteen hundred branches were open in France at the time of Ozanam's death.

Today, the Society of St. Vincent de Paul is an international organization, established on five continents and in 103 countries. Local branches are termed "conferences." There are twenty-eight thousand men's conferences, thirty-six hundred women's conferences, and six hundred conferences that are mixed. These possess an active membership of more than four hundred thousand, and the individual members often have the support of their families in one form or another. The members include persons of every rank, nation, and race.

The society has been successful in the United States. As of 1978, there were 19,500 local or parish councils of the society organized into forty-three regional councils. The national council headquarters is located in St. Louis, Missouri. In 1978, the society reported that it had aided in that year 294,633 families and made 424,712 home visits, utilizing 6,125,000 voluntary hours of service. Also in that year the society granted $7,545,000 in emergency aid and $5,637,000 in clothing and furniture.

In the United States the society is noted for its local storehouses of clothing, furniture, and other materials that it makes available to the families it serves. Often, the staff of these warehouses is composed of the handicapped and others who may be unable to find regular employment in the open community. The conferences also supply other services: regular visitation to those who are unable to participate in the general community (the aged, sick, and incapacitated—in their own homes or in institutions); funds for those who need special and temporary help; counseling of couples regarding family budgets and other matters; support of fatherless youths; summer camps for under-privileged children; religious services; homes for the chronically ill and the aged; sheltered workshops for the handicapped; programs to prevent and treat juvenile delinquency; Christian burial for the indigent; and family casework programs maintained in dioceses. By these and other means, the conferences in the United States continue and implement the work and spirit of Frederick Ozanam.

Chapter Eight

Lord Shaftesbury
Anthony Ashley Cooper
(1801–1885)

The name of Lord Shaftesbury will descend to posterity as the one who has, in his generation, worked more than any other individual to elevate the condition, and to raise the character, of his countrymen.[1]

Lord Shaftesbury, the foremost leader in social reform movements in nineteenth century England, benefited from a noble and comfortable ancestry. While some of the social welfare pioneers of the last several centuries have come from relatively poor backgrounds, this is not true of Anthony Ashley Cooper, the seventh earl of Shaftesbury.

The six lords who preceded Anthony made relatively little impression on their times. The first earl of Shaftesbury enjoyed preferment under both the Commonwealth and the Restoration governments, and he was noted for his philanthropy. Of the second earl very little is known. The third was a theologian and writer of some distinction. The fourth and fifth earls left no mark on history. The fact that the predecessors of Lord Shaftesbury were not great social leaders should not be surprising, for they were of a class in English life that, in the main, did not deem itself responsible for social leadership. They were content merely to be earls.

The sixth earl, father of Anthony Ashley Cooper, was known for the strict discipline he inflicted on his household. He was chairman of committees in the House of Lords for forty years—a vocation of responsibility. In this work he was known to be clever and generally honest, and he believed that discipline was at the heart of all moral law and personal improvement. Therefore, he reasoned, it was incumbent upon him to turn his theories into practice in his own home. There he kept everyone, especially the children, in constant fear. Seldom did he show any affection for them. Shaftesbury's mother offered the children little more in the way of emotional support and constructive aid, for she had a busy social life. Shaftesbury was born into these difficult surroundings on April 28, 1801. What his life might have been if his parents had been genuinely interested in him one can only conjecture. He was cared for by Maria Millis, a servant who had been with the family for many years. It was Maria's patient and loving attention that enabled Anthony to form the character and purpose that led to his career as a social reformer. When he was young, she recounted over and over again the stories and moral truths of the Bible. In time he came to read the Bible himself with affection and understanding.

Shaftesbury's fine relationship with Maria Millis ended when it came time for him to go away to school. At the age of seven he was sent to Manor House School, Chiswick, which catered to the children of the titled rich. Anthony was bright and sensitive, and expected to do well at his studies. The school, however, did not help him and instead presented a nightmarish version of what a school should have been. In his old age Shaftesbury held vivid memories of the Manor House School: "The memory of that place makes me shudder; it is repulsive to me even now. I think I never saw such a wicked school before or since. The place was bad, wicked, filthy; and the treatment was starvation and cruelty." The older and stronger boys bullied the smaller and younger boys, inflicting on them the devilish practices of young minds twisted by parental neglect and the lack of adequate social controls.

Maria Millis died while Anthony was attending school and he deeply mourned her passing. Anthony received a gold watch that she bequeathed to him, and he carried it with him all his life, displaying it as a means of telling friends about his affection for Maria. When he showed the watch to someone, he would say, "This was given me by the best friend I ever had in the world." Once he lost the watch while traveling; apparently it had been stolen from his pocket. He advertised in the local newspaper for the watch, and a group of thieves, camping in the area, contacted the one possessing it, retrieved it, and returned it to Shaftesbury's doorstep in a few days.

With the death of Maria, there was no one to whom Anthony could turn for comfort and encouragement. Neither his home nor school was appealing. At home he was neglected. On one occasion he stated that he knew what it was "to be left for days without sufficient food until he was pinched with starvation." He also remembered long winter nights when he was kept awake because he did not have enough blankets to keep him warm. "The history of our father and mother," he once said, "would be incredible to most men, and perhaps it would do no good if such facts were recorded." In his despair he turned more and more to the Bible. At home and at the Manor House School he spent most of his time reading it, and he found within its pages the sustenance he lacked in his family and at school.

In his thirteenth year, Anthony was sent to Harrow, another

private school for upper-class English youths. There he found the first freedom he had known outside of his association with Maria Millis. He found people who were interested in him and who gave him opportunities for learning and service. The boys at Harrow also were not oppressive as they had been in the Manor House School. In all, he spent a comfortable and happy time at Harrow.

Anthony had been at Harrow only two years when he was confronted with a tragic drama that affected the course of his thinking. The incident is effectively told by one of his biographers:

> One day, walking alone down Harrow Hill, beside the School, the lad's attention was arrested by shrill shouts. He paused to ascertain from whence the uproar sprang; and standing at rapt attention, every nerve alert, he interpreted, above a general din, the clamorous notes of a Bacchanalian song. A minute later the riddle was solved. Down a side street came a band of intoxicated ruffians, followed by a group of ragged urchins. Four or five of the party were carrying a rough casket containing the remains of a fellow-workman; and, staggering forward, they were shouting the chorus of a vulgar song. Presently they arrived at the main street; and unable to control their half paralysed limbs, in attempting to turn the corner, they lost what self-possession remained to them. Down they fell in a stupid heap, the casket crashing to earth. For a few moments Bedlam was loose. The coffin-bearers quarrelled and cursed; the urchins burst into laughter; while the rest of the party, by their jargon, increased the confusion. Finally the drunken wretches, extricating themselves, picked up the cracked casket, and, with renewed profanity, mingled with the strains of their gin song, continued the funeral march.[2]

The boy stood rooted to the spot as he watched the proceedings, then he exclaimed, "Good Heavens! Can this be permitted simply because the man was poor and friendless?" It was then that he made a vow that settled in many ways what his later life would be. He promised himself and God that he would spend his life in the betterment of the conditions of the needy and oppressed.

Soon after he was fifteen years old, Anthony left Harrow. His record there shows that, while he was not brilliant as a scholar, he was a good student. His declared life purpose was brought into play at least once during his career there. He chose a mosquito-breeding pond near the school, called "Duck Puddle," as the theme of a Latin verse. Through this effort, he was able to influence the authorities to eliminate this source of irritation and infection.

After Harrow, Shaftesbury was sent to live with a relative who was a clergyman. He stayed about two years in the minister's household, where, for the most part, he had nothing to do except read and amuse himself. Apparently, he did a lot of thinking about the vow made at Harrow, for he wrote, "There were constantly floating in my mind all sorts of aspirations." Anthony's father realized after two years that Anthony could not remain in Derbyshire forever. He had thought that Anthony should enter the army, but a friend argued against that move, leaving the earl with no clear conviction as to what his son should do. He finally decided to send his son to Oxford. Thus, in 1819, Anthony took up residence at Christ Church, Oxford. There he was tutored by the Reverend V. Short, "a kind, worthy man." Little is known of Anthony's life at Oxford except that he was a serious and diligent student. Three years after admission he was granted a degree in classics with first-class honors.

After Anthony left Oxford, the problem of what to do with himself vocationally persisted. His father had seemingly given up directing Anthony's activities, but even so there was no clear-cut course of action that either the father or the son could agree upon. So Anthony spent four years in travel, mostly on the Continent. For reading, the Bible remained his chief source of satisfaction. In his diary entries he noted that he spent some of his time versifying the Psalms and that he searched the Bible for some sort of personal and public policy or program he could present to the English people.

Anthony did not find a program for social action in the Bible, but he did conclude from his various studies that perhaps one of the ways in which he could carry out his earlier promise was to be elected to Parliament. Politics did not greatly interest him, but he wanted to initiate social welfare action, the righting of social wrongs, and he realized that one of the best ways to champion the social rights of the poor was by becoming a member of Parliament. In June 1826, when he was twenty-five years old, he ran successfully for the position of member of Parliament for Woodstock. The following November he noted in his diary: "Took the oath of Parliament with great good will . . . prayer for assistance in my thoughts and deeds."

For the first two years of his service in Parliament, Anthony did not make a speech on the floor. He was busy studying the various complexities of the legislative system and winning the confidence of the leaders of that body. In time he was appointed commissioner of the India Board of Control, and he plunged into the study of Indian problems. He came quickly to the conclusion that the custom of suttee should be abolished. (In suttee, the widow of a deceased Indian placed herself beside the body of her dead husband on the funeral pyre.) Anthony spoke fervently for its elimination. The board felt that the time was not yet ripe, but in the following year, when William Bentinck became the commander of India, the practice was abolished as one of his first steps in office.

Shortly after being appointed to the India Board of Control, Shaftesbury made his first speech in Parliament. His diary for that day says: "And so by God's blessing, my first effort has been made for the advancement of human happiness. May I improve hourly." This statement indicates how intensely religious he was. This religious sensitivity, encouraged by Maria Millis in his early years, remained throughout his lifetime as the major motivation toward social reform.

Shaftesbury lived at the same time as Karl Marx. There is every reason to believe that they were acquainted with each other's beliefs, but the reformist views of Shaftesbury did not stem from Marx's teachings. On the contrary, much of what he taught, while sympathetic to some of the goals of Marxism, was directly opposed to Marx on principle. Shaftesbury's life was God-dominated, and his aims for personal and social living derived from that fact. He was not concerned with merely an increase in material advantages of people, especially the poor; rather he saw in an increase in material advantages the possibility of raising the dignity and the spirituality of the poor. He realized that a secure physical basis to life is the best soil for the growth of religious spirit. In its deepest aspects, Shaftesbury's social reformism was ethical and religious.

Shaftesbury's social convictions were an expression of the basic Christian teaching of the brotherhood of man. Shaftesbury believed that the true Christian was one who worked for brotherhood. On December 17, 1827, he wrote: "Whether I shall ever be well off or not, God alone knows; but this I pray, that never asking for wealth should it be sent me, I may receive at the same time a heart and spirit to lay it out for man's happiness and God's glory." This statement summarizes his attitude toward personal wealth. He believed that every resource given him by God should be used to further social brotherhood. His ideas did not include the necessity of class struggle for the attainment of brotherhood; rather he wished for the application of Christian love for the creation of a spiritual brotherhood in which there would be no one with outstanding wants.

Although Shaftesbury was a member of the Established Church in England, he was tolerant of all branches of Christianity. He claimed that the achievement of the Christian ideal depended not so much on the acceptance of a common church affiliation as it did on the personal reception and expression of the spirit of Christ. At times he fought as energetically in his career for measures that benefited Roman Catholics as he did for those that favored his own religious group.

The religion that Shaftesbury professed was not highly dogmatic. In fact, it is impossible to claim that he had a theological mind. He is not noted for profound philosophical contributions to the explanation or the furtherance of religion. His religion was pietistic and evangelical. He believed in the movement of the Spirit, a belief grounded in his acceptance and use of the Bible as a divine sourcebook of inspiration. He was much more interested in right attitudes than right beliefs. Like the apostle Paul, he affirmed "salvation by faith"; but he was not hesitant in also declaring with James that "faith without works is dead."

Shaftesbury believed, furthermore, that all truth, whether gained by science or not, was God's truth. Therefore, he was willing to accept all kinds of advances in knowledge without conflict between pietism and knowledge. Religious conservatives considered Shaftesbury a conservative in essentials, but they doubted his all-embracing regard for general truth. To the radical in social affairs, Shaftesbury was a radical in his social viewpoints, but somewhat suspect in the fervor of his religious motivation. In effect, Shaftesbury sought reconciliation between religion and science (especially as it affected social reform) in a period of strife on this issue.

Shaftesbury took a moral view of political activity and made a statement that has been widely quoted: "What is morally right can never be politically wrong, and what is morally wrong can never be politically right." In Shaftesbury's practical experience, this maxim meant that he was not a political opportunist. He tried to deal with issues on the basis of their essential rightness. Then, as today, some believed that such a position is impossible under any political system. But the degree to which it can be practiced has seldom been demonstrated more clearly than in the life of the seventh earl of Shaftesbury.

Shaftesbury also believed that the law should not demand naive worship or servile acceptance. Not that he was disdainful of the power and rightness of law, but he did not conceive of law as having an uncriticizable sovereignty in human affairs. He affirmed, on the other hand, that the laws of a nation were devices by which the general welfare was maintained and increased. They represented instruments by which the actual lives of people could be affected. The purpose of Shaftesbury's pragmatic concern with law was to insure the possibility that social legislation would be used *for* the people and not *against* them. Since the law itself was not a final goal of human achievement and because it relied upon moral values beyond itself, Shaftesbury affirmed the dependence of law on religion. Thus, Christianity was the final source of social value; laws were simply to represent Christian morality insofar as that was possible.

A prominent principle in Shaftesbury's life was that of self-sacrifice. In almost every action he showed utter devotion to interests outside of himself. This point could be illustrated from many incidents in his life. Once he noticed a girl crying over her books at the George Yard Ragged School. He approached her asking, "What is the matter? Cannot you learn your lessons?" "Yes, sir," returned the girl, between sobs. "I could if I wasn't so hungry. I've had no breakfast, and we seldom get anything but bread and water." As his eyes roamed around the room, he perceived that the other children were similarly weak from hunger. Some time later, George Holland, the founder of the school, encountered Shaftesbury in another room with his head in his hands. "Oh, George," he cried, "what can be done for them? It is dreadful to see them starve like this." Within a few hours, a cart arrived at the school with soup for its four hundred students. During that winter Shaftesbury supplied soup for the school from his own London kitchen.[3]

Such experiences dotted his career. Wherever there was need, he responded almost automatically and without counting the cost to himself. But Shaftesbury is not remembered as a great philanthropist, although his charities were extensive. Rather, he is remembered for his belief that such conditions as he found in the George Yard Ragged School and elsewhere should be met not with private funds from persons of means but from the public treasury. He went so far as to insist that the social conditions making such dependence and neglect prevalent in England should be eliminated through parliamentary action. But until his aims were legislatively achieved, he remained personally responsive and helpful.

Equipped with such a religious and political philosophy, Shaftesbury stepped forward in Parliament to face the issues of his day. While his contribution to English life was broader than social legislation, it is in that area of service that he gained his reputation.

One of the first problems confronting him was the treatment of the mentally ill. Most persons are aware of the brutal ways in which these unfortunates were kept. Few reliable means of treatment were known, and the best that could be done was to provide "protective services," that is, to keep them locked up in special institutions. In many instances, as the work of Elizabeth Fry in England and Dorothea Dix in the United States show, the conditions of institutionalization were lacking even a modicum of adequacy.

In Shaftesbury's day, there was a rising popular resentment against the conditions affecting the psychotic. The work of Philippe Pinel, a French physician, in the humane treatment of the insane awoke the public conscience. The Quakers in England made a special contribution. Parliament did not ignore the situation and it had passed a series of laws to regulate the asylums used for the insane. However, most of the laws of

Parliament were ineffective, and conditions remained much as before.

In 1828, the relationship of Parliament to the problem was changed. In that year, Shaftesbury made one of his first speeches on the need for a revision of the extant legislation. This speech supported a measure introduced by Robert Gordon, which aimed to "amend the Law for the Regulation of Lunatic Asylums." Gordon was also a prime leader in legislation for the mentally ill. The bill was passed, and a new Board of Commissioners in Lunacy was appointed, and Shaftesbury was a member from the beginning. In 1834, he was made the chairman of the board and continued in that position until his death.

Shaftesbury's work in relation to the mentally ill cannot be reviewed in every detail here, because it is too voluminous. Some of his contributions, however, should be noted. Two bills that passed Parliament under his leadership in 1845 have been called the "Magna Carta of the Insane." These bills represented years of careful preparation. They repealed the previous legislation and made provision for building institutions on a county basis or through the cooperation of several counties. They required that two disinterested physicians sign a certificate of insanity before any person could be placed in an institution. Previously, a certificate of insanity was not a strict requirement, and there were people in asylums that were not formally registered. The need for disinterested physicians was as necessary then as now, because abuses in connection with institutional placement were common.

The bills also assured the permanency of the board as a regular function of Parliament. This in itself was a serious step, since it indicated that Parliament recognized the need for continual study and evaluation of the conditions affecting the mentally ill. The bills required the keeping of records, or "case books," by the institutional staff. These case records were the forerunners of modern social casework and medical case records and enabled those attending the mentally ill to treat their patients in a more scientific way. Also provided for was a degree of personal attention and treatment that had not been in practice on such a scale prior to 1845.

Shaftesbury believed that the criminally insane should be separated from the non-criminally insane. This principle, now widely accepted, was new at the time. Behind Shaftesbury's suggestion was a philosophy of social welfare that sought specialization in the treatment of specific types of problems. Shaftesbury also felt there was a need for a "Benevolent Asylum for the Insane of the Middle Classes." The existing institutions were directed mainly toward the care of the mentally ill of the lower social classes. He believed that such an institution should create a world within itself that would mirror as completely as possible the world from which the patients came. Such an environment, he maintained, would be helpful in the rehabilitation of the patients. While such an institution was not created from public funds (as public funds then were usually made available only for cases of extreme incapacity), Shaftesbury was successful in gaining the interest of several benefactors, and in 1885, the prince of Wales formally opened the Holloway Sanatorium at Virginia Water. Thomas Holloway, a wealthy merchant, expended about $1 million on the project.

In 1851, Shaftesbury shocked Parliament by his disclosures of the housing conditions in London and elsewhere. He told the members that in St. George's parish, "one of the best in London," there were 1,465 working families and 929 of these had only one room to live in, and he found one instance of five families living in a single room. Obviously, it was impossible to conduct normal family life in such an environment. Continuing his speech, he told the members of Parliament that in one temporary shelter "commonly fifty, sometimes ninety to one hundred, men are crowded in a room thirty-three feet nine inches long, twenty feet wide and seven feet high in the center." Some of the lodging houses had no beds to offer tired people. Most did not discriminate between the sexes; in some, men, women, and children lay on the hard floor. The lodging houses were filled with vermin of various sorts. Where a lodging house did have beds, it was common for eight persons to sleep in one bed. In Leeds an investigator found thirty-one persons sleeping in three beds. In general, no toilet facilities existed.

Shaftesbury did not wait for Parliament's support before doing something to remedy these conditions. He, along with others, had already been active in forming the Society for Improving the Condition of the Laboring Classes. This society maintained a variety of services for the poor, including model lodging houses, which were intended to attract the "laboring classes," that is, persons who could pay rent. Shaftesbury maintained that the overcrowded lodgings received approximately the same amount as the model houses of the society, but the society provided every man with a room to himself, a bed, a chair, and some private space. Larger quarters were provided for families in need. The model houses also supplied yards for children. The society supervised sanitary conditions closely, which enabled the tenants to attain a marked degree of personal dignity.

The effectiveness of the houses from the health point of view was proven in the cholera epidemic of 1848-49. Nearly fourteen thousand five hundred deaths occurred in one year, and these represented largely working-class people. Yet, there were only a few from the houses of the society included in that figure.

Shaftesbury believed that the problem of housing should be met by private financing. The society had invested about $100,000 in such projects and had received a fair profit. In addition to all of their other merits, the houses yielded 6 percent interest! Yet Shaftesbury realized from the experience of years that private investors were not active in providing good housing. In time, therefore, he introduced into Parliament a bill which would enable local authorities in towns of ten thousand persons or more to levy taxes for building model houses. This bill passed in the House of Lords, but was so mutilated by the House of Commons that it soon became inoperative.

Shaftesbury introduced another housing bill at about the same time that pertained to the "Registration and Inspection of Common Lodging Houses." As the title suggests, this measure brought governmental responsibility into play on the important problem of maintaining proper health and welfare conditions within housing projects. This bill proved to be one of the finest that had been passed on the subject in England, for it raised the health standards of lodging to new heights. Charles Dickens said of this bill that it was "the best Act ever passed by an English Legislature."

Lord Shaftesbury became interested in public health after visiting the East London slums. In September 1841, one of his friends, Dr. Southwood Smith, took him through the squalid White-Chapel. He was immediately impressed with several factors, one of the first of which was public health standards. He wrote: "What a perambulation I have taken today in company with Dr. Southwood Smith! What scenes of filth, discomfort and disease! . . . No pen nor paint-brush could describe the thing as it is. One whiff of Cowyard, Blue Anchor, or Baker's Court, outweighs ten pages of letterpress."[4] With such an impression, Shaftesbury went to work to improve the general health standards of the country.

Others had been interested in setting up a Board of Health to regulate health standards, and Shaftesbury gave his influence to this measure. In 1848, a bill passed Parliament providing for a Board of Health, and Shaftesbury was appointed as the board's only unpaid commissioner. The history of the board was relatively brief (1848-54), but in that time, Shaftesbury struggled for the betterment of health conditions.

His work took various forms. For one, he sought to encourage civic pride. He believed that no program of health improvement could be successful without popular support and proposed that educational campaigns be introduced to assist Britons in appreciating the value of high health standards. Another of his efforts was to establish local boards of health. These were to personalize the work of the national board and to adapt the program to local conditions. Research information also was needed to carry out the regular functioning of the national and local boards of health. Shaftesbury felt that any cause gains favor when the relevant facts are known. He was a firm believer in social research, especially in welfare matters.

The Board of Health that brought such obvious benefits to the English people failed for a number of reasons. For one, physicians were stoutly opposed to its operations. They wanted freedom to practice as they pleased. The cry of "public interference" in the lives of citizens also was raised. This meant for some that vested interests in real estate or other forms of capital were being threatened.

Shaftesbury lost a battle when the Board of Health was disbanded, but he had not lost the war. He continued to prod the conscience of England for the rest of his life, especially in his public speeches. He carried great weight in his opinions; certainly logic was on his side. In his addresses, he habitually referred to actual conditions and relationships. He knew from first-hand experience the disastrous features of disease in English life, and he never hesitated to speak out about them. He told in graphic form the ways ill health could retard the spiritual advancement of the individual. He believed that a well person could appreciate the meaning and truth of religion more than an unhealthy one. This stress upon the moral and religious implications of disease brought him many supporters from among the clergy and the lay people of the various churches.

In February 1855, Dr. Hector Gavin, a civil servant who had fought cholera for three years in the West Indies, called on Shaftesbury to discuss the disbanded Board of Health. In the course of their conversation, they touched on the topic of the terrible health conditions in the Crimea where the British Army was suffering from a very high death rate. The main cause of death was disease. The idea of trying to help the soldiers in the Crimea appealed to Gavin and Shaftesbury, so Shaftesbury agreed to introduce a bill to provide for a sanitary commission to go to the Crimea. In a few days, the sanitary commission was a reality. Its work in the Crimea is well known, especially through the activities of Florence Nightingale, another hero in the history of social welfare.

Shaftesbury was involved in the development of the Young Men's Christian Association, founded by George Williams. He was the president of the Y.M.C.A. from its earliest days until his death. He gave every help possible to the "Y" movement, and he was a close friend and adviser of George Williams. He saw in the Y.M.C.A., as did Williams and others, the possibility of helping young unmarried men lead a constructive life while living in a big city.

For several years he was president of the Social Science Congress, an organization that held considerable influence in shaping social welfare policies in England in his time. For example, it advocated the relation between public health and recreation and supported reading rooms, coffee clubs, the Y.M.C.A., public parks, lending libraries, and popular excursions.

Lord Shaftesbury believed in education as he believed in sanitation and religion, and he did not feel that education ran counter to the best interests of religious faith. In fact, he claimed, the more education an individual had, the more likely he was to appreciate the value of religion. He did not believe, however, in purely secular education, perceiving that genuine education cannot be divorced from moral meaning. He was not opposed to the development of a national program in education, but he feared any form of education that did not give an important place to the moral and religious dimensions of life.

Some political leaders of that time, as now, believed that people kept in ignorance live in tranquil bliss. They could see no reason for stirring the masses with education. Education and discontent went hand in hand, according to their philosophy. Shaftesbury disagreed with them. He believed that everyone has a right to know, and that knowledge was indispensable to the maintenance of civic standards and the improvement of the commonweal. The chief criticism brought against him by his opponents in Parliament was that he wanted too much education for the masses.

In February 1843, he delivered a challenging and stimulating two-hour-long address in Parliament on the ignorance of the ordinary Englishman. In some ways, this speech is a classic, for it compressed multitudinous facts into a clear and logical case for national action in education. He demonstrated that in 1833 there were one million children of school age in Britain receiving no daily instruction whatsoever. He asserted that many of the existing schools were no better than "pigsties" or "coal holes." He spoke of the profits of the saloons, of prostitution, and of many other of the organized social evils of the country, and he declared that Britain could not stand such waste. But, he reminded the audience, the root of the problem lay not so much in protective legislation, which would repress acknowledged evils, as in the extension of educational privileges, which would encourage people to seek a better way of life. Thus, he combined facts, logic, and moral appeal in his plea to Parliament for action in education.

His speech did not outline any specific action for consideration by Parliament. In eight days, however, Sir James Graham introduced a bill to establish local schools under the supervision of clergy from the Church of England. Many feared the influence of the established church, especially the Dissenters (Protestants who opposed the Church of England), who agitated against the bill. It finally was defeated. The effect of Shaftesbury's talk, however, remained in the minds and hearts of the members of Parliament.

Parliament did appropriate money for the voluntary schools of the country, but this sum amounted to only $200,000, while the budget for the whole government totaled about $250 million annually. Even the Royal Stables received $150,000 a year! In 1847, Lord John Russell introduced his Education Bill, which called for an appropriation of $500,000 for education on a national basis. Shaftesbury immediately threw his influence behind the bill, and it passed.

In the years following the passage of the Educational Bill came a flow of legislation providing generously for public education. Shaftesbury was behind most of this legislation, but he never took a prominent place in its advocacy, because he feared that public education would leave out the important subject matter of religion and ethics. To a considerable degree, Shaftesbury's fears were confirmed, for England developed secular education mainly through Parliamentary appropriations.

The movement toward a more secular type of public education increasingly irritated Shaftesbury. In 1870, a bill was brought up in Parliament to exclude all religious teaching from the public schools. Shaftesbury's attitude toward this is interesting in view of the way public education developed in the United States. He took a sharp stand for continuing the religious instruction then in the curricula of the English schools. Regarding the proposed bill, he declared:

> What! Exclude by Act of Parliament religious teaching from schools founded, supported by public rates! Declare that the revealed Word of God and religious teaching shall be exiled to the odds and ends of time, and that only at such periods shall any efforts be devoted to the most important part of the education of the youth of this Empire! It is an outrage upon the national feelings and, more than this, it is without exception, *the grossest violation of the rights of religious liberty* that was ever perpetrated, or even imagined, in the worst times by the bigotry of any government whatever, foreign or domestic.[5]

When it came to education, Shaftesbury declared that he would rather have the schools of Britain controlled by the Roman

Catholics than by the "secularists." The bill passed, but Shaftesbury's work did much to counteract the extreme claims and goals of the secularists in nineteenth century English education.

While he could not actively support the growth of secular education at national expense, Shaftesbury took the leadership in the Ragged Schools movement. The Ragged Schools were an outgrowth of the missionary enterprise of evangelicals led by John Pound, a crippled shoemaker of Portsmouth. Up to his death in 1839, Pound had educated over five hundred of the most neglected children in London. His work was an expression of the London City Mission. The schools were not exclusively for the poorest children, but in the main only the most deprived were taken in. The title "Ragged Schools" came to be the movement's stamp by way of the annual report of the mission in 1840, which stated: "during the past year several schools have arisen out of their labors and five has [*sic*] been formed exclusively for children raggedly clothed." In 1844, the Ragged School Union (which coordinated the activities of the various schools) invited Shaftesbury to become its president, to which he replied, "I am happy to aid you to the full extent of my power."

The Ragged Schools initially were concerned only with education, oriented toward religion and morality, as the work of the sponsoring organization would indicate. But it included more than religious and ethical teaching. The curriculum paralleled that of the public schools of the time in many respects. The schools also provided for the social welfare needs of the children and their families. In time, the schools resembled settlement houses, since they provided a number of recreational and group work services, as well as more personal services to those who were in need. The Field Lane School, with which Charles Dickens had close contact, developed a broad program of activities during the first ten years of its existence, including:

A free day school for infants; an evening school for youths and adults engaged in daily occupation; a women's evening school, for improving character and extending domestic usefulness . . . industrial class to teach youths tailoring and shoe-making; employment in the shape of wood-chopping, as an industrial test for recommendation to situations; a home for boys when first engaged in places, apart from unwholesome contamination; a night refuge for the utterly destitute; a clothing society for the naked; a distribution of bread to the starving; baths for the filthy; a room to dry clothes worn in the rain during the day; Bible-classes, under voluntary teaching, through which nearly ten thousand persons of all ages, but of one class—all in a state of physical and spiritual destitution—had heard set forth the glad tidings of salvation; various prayer meetings; quarterly conferences for committee and teachers for minute examination into the detailed working of the institution; a school missionary to supply the spiritual wants of the sick, to scour the streets, to bring youthful wanderers to the school, and to rescue fallen females from paths of sin; and a Ragged Church for the proclamation of the Gospel and the worship of God.[6]

The Field Lane School was not an exception in the number and variety of the services offered. Dozens of such schools throughout London supplied important services for needy people, though the education of children was the principal purpose of the schools.

One of the important problems that beset the schools was securing enough well-trained teachers and leaders. The government supplied no funds to the schools. They were privately financed. In the beginning, the union advertised in newspapers for young men and women to volunteer their services as teachers and leaders. The basic expenses for the school were borne through charitable contributions; but even with so insecure a basis of existence, the schools flourished. Many talented people offered themselves as workers in the schools, and the citizenry generously responded financially to enable the movement to grow. By 1870, the schools could claim 440 paid teachers in addition to the thousands giving part-time voluntary help.

Even novelist Charles Dickens played a role in the Ragged Schools movement. Those who have read his works will know how concerned he was with the poor. The problems presented by the children in the Ragged Schools also intensely interested him, and many references in his writings point directly and indirectly to the value of the schools.

In a letter to Edward Fitzgerald, Dickens wrote, "I mean to strike the heaviest blow in my power for these unfortunate creatures [the children of the schools], but whether I shall do so in the *Nickleby* or wait some other opportunity, I have not yet determined." In another letter, he wrote, "Will you have the goodness to turn over in your mind, and note down for me, as briefly as you please, any little facts or details connected with the Ragged Schools which you think it would benefit the design to have publically known?"

The Ragged Schools played upon the conscience of Englishmen. Politicians saw that there was a lack of educational facilities supported by the government and realized that something had to be done. The more the Ragged Schools grew, the more the government found it difficult to explain its failure to create an adequate program for children's education. In 1871, this situation was changed by the Elementary Education Act, which supplied the funds and supervision required for the establishment of a system of local elementary schools throughout Britain. Even after public schools were established, the Ragged Schools were needed, however, and they enjoyed a long life. In some localities where public schools were built, many children preferred to remain in the Ragged Schools.

The Ragged Schools benefited English life in other ways. Their presence stimulated the formation of the National Society for the Prevention of Cruelty to Children, the National Refuges for Destitute Children (established by William Williams), the Polytechnic Institute (founded by Quintin Hogg), and the world famous Barnardo Homes. These and similar organizations and movements owe their origins to the Ragged Schools movement.

The Ragged School Union ultimately became the Shaftesbury Society, the name adopted in 1944. Today, the Society's president is the tenth earl of Shaftesbury. The organization supports a wide range of voluntary social service projects in England: homes and camps; social casework activities clubs for the physically handicapped; mission centers; the Guild of the Good Samaritan; and other forms of welfare. Although the title "Ragged Schools Union" was dropped, the spirit of voluntary and religiously inspired social service has continued and increased.

The conditions that the Ragged Schools addressed were in large part the negative by-products of the Industrial Revolution. The invention of machinery made men, women, and children attendants in a steel trap, for they were confined to their posts for long hours. There was little time left after work for the enjoyment of other activities. In many factories, thirteen hours of work per day was common. In others, the hours spent each day tending the machines amounted to as many as sixteen. Under such a schedule, it was virtually impossible for any person to enjoy life.

Women and children were widely employed in the factories, for they provided cheaper labor than men and so were more in demand. Their plight was even more tragic than that of many men. They were not able to sustain their energy as well as the men and were thus more physically exhausted from their work. Physical exhaustion made them more susceptible to disease. The evidence shows that "man's inhumanity to man" found a strong expression in the industrial conditions of nineteenth-century England.

It is remarkable that such abhorrent conditions should have been allowed to exist for so long a time. But, during much of the nineteenth century, there were no adequate legislative safeguards against these conditions. Sir Robert Peel's act of 1802 brought some measure of control to the employment of apprentices in the cotton mills, but this piece of legislation was thoroughly ineffective. John Cam Hobhouse introduced two bills that passed through Parliament in 1825 and 1831. One reduced Saturday working hours from twelve to nine; the other provided for a maximum of twelve hours per day for all cotton mill workers under eighteen years of age. These two measures were small efforts, the latter affecting only a segment of the total industrial workers of Britain. And they were the main legislative efforts aimed at the humanization of the industrial system.

In 1831, Michael Sadler, Tory member of Parliament for Newark, introduced a Ten Hours Bill, designed to benefit children not only in cotton mills but also in textile factories. Sadler was appointed to a committee to study the problem he had raised, but at the next election he was not returned to Parliament, so his efforts were largely exploratory and temporary. The cause that he represented was not popular. Many people thought the personnel requirements of the industries hiring children could not be met by reducing hours. Some— workers and employers—believed that his measure would be an interference with their personal rights and freedom. Hobhouse, a leader in social legislation, promptly termed the measure "fantastic."

An interested cleric, the Reverend G. S. Bull, brought the matter to the attention of Shaftesbury, who felt challenged but hesitant. First, he retired to his study to pray and meditate on the matter, as was his custom. Then he consulted with his wife.

In 1830, Shaftesbury had married Lady Emily Cowper, daughter of Lord Cowper, a prominent Whig, and a niece of Viscount Melbourne, a prime minister and adviser to Queen Victoria. Lady Shaftesbury was a diligent, patient woman, who worked hard to assist her husband in his many activities. Her intelligence and social charm won many friends for her husband and his causes. They were a loyal team whose energies were largely devoted to securing legislation to aid the English people. Lady Shaftesbury advised her husband to lead the movement in favor of the Ten Hours Bill: "It is your duty! the consequences we must leave. Go forward and to victory!" With such encouragement Lord Shaftesbury gave his assent.

One of his first moves was to consult with labor leaders and members of Parliament to determine the best strategy for passage of the bill. He learned that labor was vitally interested in it, but would not force it through Parliament by strikes and riots. He also discovered that several of the leaders in Parliament would be willing to support the measure if they were convinced that it would not threaten the stability of English industry. Elections had brought about some changes in Parliament, and now there were some Liberals who were willing to support the bill.

In February 1833, Shaftesbury introduced the Ten Hours Bill, which was nearly identical to the one introduced by Sadler. It called for the following: no child under nine years of age could be employed; no person under eighteen could be employed more than ten hours a day or more than eight hours on Saturday; and no person under twenty-one could be employed at night (7:00 P.M. to 6:00 A.M.).

The facts of the case came up again, as they had previously with Sadler's bill. The evidence that Sadler's committee had gathered might have been sufficient, but some members of Parliament claimed that the committee was prejudiced in favor of labor. Therefore, a royal commission was appointed to study the problem again, and while its report was much more conservative than that submitted by Sadler and his committee, it bristled with reformist suggestions. The labor leaders, at first suspicious of the commission's work, accepted the report with little criticism.

After the report was read to Parliament, an extended discussion on the proposed bill took place. Opposition to the measure contended that Shaftesbury's bill "went too far." They wanted children protected, but they suggested that the bill make a major differentiation between workers at the age of thirteen. Safeguards should be set up to control the employment of children under thirteen, but nothing should be done to limit the employment of persons over that age. Those over thirteen, it was argued, were capable of taking care of themselves.

With this twist in the argument and the resulting strength of opposition that was demonstrated, it became obvious to Shaftesbury and his supporters that it would be impossible to pass the Ten Hours Bill. They reluctantly turned to a compromise—the Factory Bill of 1833. This bill passed. It provided that children under thirteen be allowed to work not more than forty-eight hours a week and not more than nine on any day. Youths under eighteen could not be employed more than twelve hours a day or sixty-nine hours a week. Factory children were required to attend school two hours a day. Four inspectors were appointed to see that the bill was operative. These inspectors had such discretionary powers that in many instances the bill was ineffective. This bill was a far cry from the one Shaftesbury wished for, but he was willing to accept the compromise and try it out. Labor disapproved of Shaftesbury's attitude and turned against him, and for about a year he lost his prominence in Parliament.

By the end of 1834, Shaftesbury returned to leadership in Parliament and began to attack the terms of the 1833 bill. He assembled quantities of data to show that the stipulations of the bill of 1833 were not being kept. In 1839, he succeeded in having a new Factory Bill introduced, but it failed to pass. Undaunted, he turned to the task of educating Parliament for the kinds of measures he had in mind. The best way of doing this, he felt, was through commissions to study employment problems. Two commissions were appointed, one to investigate the operation of the bill of 1833, the other to inquire into the condition of children in mines.

By 1844 Shaftesbury felt that the time had become ripe for a revision of the Factory Bill of 1833. Citing a mass of evidence, he addressed Parliament on the advantages of a revision. The new bill, the Factory Bill of 1844, included many of Shaftesbury's original ideas. Its main point, the one on which the focus of opposition was directed, was a demand for a ten-hour working day. Years of patient research paid off in his presentation before Parliament. Quietly, yet effectively, he quoted statistics and cases proving his points. Once more he combined a factual analysis with moral appeal. He showed how advantageous a revision would be even on material and self-interest grounds, but he also emphasized the importance of making decisions in relation to ethical requirements. Parliament was touched and convinced by his speech.

The opposition was led by John Bright, a noted reformer. While Bright has been trumpeted as a social reformer of distinction, he did not favor industrial reform and stood against the humane measures advocated by Shaftesbury. One of his main lines of attack was the "mock humanity" of Shaftesbury's proposals. Bright accused Shaftesbury of being sentimental and unrealistic in his attitude toward shorter working hours. Bright used a letter that had been written by a cripple named Dodd which, in effect, judged Shaftesbury guilty of "sharp practices" and "ingratitude." For a time Shaftesbury's cause seemed to be doomed once more, but when the vote was taken, his proposals were accepted by a slight margin.

His battle was not yet fully won, however, for the government was not willing to accept the views of Parliament. Because of their essentially conservative position in relation to the electorate, government leaders felt that they had to oppose the bill. There was no direct way they could do this, but by a threat of resignation, they achieved their ends. Lord Peel, the prime minister, along with his cabinet, threatened to resign, which would bring down the government. This threat proved to be too much, and Shaftesbury and his followers gave in. When the question was resubmitted to Parliament, his measure was defeated by 138 votes.

This was a crushing defeat for Shaftesbury and his forces,

but the government sponsored measure enacted in its place was an advance over the legislation that existed previously. One of the features of the government bill was that women of all ages should be considered as young persons and protected accordingly. This clause was suggested by Shaftesbury in his Ten Hours Bill; it was retained in the government measure. Thus, in a sense, this incident was both a defeat and a victory. The defeat, though great, brought at least one advantage with it: the provision for women.

Failure to achieve unity with the dominant party of Prime Minister Sir Robert Peel led to further difficulties for Shaftesbury in his efforts for other social enactments. He continued to come into conflict with Bright, especially on the issue of the repeal of the Corn Laws, a series of laws regulating the home and foreign grain trade, the last of which was repealed in 1846. Shaftesbury stood firm for the repeal of the Corn Laws and felt that he could not hold his seat in Parliament if he were required to support the other side of the question. The government forced him to choose between his integrity and his position; he chose the former without hesitation. Four days later, he resigned. But before he resigned, he made arrangements for the reintroduction of a modified Ten Hours Bill.

Shaftesbury's place in Parliament was filled by John Fielden, a member from Oldham. Fielden was a man of definite talent who agreed with Shaftesbury on many social issues. He was able to rally the forces in Parliament that formerly had supported Shaftesbury and began the campaign for the Ten Hours Bill. By 1847, when Fielden introduced his bill, the political reactions to the measure had radically changed in many quarters. Peel had resigned in 1846 because of Parliamentary opposition on his Irish Coercion Bill. This cleared the way for governmental acceptance of the measure. The labor elements in British society also had been busy during the preceding years agitating in favor of such a bill. Many members of Parliament had gotten used to the idea of a Ten Hours Bill and were willing to give their assent to its passage.

With such a favorable environment, Fielden's bill passed both houses and the government on July 1, 1847. Passage was not without opposition, but the tide had turned, and the bill was passed with a good margin of safety. Shaftesbury, who led the fight for so many years, was not in Parliament at the time the bill passed. When the tide was turning and victory seemed to be assured, many of his friends asked that he again take up his place in Parliament, but he realized that he was too late. He could not be elected in time to vote on the bill, and he did not want to hold it up. He did campaign for the measure throughout his section of the country, and his support no doubt meant much in rallying the votes necessary to carry the day.

One would think that the resulting legislation would have been received without too much comment, positive or negative, by a populace that by this time had become accustomed to the idea. But legal difficulties in the interpretation and administration of the legislation finally resulted in its nullification. The legislation had provided for a maximum number of hours for workers of different age and sex groups. But it did not specifically rule out the use of shifts or relays that might be used to dodge the intent of the bill. Shrewd employers immediately seized upon this loophole and thwarted the effectiveness of the legislation. Others rearranged the working hours of their employees so that no inspector could be present to check on the legal requirements. By 1849, the bill had been referred to the Court of Exchequer, which nullified it.

The action by the Court of Exchequer meant that the whole process of getting a new and invulnerable bill passed fell on the shoulders of Shaftesbury and his colleagues. Shaftesbury had returned to Parliament by this time and was appointed leader of the cause. There was considerable disagreement among those on his side as to how the new legislation should read. Some thought that the original intention of the nullified act should be delineated in more careful detail. Others thought that, if this were done, the resulting measure would probably not pass Parliament, since it would fail to meet the objections of the manufacturers who opposed the bill in the first place. Considerable wrangling on this issue took place with no final unanimity. In the end, Shaftesbury accepted a compromise by the government.

Shaftesbury was undecided for some time as to what course he should follow. Finally, against the advice of some of his conferees, he took his stand with the government on the compromise. Many misunderstood his motives, and rallies were held to denounce him and his "treachery." But Shaftesbury was a man of both conviction and moderation. He wanted general support, but would not buy that at the cost of what he deemed right. On the other hand, he always sought to secure the greatest possible support for any measure. His sights looked out upon the English people as a whole, rather than any one segment. Shaftesbury's methods won him followers on all sides of particular issues. He had a surprising power to integrate the varying opinions of people. His stand on the Factory Act of 1850 is a striking illustration of this.

For seventeen years, Shaftesbury worked for legislation that would protect working men, women, and children. Not always did he have his way with Parliament, the government, or his friends, but he did assist in the creation of certain benefits. All children under nine were excluded from employment in textile mills; children under thirteen were restricted to six-and-a-half hours of work per day; education was recognized as the right of every factory child; youths under eighteen were limited to sixty hours of work a week and were not permitted to work at night; women were protected in the same way as were children; factory inspectors were appointed who in time made a genuine contribution to the betterment of working conditions; no one worked after two o'clock on Saturday afternoon; and controls were created that placed human values in a more important position than economic.

In 1840, due to Shaftesbury's instigation, a royal commission was appointed to investigate the labor conditions in the mines, trades, and manufactures in Britain. This commission made its report in 1842, and while the whole report is important, its chief significance lies in the stress placed on the need for improvements in conditions affecting miners. The commission found that everywhere in Britain children, girls as well as boys under thirteen years of age, were regularly employed underground. The health conditions attendant to such work were described in great detail by the commission. Surely no child could hope for a normal physical development if his or her early life was lived in the mines. Work in the mines was strenuous and degrading for children as well as for adults. Boys were employed as "hurriers," or haulers. A chain, attached to a leather belt fastened around their waists, was attached to a "corve," or coal-sled. These boys, usually naked, would crawl on all fours over the mine's roadways of rock, often through water and mud. The hurriers represented only one type of cruel labor.

The effects of the commission's report were felt throughout Parliament. Almost everyone agreed that a terrible wrong had been permitted. The next task was to right that wrong.

It was easier to condemn than to reconstruct the situation. A week after the report had been made public, Shaftesbury was ready with a bill. The bill provided for the following: all female labor was to be withdrawn from the mines; children under thirteen were also not permitted; the apprenticing of pauper children (which amounted to a form of legal slavery) was prohibited; and only persons over twenty-one and under fifty were to be given jobs on which the lives of others rested.

In addition to these and other provisions, the bill required that a copy of the bill be clearly posted within twenty feet of the principal entrance to mines in the United Kingdom. Mine owners were made responsible for infractions of the law through a system of court punishments. The measure represented to Shaftesbury only the bare minimum of what was desirable socially, but he realized that he would have difficulty enough simply to get it passed. It did pass the Commons, however, almost in the form in which it was proposed, but it had a rougher time in the Lords. There, certain mine-owning representatives made clear to all that the new bill would cause considerable economic havoc in the mining industry. The Lords modified several points of the bill, making it somewhat weaker than the original. Finally, they too concurred, and it became the law of the land.

Shaftesbury was active in urging other industrial reforms. Some can be mentioned briefly to show the scope of his interests. His Print Works Act, which passed Parliament in 1845, brought needed relief to women and young children (sometimes as young as four years old) employed in calico-print factories. The gains Shaftesbury had earlier achieved for certain factory workers were improved by the acts of 1864 and 1867, which extended the government control over all previously uncontrolled industries. The first covered only six additional industries, but the second extended protection to the laborers in all industries.

Shaftesbury believed that too many young children and

women were employed in agriculture. His bill to remedy the situation never passed, but it encouraged the government to introduce measures that accomplished almost the same beneficial results. Even children forced to work in brickyards and as chimneysweeps were aided by legislative measures introduced by Shaftesbury.

Shaftesbury was approached on several occasions by prominent social reformers to take up the cause of the abolition of opium. Responsive to all social needs, he plunged into the struggle against opium.

In 1775, Warren Hastings, governor general of British India, had laid down the following inconsistent rule regarding the traffic of opium: "Opium is not a necessity of life, but a pernicious article of luxury which ought not to be permitted, except for purposes of foreign commerce only, and which the wisdom of the Government should carefully restrain from internal consumption."[7] How was it possible to permit the international trade of opium and yet successfully ban it from "internal" consumption? As the history of recent times shows, there is no way.

The opium trade between Britain and China in 1840 amounted to about $20 million. Shaftesbury's arguments against the opium traffic were many and effective. He stood always on moral and religious grounds and constantly reminded his hearers that opium did not enhance personality when used indiscriminately as a drug. He felt that Christianity was basically opposed to its use, and he argued that opium trading with Oriental countries to which Christian missionaries had been sent created a basic dichotomy of responsibility. Either one or the other should be stopped. Furthermore, he said, the government was actually helping the opium traders by the protective measures that it had passed benefiting the growth of the opium industry. Opium trading had actually become a monopoly on the part of certain British individuals. The securing of the opium from the Orient often led to violence, underhanded methods of dealing, and the bribing of government officials. Finally, the growth of opium trading had negatively affected the trade of more stable materials, such as cotton, between the nations. Figures showed that traders favored the more lucrative opium trading over other products.

Although Shaftesbury spoke on many occasions in Parliament against traffic in opium, he was unsuccessful in establishing restrictive legislation. The governments involved made too much money in taxes, and private investors had too much at stake to change an advantageous situation. In time Shaftesbury realized that a great deal more social preparation was required before a bill would find acceptance. He therefore turned his attention to the task of building up public opinion in his favor. For the rest of his life, he was the head of the Anti-Opium League and president of the Anglo-Oriental Society, which were concerned with "the suppression of the opium trade."

While Shaftesbury was not known as a temperance worker, as some were in his time, he did perceive certain evils in the excessive use of liquor. He did not crusade against liquor as he did against opium, but his stand was made clear on many occasions. He strongly believed that alcoholism was one of the greatest social evils and that it required legislative regulation.

Shaftesbury spent the last twelve years of his life in relative solitude. After the death of his wife in 1872, he sought to lose himself and his loneliness in his work, but he no longer had the stamina to continue his traditional roles. Increasingly he looked to others younger than himself to provide the actual leadership in social reform. But he remained as a "grand old institution" and was held in respect by the British as a man who had led them to a higher status as individuals and as a nation.

In 1885, the Duke of Argyll, addressing his fellow peers, said: "My lords, the social reforms of the last century have not been due mainly to the Liberal party. They have been due mainly to the influence, character, and perseverance of one man—Lord Shaftesbury." Endorsing this statement, Lord Salisbury exclaimed, "That I believe is a true representation of the facts."[8] He remained until his death the nominal leader of many organizations and movements for social improvement.

Shaftesbury died on October 1, 1885, at Folkestone. The dean of Westminster had asked him if he would be willing to be buried in Westminster Abbey, but he had declined. A service was held in his honor and memory in the abbey, however, and many thousands of Londoners turned out to pay homage to their friend. He was buried beside his family in the churchyard of St. Giles Church, Dorset.

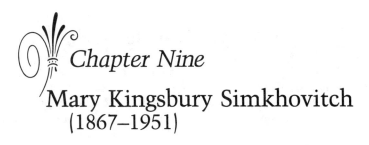

Chapter Nine
Mary Kingsbury Simkhovitch
(1867–1951)

If I, too, have learned anything throughout these many
years, it is surely this, that it is our common life that
matters, and that to stay apart from it is the death of art,
of politics and of religion.[1]

Mary Kingsbury Simkhovitch, founder and director of Greenwich House in New York City, came by her interest in social welfare through a number of influences. Among these were her home life, religious leaders, teachers who saw the whole of life's problems rather than their small corner of human knowledge, and loyal and thoughtful friends.

Mary Kingsbury's ancestors came to America in the late seventeenth century and made their home in Bridgewater, Massachusetts, and young Mary made frequent visits there from her own home in Chestnut Hill near Boston. It was at Bridgewater that Mary's mother went to church with her grandmother. The story is told that the minister stood an hourglass on the pulpit, turning it over as he began his sermon. When it had run out he would turn it over again to make sure that the congregation got its full two hours' worth of New England preaching.

Mary's grandmother urged her to study music, so, along with her four cousins, Mary took piano lessons from Ellen Whittlesey, who sang in the Congregational church choir. Mary's father was choir director and also sang tenor. Ellen Whittlesey was something of a "progressive" educator long before the formal rise of that movement. She taught Mary to listen to all sorts of musical sounds such as the songs of birds, the surf beating on the shore, and the twanging of taut wire. Mary learned to sight-read by singing duets. Biographies of musicians were required reading, so that Mary might know not only the music, but also the personal and social background out of which it had come.

At age fourteen, Mary joined the Congregational church in nearby Newton Centre. Of this she later said, "I suppose I may have been the last of my generation to be asked if I were willing to be damned if it was God's will." But little of her early religion was so dour as this. For the most part, religion caught her interest so firmly that, throughout her life, it was a source of comfort and stimulation.

Professor Nash of the Cambridge Theological School presented Mary with a more liberal and socially oriented theology. (His great-grandfather, while listening to a sermon on eternal damnation, arose from his seat, stamped down the aisle, and shouted, "I don't believe a word of it!") Professor Nash's book, an important one for the times, *Genesis of the Social Conscience*, appealed to Mary.

The church Sunday school introduced her to some of the social service aspects of city life. One Thanksgiving morning, the members of her class went to a tenement on Kneeland Street in Boston. There they visited a poor woman who lacked food and fuel. The class gave her some coal and a turkey. This scene left its imprint on Mary's impressionable mind.

When Mary was fifteen, her father left the State House where he had been employed to become city clerk of Newton. High school in Newton strengthened Mary's understanding of the relationship of the past and the present. Solid study also had its lighter aspects, such as the time when Mr. Kent, a sarcastic but kindly mathematics teacher, said to Mary, "Yes, yes, that is the right answer, but it is exactly as if you had gone to Worcester *via* Europe and Asia!" Many of the high school students occasionally went to Boston to hear the renowned Episcopal preacher Phillips Brooks during Lent. Mary came under his spell and accepted his religious philosophy, which called for a commitment to personal and social change.

Mary's parents were her mentors during her early years. Her mother was an intellectual person who stimulated Mary's love for reading. Of her mother, Mary later wrote: "Widely read in many languages she exemplified the old literary culture now passing away and indeed deprecated by a generation too engrossed in the violent passions of world conflict to sympathize with the detachment of more innocent years." Her father was kindly and wise. Their walks and their informal conversations gave Mary a concern for the public interest to which her father had devoted many years.[2]

High school finished, Mary looked toward college, and Boston University, seven miles away, was her choice. Mary enrolled in 1886 with her friend Ida Davis. After an initial period of adjustment, both were "rushed" by the various sororities and were finally accepted into Kappa Kappa Gamma. The sororities at Boston University were very snobbish. They selected their members for their class position, intellectual ability, and religion. (The schools of medicine and law were broadly nonsectarian, but the undergraduate college, like the theological seminary, was strictly denominational.) But the sororities did encourage an *esprit de corps* and, through it, aided scholarship. Mary later mentioned the benefit which came, especially to the newer and younger members of the college, from the intimate association with the older and more knowing students within the sororities.

The college, being small and featuring small classes, enabled Mary to have close contact with her teachers. Among those she came to know well were several who influenced her thinking. Professor Thomas Kindsey was one of these. He was primarily a teacher of Latin, but the range and depth of his scholarship attracted her to whatever course he might teach. He involved his students in his research, and Mary was thrilled with this sense of collaboration with him. "For one whole season," she said, "I was given the task of analyzing all of the *qui* clauses with the subjunctive in Ovid, Propertius, and Tibullus." Mary chose teachers rather than subjects.

Professor Borden Parker Bowne was another teacher who had great influence on Mary. As a professor of philosophy, Bowne founded and developed the "Personalism" school of American thought. His ideas ran counter to the Spencerian-Fiske (Herbert Spencer and John Fiske) conceptions of philosophy, dominant at that time, which rested on pervasive, impersonal, evolutionary force as a cosmic principle. Bowne was unexcelled in his ability to analyze the faults in his opponents' thinking. He first destroyed in order to build, but even when he was building, he was cautious. Mary learned from him the need for the utmost care in dealing with intellectual problems and for careful and sound reasoning, and she also absorbed some of his social interests. Religion, because of its personalistic implications, had for Bowne a vital social meaning.

The Brotherhood of the Carpenter ranks as another potent contributor to Mary's intellectual life. This was a congregation led by the Reverend W. D. P. Bliss, who was also the editor of the *Encyclopedia of Social Reform*. An Episcopalian, Bliss held strong social convictions. The brotherhood was established in 1889 and met in a bookstore. Upstairs were a reading room in the front and a chapel in the back. Discussions of social problems were held at Sunday supper meetings in the basement of the building, and these attracted not only Mary Kingsbury, but others who were led through this association to take part in the social movements of the day.

The "federal unions" in which manual and nonmanual

workers held common membership also appealed to Mary. The headquarters in Boston for the unions was Denison House, a pioneer Boston settlement house, which also served as a place for discussion meetings and other activities. It was here that Mary's social sense was strengthened and enlarged. Here she met Vida Scudder, Emily Balch, and others who achieved positions of social leadership.

While playing the organ for a Saturday children's service, Mary came into social contact with blacks for the first time in her life.

> The members invited me to their homes, and when I saw the primitive wooden houses in the rear of Beacon Hill with yard toilets and no bathing facilities I was amazed. "Who owns this house?" I asked the mother of one of the club girls, and in reply I discovered that the owner was a senior warden in one of Boston's oldest parishes! This certainly was strange, I thought. How could that be?[3]

Mary could not forget the living conditions of her black friends.

After college graduation in 1890, Mary taught Latin at Somerville High School, but she did not really succeed as a teacher. She lacked the patience to deal with slow pupils and to grade daily papers. After two years of teaching, she decided to go to Radcliffe College for graduate study. Radcliffe featured quite a different social atmosphere than that of Boston University. Radcliffe students were permitted to attend Harvard University as "extras," and this created an opportunity for new intellectual pursuits. In addition to her studies, Mary continued to work with black children in Boston. She lived with the family of the Reverend Charles Tiffany, a Unitarian minister and an editorial writer for a Boston newspaper.

While at Radcliffe, Mary Kingsbury studied the medieval guild system with Professor Gross, the history of philosophy with Professor Palmer, sociology with Professor Edward Cummings, and economic history with Sir William Ashley. Ashley, who called Harvard a "Unitarian high school," was an indefatigable worker and expected all his students to be the same. Before he returned to England, he taught Mary how much economics and history need each other and what strong forces they are together.

At the end of that year at Radcliffe, Mary was awarded a scholarship by the Women's Educational and Industrial Union to study in Germany. That experience was to enrich her life in many ways. She and her mother sailed on a Dutch liner for Antwerp, then visited The Hague, Scheveningen, Haarlem, Amsterdam, Cologne, and other cities on their journey to Berlin. Mary wanted to improve her German language skills, so with her mother she spent time first in Eisenach and then in Weimar. In Weimar they stayed in the home of an historian, who impressed them with his love of scholarship, and they visited Goethe's home and other shrines of culture.

Reaching Berlin, they settled down in a pension on one of the main streets of the city. Parades and other street activities entertained the newcomers, and nearby was the Tiergarten, a public park, where they could read in seclusion and comfort.

Soon Mary renewed her friendship with Emily Balch, who was also living in Berlin, and the two spent many hours together reading and discussing their studies and their experiences. It was not possible for them to be enrolled formally in the German universities, because women were not officially accepted for higher education. But they were allowed to attend the seminars and lectures. Schmoller and Adolf Wagner impressed the Berlin students of that time. Schmoller was known for his "historical method," and his respect for detail helped his students realize that there is no firm and permanent knowledge that is not rooted in particulars.

Politics was more important than methodology to Adolf Wagner. Students heard him discuss the danger from the East (Russia) and the hope that Germany would some day come into a very strong position on the Continent. He especially disliked sociology. Mary Kingsbury told of one occasion when she was called upon in his seminar to review some sociological materials. Wagner sprang from his chair and shouted, "Ja, die Soziologie! Was heisst, aber, die Soziologie? Das Heisst, meine Freunde, die Amerikanische Wissenschaft!" (What is sociology? That, my friends, is the American science!) With that blast, he looked fiercely around the room to see that all were completely squelched.

Aside from such outbursts, Wagner was a kindly man and attracted students from all over the world. In his classes were Sonya Daszisskaia, who later became interested in labor legislation in Poland, Bertrand Russell and his American wife Alice Pearsall Smith, and Walter Weyl, Frank Dixon, and Peter Struve, all from the United States. Also in the group was a Russian, Vladimir Gregorievitch Simkhovitch. Mary and Vladimir became close friends, and before she returned to the United States, they were engaged.

Other teachers also held her interest: Professor Sering, who lectured on American agriculture; Georg Simmel, one of the early social psychologists; and Professor Bastian, a famous anthropologist, who was noted for his red flannel "chest protector" and his love of his subject. Students and teachers took part in the social and economic debates of the period, discussing problems of free speech, socialism, industrial development, and other subjects with considerable zeal. It was at this time that Mary first saw a woman smoke—she was the widow of a general from Hanover.

Travel was also a part of Mary's education. Between terms, Mary and her mother toured Italy with friends. Short trips to Dresden and to nearby mountains, Nuremberg, and other places provided pleasure and intellectual stimulation. At the end of Mary's final semester, they went to Paris and London. Mary's mother returned home, leaving Mary in the company of Emily Balch to attend the last great International Socialist Trade Union Congress. Emily had a press ticket, and Mary got a ticket from a London friend of Karl Marx. Some of the great socialist and labor leaders of the period attended the Congress, including Jean Leon Jaures, the Avelings (Marx's daughter and son-in-law), Sidney and Beatrice Webb, Bernard Shaw, Charlotte Gilman, and Ferri. The Congress failed to accomplish very much, but it must have been interesting to watch.

On her return to the United States, Mary spent a year in New York attending Columbia University, where she studied with Seligman, Giddings, Clark, and James Harvey Robinson. For a time, she lived with Anne O'Hagen, a writer with the now defunct *World,* but her interest in sociology and social problems led her to accept an offer to live in the College Settlement. She had been interested in settlement house work since her early days in Boston. At first, the idea of a church settlement appealed to her, but she later grew to believe that church dogma and the experimental requirements of the settlement could not be combined, and she turned more and more to the conception of a settlement house operated on a nonsectarian basis. This did not mean that the settlement was to be antireligious; it simply meant that it should be objective and impartial, dealing with people according to their needs rather than their religious status.

On a long summer holiday, Mary traveled to London to study at the British Museum. She returned to New York City in September 1897 and moved into 95 Rivington Street, ready for work.

On the first night in the College Settlement, a shot woke her from sleep. Looking out the window onto Allen Street, the heart of the red-light district, everything seemed silent. Then she heard cries and the rapid steps of policemen. But it was just a disturbance, and Dr. Robbins, her superior at the settlement, hardly mentioned the incident. In time, Mary became used to all sorts of bizarre happenings.

The settlement was located in a crowded section of the East Side of New York City. The house itself was a beautiful old dwelling with two main rooms on the first floor. In the spacious backyard was a playground—one of the first in the city. Opposite the house was a wooden tenement. Emily Wagner began a music school in the front basement of the settlement, but soon her classes were so popular that she moved them to the tenement across the street. Later Wagner's school joined with the University Settlement Music School and finally emerged as the Third Street Music School Settlement. The front room of the College Settlement was a library and assembly room. The back room, the residents' dining room, was also used for club meetings, parties, dances, and other gatherings.

Mary felt she should learn something about the life and customs of the people with whom she was dealing, so she read history and studied different languages. Because a large number of Jews lived on the East Side, she began learning Yiddish, making enough progress to read Yiddish newspapers and attend the Yiddish theater.

After a few months of apprenticeship, Mary took over the responsibility of running the settlement. Her special task was the Sunday Evening Economics Club, which she started her first winter there. From this club, and others like it, have come some of the nation's leaders in many fields of activity: judges, teachers, actors, musicians, and playwrights.

The East Side was quite different from that area today. Unemployment, disease, political corruption, and other evils were evident everywhere. Reform movements rose at various times, labor unions were initiated as a means of improving the economic well-being of the people, and "good government" organizations sprang up with persistent regularity to help lift the political standards of the community. The first Seth Low mayoralty campaign was run during Mary Kingsbury's first year at the settlement. Low, standing for reform government, caught the enthusiasm of the people. The College settlement, like others near it, was interested in these movements, but it also was concerned with other fundamental human "rights"—the opportunities for children to play safely and freely, for people to assemble in discussions of whatever they felt to be closest to their own welfare, and for those who were unable to provide for themselves to secure necessary support.

The East Side gradually changed as floods of new immigrants concentrated there. The earlier immigrants, predominantly Germans, migrated northward, although there were always some who remained and others who were added from time to time.

The College Settlement was almost next door to the oldest settlement in the United States, the University Settlement, and the two organizations often worked together. Stanton Coit inspired many with his work at the University Settlement. One of the boys in the Social and Educational Improvement Club was Henry Moskowitz, who despite his impoverished youth became one of the welfare leaders of New York City and later of the state of New York. Three of the other members of the S.E.I. Club formed the Downtown Ethical Society in 1890, which later became Madison House, another settlement. Despite the harrowing, frustrating conditions on the East Side, the settlements, along with other agencies and organizations, helped many young men and women to constructive careers within the life of the city, state, and nation.

Mary Kingsbury spent only one year at the College Settlement, and then she accepted an invitation to be head of the Friendly Aid House, which was supported by the Unitarian Church of All Souls. Their goal was to establish cooperative relations with the lesser privileged groups on the nearby middle East Side. The leading forces in the church at that time were two brothers, Norton and Warren Goddard. Norton Goddard was a man of means, a Republican, who had built and maintained a clubhouse called the Civic Club, which attracted workingmen. Throughout his life Norton Goddard sought political reform using the methods of the political party in power to accomplish his ends. Ultimately, his work proved to be of little permanent value, because it did not have the genuine acceptance and active support of others.

Warren Goddard was not so much interested in politics as in changing the social structure itself. He believed that if members of the various classes were brought together for the enlightenment of all, social progress could be made. His methods were not always practical, but his motives were high.

The Friendly Aid House was operated by church-minded people. To them it was a charity that should be carefully controlled in all of its aspects. Symbolic of this control was the board room, closed to all but board members of the house. Free speech early became an issue in the management of the house. Mary Kingsbury had invited Edwin Mead of Boston to speak on the independence of the Philippines—in her own apartment. This meeting was canceled because it was felt by the board to be somewhat treasonable to question the integrity of President William McKinley's stand on the issue. The University Settlement, however, welcomed Mead. This experience taught Mary Kingsbury the lesson that a settlement, in order to fulfill its own distinctive functions, must be free from all domination—even though those in control might be charitable or well meaning. The experience confirmed her earlier view on the need for nonsectarian settlements.

At this time there were no public playgrounds in the middle East Side. Mary had had some experience with the Outdoor Recreation League, which helped in establishing Seward Park. For the middle East Side, similar parks were needed, and for years she worked to attain them. She began by obtaining two lots adjoining the house for a playground, the Kips' Bay playground.

In January 1899, Mary Kingsbury and Vladimir Simkhovitch were married at the Chapel of the Incarnation on east Thirty-first Street. They had met in Berlin as students and were engaged when Mary returned to the United States. Vladimir came to the United States in 1898, and attended Cornell University as a foreign fellow. He became a professor of economics at Columbia University and was associated with the university the rest of his academic life. Many noted persons came to their apartment on the upper floor of the house, including Henry Lloyd, President Thomas Masaryk of Czechoslovakia, Herbert and Elsie Parsons, and James Harvey Robinson.

Church control over the Friendly Aid House was a constant source of irritation to Mary Simkhovitch. Finally, in 1901, the break came. The Friendly Aid House continued after Mary left under the name of the Warren Goddard House, and it changed in aspects other than name. The policy of administrative freedom for which Mary stood became the accepted rule of the house, and it survived to accomplish much good in its location.

But Mary Simkhovitch had made her decision. What she sought was the establishment of a truly free settlement, so she gathered about her the founders of what was to be called the Cooperative Social Settlement Society. Among the incorporators of the society were Henry C. Potter, then the Episcopal bishop of New York City, Eugene Philbin, a prominent Roman Catholic layman, Carl Schurz, Jacob Riis, Felix Adler, and Robert Fulton Cutting. These persons represented a variety of viewpoints on social improvement, but they were bound together for this enterprise by the philosophy of the society's founder and the needs of the community.

In the summer of 1901, Paul Kennaday and Mary Sherman, representatives of the incorporating group, searched for a neighborhood in which the new settlement could be placed. They decided on Greenwich Village, the old Ninth Ward, on Manhattan's West Side. Jones Street was chosen as the most suitable street within the Village—the most densely populated of the lower West Side streets, having fourteen hundred people in a block. A survey showed that twenty-six nationalities were represented in the community. The people were mostly Irish with Italians and blacks also present in abundance. The street featured five saloons, nine boarding houses, and dilapidated tenement houses. Number 26 Jones Street was the place chosen for the new venture. Once the decision was made, Mary Simkhovitch secured the first year's lease for $1,200.

The house needed alterations, so walls were torn down and partitions erected and the whole place was painted. The house was three rooms deep. The top floor was divided up into small rooms to house the women resident workers. The men stayed at a nearby residence. Their first meal together at 26 Jones Street was served on Thanksgiving Day, 1902. Mary Simkhovitch moved into the house with her family, including her baby, and the place was given the name Greenwich House.

The new settlement house was democratically administered from the very start. Policies for its management were arrived at after all interested persons and groups were taken into account. As Mary Simkhovitch said, "Those who paid the bills, those who were doing the work and those with whom and for whom the work was being done formed in our minds a necessary network, a real union."[4]

The neighborhood residents were not united in any way at the time of the founding of Greenwich House. Under the leadership of Mary Simkhovitch, the society aimed to make "this Village the best place in which to work and live in New York City." The group met in the "coffee room" in the basement of the house. They called on delegates from every organization in the neighborhood, in addition to the individual members and prominent persons in the city. The society instigated such improvements as the Barrow Street recreation pier, the Carnegie Library in Hudson Park, now a repository of Simkhovitch's writings, and the hall for Public School No. 3, and they worked with other organizations in the Village. Child labor was a common problem on the street. The Child Labor Committee and the Consumers' League used information provided by Simkhovitch's group to fight this evil. One of the characteristic features of the settlement house movement was its concern for the community. Whatever influenced the lives of people in the neighborhood was investigated by the settlements.

The first year's expenses came to about $2,800. This included only one salary, an honorarium of $400 paid to one kindergarten teacher. Everyone else paid his or her own way, including the head of the house. Mrs. J. Pierpont Morgan was the first benefactor.

The first year in the Village gave the staff perspective on the tasks that lay ahead. It also gave them some understanding of the people with whom they were working. While the Village had been settled by the Dutch very early, it did not receive its name until 1664. Until 1807, it had been a relatively small residential district containing the homes of many famous men of the period, including Thomas Paine, patriot and social philosopher.

After 1807, the Village began to grow. New immigrants came into its borders, bringing with them their problems. The Village had a very high death rate due to disease. Houses were inadequate for modest family living and contributed to the poor social conditions of the area. The streets were irregular, many of them following the cow paths of the Dutch colonial period. The coming of the Ninth Avenue elevated train also brought problems such as commercialization of the neighborhood and an exodus of higher income families.

In contrast to the Village of today was the self-contained Village of yesteryear. In former times, most of the people in the Village lived and made their living within its boundaries. This created a kind of protection for the community. The churches, too, played an important role in community affairs. Many of the churches conducted programs that approximated those of the settlements, and church leaders were active in assisting organizations to improve the Village.

The years from 1901 to the outbreak of the First World War were relatively progressive and hopeful years for Greenwich House. During this period, despite the ups and downs of political circumstance, progress was made politically through several reform governments. The leadership of William Travers Jerome, district attorney in Manhattan from 1902 to 1909, aided the forces concerned with law and order and did much to support social morality. The State Tenement House Commission helped improve housing in the Village. It was composed of building inspectors who had not lost their "missionary spirit" and were eager representatives of high standards of housing. Through the efforts of the commission, the provision for courts to replace the older airshafts became one of the notable advances in the housing legislation of that time.

Settlement workers spent a great deal of time in court, where family quarrels often came to a head. One woman was compelled to feed her husband in one room and their son in another because of the constant strife between them. Many girls were too strictly disciplined by "old-fashioned" parents. Whatever the difficulty, Greenwich House stood by its friends. Mary Simkhovitch said concerning such work, "Jones Street was not a melting pot! It was rather a boiling kettle."

Not all of those who had contact with Greenwich House developed into fine men and women. A few ended their careers in Sing Sing and some died at the hands of rival gangsters. But many used the challenges of the neighborhood and the resources of such organizations as Greenwich House to build vocations that were the pride of the neighborhood. Mary Simkhovitch told of one boy who didn't want to go to school and would hide under his bed to escape going. A friend was hired to rout him out and drag him to school before the clock struck nine. All this for the sum of ten cents a day!

The resident workers at Greenwich House were devoted to the neighborhood and the house. Many later came into positions of responsibility. One became the president of the University of Nevada. The house also served as a match-maker for both workers and neighborhood residents. One boy told of what the house had meant for him in these words: "But the chief value of the House to us boys is that here we have met our wives."

Greenwich House believed in publicizing its studies of the neighborhood, and a number were published: Mary Ovington's *Half a Man*, a study of Negro life in New York (1911); Elsa Herzfeld's *West Side Rookery*, on local housing (1906); Louise Hyman's *Industrial Survey*, on factory work (1912); Mabel Nassau's *Old Age Poverty in Greenwich Village* (1915); and Emily Dinwiddie's *Tenant's Manual*, a directory of useful social information (which later appeared as the *Social Worker's Handbook*). All of these served some purpose in connection with the broader objectives of Greenwich House and its community responsibility.

Greenwich House did not believe that it should seek benefits for its neighbors through an increase in its own facilities or power; rather, community benefits were sought from the appropriate departments of government and from private organizations. This practice was a cornerstone in the community policy developed at the House and evident also among the other settlements of the city. If more play space was needed, the House would join with its neighbors in urging those organizations and departments, private and public, that held responsibility for such matters, to act, leaving the final disposition of the problem to the "outside" individuals and groups.

The arts had been a concern of Greenwich House from the beginning. In 1906, one of the residents provided a scholarship for musical training, and in time, music became one of the dominant activities of the House. Its own music school began at 18 Jones Street (16, 18, and 20 Jones Street were purchased in 1909). Later, in 1913, the work had so expanded that 46 Barrow Street was purchased, a building that still houses the Music School of Greenwich House. Drama also was popular, and the pageants and plays are still recalled by some as instrumental in developing dormant acting talent.

In this period of Greenwich House, Mary Simkhovitch believed three activities were important: the Congestion Committee's work; the fostering of school social centers; and the Greenwich Village Improvement Society, which promoted community spirit through local festivals. The Congestion Committee was formed in 1907, largely through the support of Florence Kelley. The basic idea of the committee was to show, through meetings and demonstrations, that overcrowding was responsible for many of the city's ills. Through an exhibit held in March 1908, which attracted wide attention, the views of the committee won state and even national support.

The school social center movement in the city received its impetus from the Greenwich Village community. It began when a committee from the Church of the Ascension formed an organization to advocate the use by adults of Public School 41 in the evening. The Board of Education accepted the committee's plan, and the new facilities attracted many people. A variety of activities geared to special interests and capacities were provided, and in time, programs of a similar nature appeared in other schools and centers. Festivals brought together the various groups that composed the neighborhood, and this unity led to other activities on the part of the neighbors aimed at the general improvement of the community. The Greenwich Village Old Home Week was the biggest of these festivals, and it brought many prominent people from various fields into the Village.

The growing work of Greenwich House made the cramped quarters of the old building inadequate. New quarters had to be found if the work was to go on. Through the generosity of Anna Woerishoffer, whose daughter had been associated with Mary Simkhovitch in the early days of Greenwich House, a new building was erected. In every way it was more suitable to the work than the old, makeshift arrangements. Today, there are only a few visible traces of the old center on Jones Street. The men's residence as well as certain group activities still are housed at 18 and 20 Jones Street. The old houses at 26 and 28 were sold to former residents of Greenwich House who formed the first cooperative housing project under New York State law. Number 16 became the Greenwich House Workshops. The new Greenwich House opened formally in January 1917.

The opening of the new house was an important event for its leaders, and it coincided with an even more important event, the entrance of the United States into the First World War. The fact that the country had entered the war brought complications to the operation of the house. Some argued against the project of the new house on the grounds that it was inappropriate during wartime, but those who saw no conflict between expanding social services and the war effort won out. Some settlement house leaders were pacifists, but most workers at Greenwich House believed that entering the war was necessary on the grounds that it was the lesser of two evils. They felt that they had a responsibility to work even harder to show the merits of the settlement house.

Settlement houses usually refused to become recruiting stations, but they wanted to help in civilian ways. Some of the workers left to take a more active part in the war; some joined the armed forces, while others worked for the Y.M.C.A., the Y.W.C.A., and the Friends. Mabel Spinney, Simkhovitch's associate, headed the Food Administration for the West Side in Manhattan.

Greenwich House programs were affected in various ways by the war. The amount of coal needed to heat the building was so large that it was not until the Fuel Administration took up residence that there was fuel enough to maintain all the activities. Knitting items for the troops became popular, along with victory gardens. The War Service Bureau was established to help the neighborhood in many ways—with the mail, with information about various kinds of war-connected payments, and so on. The Red Cross had its offices for the Village in Greenwich House. Special meetings on various topics were often held. A military census of men available for wartime service was conducted for the Village by residents of the house, and Liberty Loan drives became a familiar part of the program, with their attendant speakers and financial campaigns.

A wealthy neighbor, Mr. Personeni, loaned the house his property on Staten Island for a day-camp and garden. About a hundred boys went there each day to take part in activities similar to those of a modern work camp. And the president of Greenwich House, Herbert Parsons, loaned his country home, Lounsberry, to the girls' club for their use.

During the war years, Simkhovitch worked on the Mayor's Committee of Women as chairperson of the subcommittee on social welfare. This committee included many of the most prominent women of the city, directing those welfare activities for civilians. The war drew many women into industrial and other kinds of employment in the community. Often children were without adequate care while their mothers were working. The idea of the nursery school was just beginning to take hold, and Greenwich House, in conjunction with Teachers College, Columbia University, started such a school in 1920 with the help of Mrs. R. J. F. Schwarzenbach.

A "Learn English Campaign" was attracting the interest of many immigrants who saw in it a means of identifying themselves more closely with American patriotic ideals. The Board of Education ran classes, but there were so many non-English speaking people, especially in neighborhoods such as Greenwich Village, that there was need for increased efforts and facilities. The House took part in this movement by supplying classes in English as a second language.

Following the war years, a period of reaction set in. Young people of New York City and elsewhere had always been attracted to the Village, and many of them made names for themselves in the arts, in politics, and in the humane services. Some, like Daniel French, Jonas Lie, John Sloan, Victor Salvatore, Jules Guerin, Robert Blum, George De Forest Brush, and Herbert Adams, settled in the Village before 1920. The freedom of the Village became nationally and even internationally known. "Art" became the dominant intellectual pursuit of the Villagers, and Bohemianism was looked upon as one of the rights of the newfound freedom.

The problems and possibilities of Greenwich House were to some extent determined by the social changes that occurred after the war. What had been considered poor housing became, after the influx of the newcomers, good housing when a few rearrangements were made to change a basement into a "studio." The prices of most things in the Village rose in keeping with the new circumstances. Housing fitted into this trend, seriously affecting the old time residents. Restaurants and nightspots of various kinds sprang into being and new problems came with them. The former insular condition of the Village was changed. The rise of technological inventions, such as the movies, changed the community's relationship to the settlement house.

Prohibition, with its accompanying evils, wrought further havoc in the community. Mary Simkhovitch said of speakeasies, "There one could find on a Sunday a policeman dining with his family in innocent domesticity at the proprietor's expense." Protection of undercover activities was widespread, and many who dealt in such activities became rich overnight. To a large extent, all of these things were made possible by the economic boom of the 1920s.

This period was not without some benefits, for many of the old-time Villagers now had continuous work and were able to provide themselves and their families with the necessities and even some luxuries. They also had the opportunity of sifting the old and the new. They saw about them the conflict between what the Village was and what it now had become. Many came to see that there was some good in the old and some bad in the new. For example, the emergence of theater groups in the Village provided significant and lasting influence on the life of the Village and the larger city. The Washington Square Players, the Provincetown Playhouse, and the Greenwich Village Theater set standards for theater participation that gave experimental-ism in the theater new meaning. The Museum of Modern Art conserved the best of the newer art works.

In the last years of the war and in the postwar period, influenza became a new health problem. Lillian Wald, leader of the Henry Street Settlement, and other leaders organized to spread information about the disease. The work of this group did much to decrease the death rate from influenza among the people of the whole city.

In 1928 the workshops of Greenwich House were opened, 46 Barrow Street was purchased to enlarge the music school, and the new swimming pool in Hudson Park was opened. In 1929 Greenwich House established a co-operative relationship with Columbia University. The trustees of both institutions entered into an agreement whereby there should be no financial respon-sibility on the part of the university for the work of the house, yet there would be joint activities undertaken from time to time. It was also arranged that, if the society supporting the house should at any time be dissolved, the university should become the residuary legatee. This tie between the settlement and the university was appropriate, for a settlement can be a constructive experimental field for a university. Likewise, the settlement needs the kind of intellectual orientation that a university can provide.

Mary Simkhovitch was hospitalized in Hartford, Connecti-cut, in October of 1929, the time of the great stock market crash. Like everyone else, she did not immediately grasp the full significance of the crash. Many people viewed it as a temporary set-back and looked each day for a reversal of the downward turn. But there was no reversal—it continued to go downward, bringing more misery and disappointment. After the crash came widespread unemployment, and committees—local, state, and federal—were established to meet the needs of the unemployed. But no one seemed to be able to supply what was needed to right the situation. Public relief seemed the only answer.

Greenwich House channeled requests for assistance to vari-ous government agencies and gave emergency help to the extent it was able. Greenwich House was not exceptional in this; all sorts of organizations, church, fraternal, educational, and other-wise, came to the rescue of people in need. Homeless men formed a "jungle" community in the Village on West Street at the corner of Charlton Street, one of the blocks cleared by the New York Central Railroad for its tracks. They erected their homes over the open basements that remained after the houses had been demolished. Most could scarcely be called homes—they were without heat or light and with very poor ventilation. Simkhovitch described one in the following way: "One of these looked like an overgrown coffin on stilts. It was raised about a foot off the ground, was hardly high enough for a man to sit up in, and was perhaps four or five feet wide and ten feet long. It had neither heat nor light."[5]

The necessities of life were secured by these men by whatever means were available. Most of the men were single, although there were a few married men who had sent their families elsewhere while they tried to get work in the city.

During the depression of the thirties, the House became an active center for those people who, because of their circumstances, could not afford more expensive recreation and amusement. The program included club meetings, dances, weekend trips, and chess tournaments. The various specialized parts of the House, like the workshops and the music center, provided activities, and artists and lecturers that came to the House to speak on topics of the day were received by large audiences. In 1930, the House secured a camping site seven miles from Poughkeepsie on the Hudson, and it was named in honor of a former president of the board of trustees, Herbert Parsons. Through the years this camp provided for a large number of children who otherwise might not have been able to enjoy the pleasures of camping. In 1933, approximately ten thousand people used the facilities of the House each week.

The depression encouraged Greenwich House to make and keep important contacts with other agencies, both public and private, that were concerned with the welfare of the Village. The house did several significant studies of neighborhood conditions during this period. As the depression waned and better economic conditions became more widespread, the changes in the organization of social life became more evident. Labor conditions, for example, had changed considerably. In place of the relatively unorganized labor force of the previous years were active, influential labor unions. The status of women had improved and they were found in many occupations and activities previously not open to them. Public education had grown significantly. The participation of government in various spheres of activity had increased and improved: public recreation, public health programs, and public welfare arrangements particularly were on the increase.

The work of Greenwich House was affected by these changes, but certain principles were held to despite the changing circumstances. Change was not feared or regretted but used as an ally. This meant that the programs of the House underwent constant revision; some activities survived, and others fell by the wayside.

Experimentation was another principle that aided the growth of the House. Settlement house work is based on experimenting, and no methods are accepted as final or absolute. The ability to try new ways of meeting needs is one of the marks of intelligent leadership within the field. In some instances, the experiments of the settlements have been so successful that they have been incorporated into public programs. The case of the workshop program of Greenwich House is an example. Developed under the auspices of the House, it later became a part of the public school system. In February 1935, the workshop program was given over to school authorities for a five year period with a view that, if it were successful, the program might be used elsewhere. For its first year, the workshop was accepted and classified as a vocational school.

During the period before the Second World War, the programs of the house continued to change and develop to meet the needs in the community. During the war years, Greenwich House again aided the war effort by assisting other organizations, both private and public. To some extent, the wartime program was similar to that maintained during the First World War.

Following the war, the relations of the House to the community changed somewhat due to the pressures of the new era. Today, Greenwich House still serves the needs of its neighbors. It performs a number of services: the child-care center provides all-day care for children of working mothers; the group work department offers a full program of educational and recreational activities for all ages; a full daily program for senior citizens is offered in arts, crafts, films, discussion groups, table games, sewing, and so on; and the counseling center provides casework, group psychothcrapy, and counseling for narcotic addicts and their families—a problem which has been on the increase in the recent years in the Village.

The Greenwich House Music School continues to provide a comprehensive program in music education. The Pottery School, one of the largest in New York City, offers a full range of courses to both the beginning and the advanced student. Embracing Simkhovitch's strong interest in drama, the Theatre Department features activities in all phases of theatre work for children and adults. Finally, the Greenwich House Camp at Copake Falls, New York, serves about two hundred children for two months in the summer. Through these and other ways, Greenwich House today continues as a lively, changing social welfare resource in its neighborhood.

Mary Simkhovitch formally retired on March 5, 1946. After retirement, she remained for periods of time in the city, working with one organization and another for the general good. But retirement brought some letup from the vigorous life of a community leader in a great city like New York. Her death on November 16, 1951, came at the close of an active career of helping others.

A few years before her death Mary Simkhovitch commented, "My grandfather was a quiet but a just man, much respected for his substantial judgment. It was said that Isaac Kingsbury's apples, like George Washington's, were never opened for inspection at the market—his name on the barrel was enough."[6]

So it was with Mary Kingsbury Simkhovitch—her name was a guarantee of quality in social welfare.

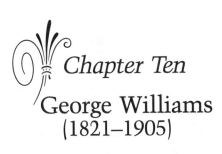

Chapter Ten
George Williams
(1821–1905)

The Y.M.C.A. is one of the greatest inventions of modern times. It has been the means of providing comfort and encouragement and protection to hundreds of thousands of young men who are to be the future merchants of this country and upon whom this country will rest for its character and even for its safety.[1]

George Williams, the "Father of the Red Triangle," was the youngest of the eight sons of Amos and Elizabeth Williams. He was born on October 11, 1821, in Ashway Farm, Dulverton, in the county of Somerset, England.

The Williams family were children of the soil. For generations they had known the hardships and the virtues of farming. Being some twenty-five miles from the nearest town of Bridgwater, they early learned to rely on themselves. The farm on which George was born and raised was isolated even from the surrounding farm country, and it bordered on a pathless moorland.

The life of the Williams family was similar to that of other farmers in that time. The age of agricultural machines had not yet dawned; one's own physical strength was a major asset in wresting a living from the earth. What could not be gotten from the ground was sought in the streams and forests. Red deer were favored game for the farmer-hunters. It was not unknown in the Williams's district for men to be hanged for stealing sheep. Coarseness in human relations paralleled the rigors of making a living. George was influenced greatly by his mother, Elizabeth, a small but sturdy woman, who worked tirelessly, for the well-being of her family. While Amos Williams's influence on the development of high moral standards in his children was considerable, Elizabeth was the main source of moral encouragement. She was always willing to help those in need. This spirit probably laid the foundation for her son's later activities.

George's early life was not eventful. He did not study late into the night to accomplish his education. He was an ordinary, spirited, hard-working boy, who grew up in a fashion normal for the environment in which he found himself. He was, however, the life of his family. Being the youngest, George enjoyed an element of liberty denied the rest of the children.

George's formal education began in an old-fashioned school on Dulverton High Street, a four-mile hike from the farm. Later, George attended the grammar school at Tiverton. The records of that period show that these schools were simple in their educational menu and harsh in discipline. Sometimes Amos Williams would accompany his son to Tiverton. On one occasion a neighbor took Amos's place, and as they were returning home and nearing the Williams farmstead, the neighbor gave George a shilling. He never forgot this favor; years later when the son of that man came to London and applied for a job at the business that George then managed, he was met warmly and given an excellent position. Williams constantly inquired after his welfare and did everything in his power to advance him.

George was baptized and confirmed in the Church of England and attended the Dulverton church along with his family. But few were greatly inspired by the Established Church of the time. Many of the clergy were "sporting parsons," who gave primary attention to the sports and hunting. Of one of these ministers, it was written:

> Parson Gale was one of these ecclesiastics who looked upon his preferment and his parish as a layman of the present day looks upon a sporting manor and a hunting box. There were few men between Bodmin and Barnstaple who could vie with the parson in tying a fly, tailing an otter, handling a gamecock, using the fists, cudgelling, wrestling, and, on occasion, emptying a gallon of cider or a jack of double ale.[2]

George saw that sports were held in high esteem. Prizes for village sports were displayed in a place of honor in the community. He often watched the wrestling and running matches that were held immediately after church services.

In rural England, the early nineteenth century was a period of inflation, which drove many rural children from the farms into the small towns and cities. The attractive and relatively luxuriant life of the urban centers also held their appeal for young minds. Many people dreamed of leaving the farm to create a fortune in the big city.

After leaving school at the age of thirteen, George continued to work on his father's farm, but he did not like the work. His mind was filled with the unknown prospects of distant places. According to his own account, one event helped him to make his decision to leave the farm. One day he was leading a cart of hay back to the barn. Clouds were coming over the hill, and all speed was needed to bring the precious cargo home before the storm. He was not watching his horses closely and suddenly the cart overturned. Horses, hay, and George ended up in the wayside ditch.

George's family encouraged him to work in one of the nearby towns. A brother in Dulverton was consulted about the opportunities in that town, and it was to a draper's shop (a dealer in cloth) in Dulverton that George finally was brought by his father on one summer evening in 1836. As an apprentice to the draper, George had entered "the world."

One of the advantages George was granted by biological inheritance and home upbringing was a sound body. Throughout his eighty-four years he was active and seldom suffered ill health. He was able to devote himself with boundless energy to his visions for human betterment and still have sufficient time and will to manage his business and home responsibiliies with success.

Later in his life, Williams said of his early years, "I entered Bridgwater a careless, godless, swearing young fellow." Religion and morality had no firm grip on his conscience at the time he began his work as an apprentice to the Dulverton cloth seller. Most of his time was taken up with work, and he apparently thought little about the weightier problems of life. Little is known about his work beyond the fact that he was successful. The draper, Mr. Holmes, appreciated the eager farm boy who wanted to learn the business from top to bottom. Holmes answered his questions and gave him opportunities for learning the trade. George was particularly successful in selling goods to women customers. And the other workers in the establishment liked him.

Twenty-seven assistants worked in Holmes's shop, since he was the chief tailor in the district. All of the men "lived in," that is, according to the custom of the times, all received room and board from their employer. The system had many disadvantages, but also some benefits. In some instances a family atmosphere aided boys such as George to overcome the loneliness of city life. Living with a large number of men also gave boys an introduction to various types of personalities. This experience alone socialized George more than all of his previous education and experience.

Holmes was a member of the Zion Congregational Chapel in

the town of Dulverton and required that all of his workers attend the regular church service on Sunday morning. In fact, so strict was he that clauses were written into the assistants' contracts, a practice that was common at that time. George's mother looked on this restriction with some annoyance, as did George himself. His mother told him to obey his master but to make up for it by attending the services of the Established Church on Sunday afternoons.

While religion was not the central concern of George's life at this time, it did have its place. On one occasion he remarked in reference to those days, "I felt that there was a difference between me and those other assistants, and I tried to discover what it was." He also developed some knowledge of Unitarianism, popular in many of the rural areas in England at that time.

One Sunday morning in the winter of 1837 (he was sixteen years old), George sat alone on the back seat of the little Congregational chapel. The minister, the Reverend Evan James, who was popular with the young men of the town, was the preacher. No one now remembers the text of the sermon, but it changed Williams's life. It was one of the most moving experiences he was to know in all his life. He saw that there were two ways set before him, the life that he had been living and a life of absolute devotion to the will of God and the service of his fellowman. From that moment on, he knew he was part of a moral economy that required his utmost energy. His own description, couched in the language of religious expression now almost defunct, was as follows:

> It is not easy to forget one's first love. I first learnt in Bridgwater to love my dear Lord and Saviour for what He had done for me. I learnt at Bridgwater to see the vital importance, the tremendous importance, of the spiritual life. I saw in this town two roads, the downward road and the upward road. I began to reason, and said to myself, "What if I continue along this downward road, where shall I get to, where is the end of it, what will become of me?" Thank God, I had kept in the clean path; nevertheless I was on the downward road. I saw that this road would certainly lead me to spend my eternity with the devil and his angels, and I said, "Cannot I escape? Is there no escape?" They told me in this very town of Bridgwater how to escape—Confess your sins, accept Christ, trust in Him, yield your heart to the Saviour.[3]

George Williams was admitted to membership in the Congregational church on February 14, 1838. From the outset, he
was active in the church, believing that his new experience
created obligations to take part in its program. Soon afterward
he joined with others in forming a Bible class, and later he
became a Sunday School teacher.

George Williams continued to grow spiritually through the
years. Yet, he also learned to be tolerant of the religious views of
others and to make concessions when necessary. For a time
Williams admired a popular American preacher, the Reverend
Charles G. Finney, who captured Williams's mind and heart
through his vigorous sermons. Thomas Binney, whose pulpit
was at that time the most influential in London, also held
Williams enraptured with his message of the love that the
Christian owed to his fellowmen. Binney's view of religion
emphasized to a surprising degree the commitment to service
that Williams's own life came to exemplify. Finney gave Williams a taste for theological speculation, but Binney increased
his affection for mankind.

George Williams's apprenticeship ended when he was nineteen. His older brother Fred had been in the employ of
Hitchcock and Rogers, a draper's firm in London. By the time
George left Mr. Holmes's establishment, Fred had a shop of his
own in the small town of North Petherton, a few miles from
Bridgwater. For about six months George worked with his
brother. Then, in October 1841, Fred took him to London on a
buying trip, and there he went to work for George Hitchcock.
For the first few years Williams worked behind the counter. One
day a buyer was seen cutting off a piece of silk and hiding it in
his drawer. He was dismissed, and George Williams took his
place. "I succeeded so well," George commented on the following years, "that in a few years' time I had increased the turnover
more than $150,000 a year."

Hitchcock and Rogers were not wholly confined to retail
trade, although that was their principal activity. Hitchcock,
who was to figure so prominently in the life of George Williams,
was a "self-made man." Born and raised in Devonshire, he had
started as a tailor's apprentice and had learned the trade from the
bottom up. After years of experience, he had entered into a
partnership with Mr. E. Rogers and located the firm in St. Paul's
Churchyard, London, a leading shopping center. Rogers was

compelled to retire from the business at an early age and left the direction of the whole business to Hitchcock. By the time George was hired, there were about one hundred forty employees.

The work in the shop was not especially hard, but it was long. In the summer months the workers were employed from seven o'clock in the morning to nine o'clock in the evening. In the winter months they stopped an hour earlier at night. There were no labor organizations, and each worker had to sign a contract that allowed the employer to discharge him for any reason at any time.

Hitchcock expected his men to attend religious services, but he did not check on their attendance. The men lived within the work establishment. In George's firm small rooms were provided for the men. In each room were two or three beds and two persons slept in each bed. Near the shop was a pub where the men spent the few hours they had for leisure. Some brought liquor into their rooms, and a surreptitious party life flourished on a modest scale.

A general need for moral improvement on the part of the workers existed, although they were not especially corrupt. The fact is that the young men did not have enough free time to get into serious difficulties, unless they were determined to do so. In the main, the "sins" of George's associates were the moralistic ones of lying, petty stealing, dishonesty in business, and excessive drinking.

George Williams was not interested in simply helping others avoid the minor temptations of city life; he had a more positive contribution to make. He wanted all young men to know the uplifting experience that he had had in Bridgwater. He wanted them to have the "abundant life." After George had been at Hitchcock and Rogers for three years, the place was completely changed. At first it was difficult for any man to be a Christian; after Williams did his work, it was difficult for a man not to be a Christian.

The spiritual life of George Williams, however, was not always serene and positive; at times he fell into periods of despondency. On the flyleaf of his diary, he wrote, "February 5, 1838. Joined the Church at Bridgwater, and since that period proved an unworthy member." He was not living up to the high standards he had set for himself. He tried to keep the flame of his earlier religious experience burning brightly. He attended all sorts of religious services. Sunday, his one free day, was taken up almost completely with church meetings of various types. He practiced a methodical plan of increasing his spirituality. His private devotions began early in the morning, before others were awake. He read the Bible regularly, along with other books on religion. Williams was not a scholar; rather, he was concerned with devotional values and had a nearly uncritical attitude toward many of the religious teachings of the time. He believed in freedom of religious conscience. One of his friends told of his views on sectarian religion:

> One Sunday evening four young men were standing talking outside Messrs. Hitchcock & Rogers before separating each to go to his chosen place of worship. George Williams was one, I was another. It happened that four sections of the Christian Church was represented by us; but this was unnoticed by all excepting George, who, without a word, suddenly threw his arms around our necks, drawing us closely together, and said, "Here we are Churchman, Baptist, Independent, Wesleyan—four creeds, one in Christ. Come along."[4]

Williams had a few interests besides religion, and for some time he took piano lessons from a private teacher. There is no record of his being an outstanding student, but at one time, he noted that he had gotten beyond "the lark." He also enjoyed elocution (public speaking) and joined a class in that subject. He felt that it would contribute to his success in winning converts to Christianity. He also tried to attend as many lectures as possible on a wide array of subjects.

George found time to visit his old home in Somerset, and he preserved his ties with the people there throughout his life. In later life he acted as an examiner in the local school, and he was invited to preach in the local congregations.

His work for Hitchcock, however, was not slighted by his manifold interests. In time he was the second in command of Hitchcock's prosperous enterprise. Through all of his advancement in the business, he held to the conviction, in true Calvinist spirit, that his life was being favored by God because of his faithfulness to spiritual ends. In fact, the religious views of

George Williams represent a combination of spiritual insight supporting a commercial ethic, which was characteristic of this period in England. To Williams, good religion went hand in hand with good business and vice versa. The man who was successful in business was, in a sense, approved by God, and one of the first marks of divine displeasure was lack of success in business. His was a businessman's ethic clothed with the appropriate guise of practical Christianity. Business morality as an adjunct to vital religion is expressed in the following statement:

What is my duty in business? To be righteous. To do right things between man and man. To buy honestly. Not to deceive or falsely represent or colour.

What is my duty to those under me? To be kind, patient, winning, and respectful. When I see a fault, to call the party aside and talk to him rather than rebuke him before others.

Oh, my soul, do all under me think I am sincere? Where is the difference in my daily actions from another man's? Am I more kind, more forbearing? Do the wicked glorify God on my behalf?

What ought I to do? Constantly repose on God. He tells me to be careful for nothing, but in everything by prayer and supplication make my requests known unto Him.

How short of that have I lived. How ought I rather to have felt that He who placed me in this situation will give me wisdom and strength to glorify Him in its midst. Oh, for a stronger faith in God. What have I to doubt or fear? Yea, by His help I will not. I would be righteous and holy in business, doing it as for Christ.

"Oh, Lord, Thou hast given me money. Give me a heart to do Thy will with it. May I use it for Thee and seek to get wisdom from Thee to use it aright."[5]

The beginnings of the Young Men's Christian Association can be traced to prayer meetings directed by Williams in Hitchcock's London establishment. Some of the one hundred forty employees were interested in establishing a "prayer circle," and they met in George Williams's room. Of those early prayer meetings Williams said, "We met, our numbers grew, and the room was soon crammed. In answer to prayer, the Spirit of God was present, and we had conversion after conversion."

The object of the little group was to strengthen the members' spirituality and to win converts. Their method was relatively simple; they would choose one of their comrades at work as a likely candidate for conversion and then pray for his soul. They also approached the person and invited him to their meetings, telling him what their intentions were. Sometimes those who were approached refused. But others were attracted and visited the group to see what it had to offer.

In time the membership grew. At the beginning there were twelve members. Within a few months twenty persons had come under the influence of the personality and religious views of Williams and his friends. By the end of the first year, twenty-seven individuals were present. Aside from prayer, the meetings featured a reading from the Bible and a discussion of the writings of Charles Finney.

The strategy of the group was directed by young Williams, and he took pains to be tactful in his approach to others. His advice to his followers on one occasion shows his own approach: "Don't argue, take him to supper." He felt success could come from associating with his unconverted friends on a social basis before broaching the subject of religion. One influential member of the business scorned the group, believing them to be effeminate and weak, so Williams invited him to an oyster supper with the group. He was so impressed that he joined them.

In time the group felt that it was their obligation to approach their employer, Hitchcock, with the suggestion that he, too, might become a vigorous Christian in sympathy with their objectives. Williams initiated a series of private discussions with Hitchcock, and in time Hitchcock came out openly in favor of the group. This, indeed, was a significant triumph for Williams and for the group.

As an expression of gratitude, Hitchcock, in the fall of 1843, appointed a chaplain to conduct morning worship for the group. In time, Hitchcock accepted the presidency of the group, then called the Young Men's Missionary Society, and throughout his life, he supported the group financially. In the fall of 1843, in recognition of his unfailing personal support, the members presented him with a Bible.

Williams's success led him to consider seriously foreign missionary work as a life career. He joined several missionary projects and societies in London, but he felt that his life might be more devoted to God if he were to leave London and live in some mission field. A friend dissuaded him from this move, however, pointing out that Christian young men were sorely needed in the business life of the great city of London. He also convinced Williams that he already held responsibilities of no small import and that he should not run out on them. So, instead of becoming a missionary to a foreign land, Williams became a missionary of a kind in his own country.

Up to this point, the religious work of Williams and his friends was confined to their own business house. They began to feel, however, that the type of activity the group conducted so well might have an even wider appeal. As Williams crossed the Blackfriars Bridge in London one day, he mentioned to a companion that it would be a good plan to include in the group persons who worked at other shops. June 6, 1844, was decided on as the day for a general meeting to discuss with representatives of other shops the possibility of establishing a broader association. The response was positive. In fact, informal organizations existed already within other groups of workers. James Smith, a leader of one of these groups, immediately wrote to Williams that he would be happy to cooperate, and other groups also responded.

At the meeting to form the new association were twelve men: George Williams, C. W. Smith, Norton Smith, Edward Valentine, Edward Beaumont, M. Glasson, William Creese, Francis John Crockett, E. Rogers, John Harvey, John C. Symons, and James Smith. No account exists of the exact nature of this meeting, only that $3.60 was collected to meet expenses. Edward Valentine's account of the meeting is terse:

> Thursday, June 6, 1844, met in G. Williams's room for the purpose of forming a society, the object of which is to influence religious young men to spread the Redeemer's Kingdom amongst those by whom they are surrounded. Mr. Smith, of Coram Street, President; Self, Treasure, *pro tem;* Creese and Symons, Secretaries. Committee, those there present belonging to us.[6]

A second meeting, at which twenty members were present, was held "for the purpose of carrying into effect the system of introducing religious services into drapery establishments throughout the Metropolis." Each week the group met to solve the problems of expansion. At first the meetings were held in Williams's room, but as the membership grew, the group moved to a room at St. Martin's coffee house, for which they paid seventy cents a week.

At one of the early meetings, a circular was written and sent to all tailor establishments in London. It stated the objectives of the new organization, and because of its importance to the early life of the movement, it is reproduced here in full:

> Dear Friends,—Suffer us to bring before your notice some important considerations, to which, for some time, our minds have been directed, and which intimately concern the eternal welfare of a large class of our fellow-mortals.
>
> We have looked with deep concern and anxiety upon the almost totally neglected spiritual condition of the mass of young men engaged in the pursuits of business, especially those connected with our trade, and feel desirous, by the assistance of God, to make some effort in order to improve it; and as we regard it to be a sacred duty, binding upon every child of God, to use all the means in his power, and to direct all his energies, in and out of season, towards the promotion of the Saviour's Kingdom, and the salvation of souls, we earnestly solicit your assistance in the great and important undertaking we now lay before you.
>
> We have seriously and carefully consulted as to the best means by which to accomplish so great a work; and we have come to the decision—we trust by the direction of the Holy Spirit—that there is nothing so calculated to discountenance immorality and vice, and to promote a spirit of serious inquiry among the class in which our lot is cast, as the introduction of some religious service among them, which they shall be invited to attend; and as of the various means in use for the salvation of souls, among the Church and people of God, prayer has been of all others the most honoured, we would suggest that the service thus introduced should largely, if not entirely, consist of prayer.
>
> We shall not be surprised if such a proposal as this be reckoned by some a Utopian scheme. And we expect that from many who name the name of Christ we shall meet with considerable opposition. We are likewise aware of the numerous difficulties which in many places will present themselves, and the obloquy and contempt which such a procedure will bring down upon the promoters and supporters of such an attempt, from the irreligious members of some of our large establishments. We have calculated upon all

these difficulties and shall not be surprised or discouraged if we behold them increase, but we hope that these things, instead of discouraging us in the great work we have commenced, will only induce us to increase and redouble our efforts. Shall it be said that the followers of the Lamb are afraid to incur the frown and censure of the world? Shall it be said that the ridicule of the world prevented the use of the means such as those to which we have adverted? Shall persecution—for we shall doubtless be called upon to suffer it—keep us back from attempting the salvation of souls? We believe that every true Christian will answer—"No."

A society is now formed, the object of which is the promotion of the spiritual welfare of young men engaged in the drapery and other trades, by the introduction of religious services among them. We earnestly entreat your Christian co-operation in this great work; and in order to lay before you fully the plans and views of the society on whose behalf we address you, a deputation from the Committee, prepared to give you all the requisite information, will wait upon you at your earliest convenience, when we hope to hear of your hearty concurrence in our plans. We shall feel obliged by your informing us, as early as you can, the time and place at which the deputation shall wait upon you.

[Signed]
JOHN SYMONS
WILLIAM CREESE[7]

At the fifth meeting, a name for the group was discussed. Up to this time several names had been used, the current one being the Drapers' Evangelical Association. Three names were suggested: the Berean Association (a reference to Acts 17:11, 12)[8]; the Christian Young Men's Society; and the Young Men's Christian Association. The last found the most favor with the group and has been used to this day.

Within a short time, the group had expanded greatly. The room at the coffee shop was now too small, so another room was rented at Radley's Hotel at a cost that some of the members felt was extravagant. Williams, however, was not concerned with costs; he believed that, if an idea were good, it would find financial support. The room at the hotel became the group's headquarters until the building was demolished five years later.

Much of the success of the group was due to the quality of

the personal relationships the members had with workers in the various draper's organizations in London. Williams devoted a large amount of his time to these relationships for the new association. They were especially important because of a number of objections to the new movement. Some people believed that the association was organized to circumvent the sectarian differences of that time. (Of the twelve founders, three were Anglicans, three Congregationalists, three Baptists, and three Methodists.) Resistance to the association was encountered among the leaders of the Established Church, who felt especially threatened by it. Williams replied that the association had no pretense at reconciling different sects. It was solely a nonsectarian enterprise with no designs on any denomination.

Again, some people thought that the association was chiefly an offshoot of the Metropolitan Drapers' Association, a labor organization in the forefront of the fight for shorter working hours. To these, Williams could easily point out that the association had different purposes in mind, although it did not oppose shorter working hours. (In fact, throughout his life, Williams was a consistent advocate of shorter working hours.)

At the beginning, fourteen business establishments came in with Hitchcock's plan for the association. Each held its own religious services, and weekly services were held in Radley's Hotel, "from which gatherings the members of the Association separated to their various places of business strengthened and cheered by such fellowship for the difficult task of keeping their flag flying in dormitory, shop, and warehouse." At this time, the Y.M.C.A. had no social program, but each meeting was preceded by a simple tea. Seedcake was served, and conversations were encouraged about various topics of the day. These sessions were preliminary to the more serious activities to follow. Prayer, Bible reading, and discussions of spiritual topics were the main diet of the group. Missionary activities also comprised a notable part of the association's activities.

The association early established a Bible class with Williams as its teacher. He held this position for years. While he was not a brilliant speaker and was not truly learned in religious matters, he was able to win the cooperation of his listeners by his forceful, sincere, and personal appeal. He sought always to speak directly so that each person felt that he was speaking just to him. This enabled him to gather a large following.

In time the somewhat narrow purposes of the association were modified. The guiding committee added courses of lectures modeled after those of the mutual improvement societies, groups of young men who sought informal educational opportunities. Some objected to this development, believing that it was detrimental to the original intentions of the association. Williams felt that almost any activity could be utilized by the association if it met the genuine needs of the members and if it led to the possibility of further conversions. He did not believe that such activities had merit simply in themselves but that they should be directed at increasing the spirituality of the membership.

The association eventually admitted as associate members those who had not been converted. Opposition arose to this development, but Williams argued that the function of the association was to attract outsiders as well as to strengthen the spiritual life of those who were members. He believed that unconverted persons should enjoy the benefits of the association to some degree so that they might be brought in time to understand the full program.

One of the high points in the early life of the association was a tea-meeting held in the hotel headquarters on November 8, 1844. The association was only five months old, and 161 men attended. In March of the following year, another social meeting was held, and about three hundred attended. The meetings regularly increased in size, so a new West End branch was opened. In 1845 a salaried secretary, or missioner, was hired. Thus T. H. Tarlton became the first paid official of the Y.M.C.A. Tarlton was a member of the group and had been a city missionary. The salary the association was able to afford was not as much as his past income, but so great was his belief in the new work that he was willing to accept the position. Tarlton and Williams were loyal friends, and together they went about organizing the association. Williams had the ideological strength, while Tarlton's strength was organizational tactics.

The *First Annual Report* of the Y.M.C.A. was presented at a tea held at the hotel in November 1845. This review of activities showed that the association was on a fairly solid and permanent footing. With careful guidance, it well might grow into an agency of wide influence. Extending the work of the association was discussed and Williams explored many possibilities for expansion.

In the years that followed the establishment of the association, George Williams's public actions became more widely known than ever before. He was involved with almost every aspect of the development of the Y movement and lent a personal touch to many of its features. It was Williams, for example, who championed the policy, which later characterized the Y.M.C.A., of having prominent speakers from various fields of public and scholarly life address the members. Exeter Hall in London, a part of the expanding program of the association, was made famous, in part, through the many excellent public talks held there. More eminent persons assembled at the hall in those early years than at any other single place or under any other single auspices. Among those notables were the lord mayor of London, Samuel Morley, George Moore, and statesman and reformer Lord Shaftesbury. In 1848, Shaftesbury was at the height of his political power and had successfully supported the Public Health Act and other social legislation. He knew Williams personally, and as time went on, the two grew close in their interests and outlooks. This friendship led to many advantages for the association. Lord Shaftesbury often consulted with Williams about legislative matters, and Williams, in turn, depended greatly on his "best friend" for help with the Y.

When the Y.M.C.A. moved to larger quarters on Gresham Street in 1849, the question of the nature of membership and activities came up again. Some felt that the members should be only those who were avowed Christians. Williams felt that conversion was an important goal of the association but that all should be permitted to use its facilities—with certain provisions as to desirable conduct—with the hope that they would be attracted in the end to the Christian way of life. Critics had considerable misgivings about this point of view, but it finally won out.

There was more opposition to the activities. Some critics felt that the members should not have so many activities available to them—for example, swimming—saying that there was no possibility of tying up these activities with the Christian life. Others felt that the library was a waste of assets to an openly Christian organization. Williams, of course, disagreed with these views. He felt that such activities helped attract young men to the fuller implications of the Christian religion, and that even on a minimal basis they helped young men, whether Christian or not, to escape the more serious sins of the city. He also felt that the primary emphasis in the Y should not be on what should *not* be done. Rather, he thought that the important question was, What shall we do to win young men? This question guided the positive, constructive, appealing program the organization ultimately adopted.

The Great Exhibition in London, in 1851, was viewed by the controlling committee of the association to be an ideal occasion to publicize the merits of the Y to a wide audience. People traveled from all parts of the world to see the exhibition, for it epitomized for that time all of the splendid, if somewhat naive, hopes that the generation had for the future. Here was an opportunity to spread the benefits of the Y.M.C.A. to other parts of the world. The Y leaders organized group meetings at which the association's structure and purposes were outlined. The members distributed 62,000 pamphlets to visitors, many of whom took the information back to their home countries and started groups modeled on the original London organization.

Once, while on a business trip to Paris, Williams learned that the city had no Y.M.C.A. He called a convocation of the Protestant clergy of the city and described the Y movement in London and elsewhere. They were interested. In 1852, the first Y.M.C.A. in France was formed in Paris, and soon more branches opened throughout France. One visitor at the original Paris meeting was a citizen of Holland, and when he returned home he helped create a Y.M.C.A. there.

The association grew rapidly from a relatively small organization located in London to one that embraced the whole of England and its possessions, and spilled over onto the Continent and the New World. In London, a new headquarters location was secured on Aldersgate Street. At the opening it was estimated that upwards of 6,000 had joined the Bible class from its inception and over 500,000 had attended the public lectures.

The association leaders in various parts of the world decided to have a meeting, and Williams was one of the fifteen English delegates to the first conference in Paris in 1855, which marked the official beginning of the world-wide Y.M.C.A. movement. Here it was declared that the affiliated bodies in the various parts of the world should be "one in principle and one in operation, preserving independence of organization and modes of action." Here also the purposes of the association were stated in a resolution:

> The Young Men's Christian Associations seek to unite those young men who, regarding Jesus Christ as their God and Savior according to the Holy Scriptures, desire to be His disciples in their doctrine and in their life, and to associate their efforts for the extension of His Kingdom among young men.[9]

The Paris conference did not solve all of the problems of the burgeoning organization. Some groups did not wish to enter into a controlling relationship with the parent organization. These, so far as it was possible, Williams visited to explain the values of being attached to the central body. Many were convinced, but some remained aloof.

In 1855, Tarlton retired as administrative head of the Y.M.C.A., and Edwin Shipton was appointed in his place. While Tarlton was noted for his organizing powers, Shipton was no less capable. He left a profitable business connection to serve the Y.M.C.A. in the time of its greatest expansion. He was able to meet people with ease and efficiency and was an enthusiast for the work, inspiring many of his co-workers.

Because the organization was so successful in the molding of young people's opinions, politically minded persons often wished to use it to their own advantage. Williams would not condone this and, despite the fact that he held definite political views, he realized that the movement would be lost if it gave its sanction to a particular political movement or party. For him the primary work of the association was religious. He worked very hard to keep out all political interference. Although Williams did not drink alcoholic beverages and believed that all men should abstain, he did not wish the association to be used as an instrument for this cause either. He believed that the Y should take no aggressive stand on any public or sectarian issue.

In 1863, Mr. Hitchcock died; from the inception of the association in his establishment, he had been a strong supporter. In his last years, the main responsibility for his business had fallen on the shoulders of George Williams, who had been made a partner. Williams had married Hitchcock's daughter, who came to be of great help to him in his ventures. Upon succeeding to full ownership of the Hitchcock business, Williams assumed the financial responsibilities of the Y.M.C.A. that formerly fell to Hitchcock. Williams had been noted for his contributions, but now he became the chief supporter. Whenever a local group was in financial straits, Williams could usually be depended on to relieve the pressure. He also gave money to start branches in new communities.

The association continued to have problems as it increased in size. At the conference held in Edinburgh in 1874, criticisms were tactfully and patiently answered by Williams and other leaders. Again, some accused the association of favoring one religious denomination over others. Other critics complained about organizational aspects, and still others continued to challenge the nature of the activities. While conferences were held in various cities during the succeeding year, it was largely to the credit of one held in Edinburgh that the most basic problems of the organization were solved. Groups not in agreement with the association broke away at this time.

The work of the association expanded rapidly. Additional branches were established throughout England, and local units were in time found in almost every part of the world. In many places, the meaning of the Y.M.C.A. was adapted to meet special circumstances. In London, for example, special Y's were established for particular nationality backgrounds. In 1873, special work was begun with travelers at Paddington Station in London, and later the Sunday evening crowds in Hyde Park were included.

The Y.M.C.A. regularly gave assistance to American evangelists who visited England. Charles G. Finney was sponsored by the association and reached wide audiences, and in 1873, Dwight L. Moody was sponsored by the association. Moody and

Williams became fast friends. Moody believed the Y movement was an important instrument in the revival effort he was helping to shape. He said on one occasion that he owed more to the association than to any other organization for his conversion and spiritual development. He pointed out that in the large cities the employer had been responsible for the social and spiritual well-being of his employees but that now it was the obligation of Christian organizations like the Y to provide guidance.

Williams attended Y conferences throughout England, and usually he was invited to preside at these meetings and to give his opinion on the weightier issues. He entered into the details of these conferences with enthusiasm and interest; he felt that they were heart-warming experiences comparable to church meetings. Williams is said to have converted five young men at one such conference, all of whom later entered the Christian ministry, one in the Church of England, one as a Methodist, two as Baptists, and one as an Independent.

Williams's success in personal relations was due in part to the fact that he was singleminded in his affection for the association and its programs. He said, "Let us be men of one idea! We have—I know I have myself—too many irons in the fire, and our energies are scattered and worth nothing." He continually aimed at one goal: advancing the work of the association. In his later years, even his business became secondary as he devoted increased time to youth activities.

In 1880, several noteworthy changes were introduced into the London association. For one, Shipton retired as the executive and was followed by W. Hind Smith. Smith had been an active provincial secretary since he joined the association at the time of the Edinburgh conference and he had advanced the association's cause during the years with considerable skill and ingenuity.

In that year also the purchase of Exeter Hall began, one of the chief aims of Williams. The hall was built in 1831 to provide a meeting place for philanthropic and religious societies, and during its brief life it had hosted a succession of outstanding events. Here Mendelssohn's "Elijah" was first performed. Here, too, the prince consort made an appearance in 1840 to protest the slave trade. But by 1880, the hall was up for sale. Williams recognized that the London Y was expanding beyond the most fanciful dreams of its founders and saw the possibilities of the hall for the movement. The price—the equivalent of $125,000—was an especially large sum, but Williams was determined that the association should have the hall. He believed that five men should be contacted to contribute $25,000 each to the fund and that he should be one of the five. Carefully scrutinizing a list of favored friends of the association, he picked four other men and visited them. These were: Samuel Morley, R. C. L. Bevan, the brothers Denny, and H. D. Allcroft. He did not meet with a single refusal. The hall, which meant much to the fuller development of the London Y, was secured and opened in 1881.

The purchase of the building attracted many new members, for the number and variety of activities were now increased. In 1882, the year after it was opened, the hall housed the Ninth International Conference, attended by 338 delegates from sixteen countries. This meeting created the National Council, a body to which the local Y's within England could look for national leadership. In time, national councils were formed elsewhere, which looked to the International Conference as their coordinating body.

Lord Shaftesbury had been president of the association until 1886, the year of his death. The next president was George Williams. In his presidential address, given that May, he said:

I am greatly indebted to the Central Association, and to all the friends of the Association, for the great honour conferred upon me, in placing me in the position of President of this great institution. I do confess to have taken a great interest in the movement from its very commencement. I do humbly thank God that I have been permitted and spared, not only to cooperate in the work in England, but to see its wonderful growth on the Continent and throughout America. No one, I think, can well estimate the enormous advantage which the Association has been to a very large class of the community—in the United States and Canada as well as in Australia, and in various other parts of the world. Now we are met together under very new circumstances. Our great Moses has been taken up. We thank God for his life. It was a life lived for the welfare of the United Kingdom of Great Britain and Ireland. The results of what he did must be abiding, must continue: and I do hope and pray that now he has been taken up, God will raise up hundreds of Joshuas to carry on the various and multifarious associations in which he took such a lively interest.[10]

In 1887, Williams was pleased to return to the town of Bridgwater to dedicate a Y building named in his honor. Like many famous men who return home to visit the scene of their early days, Williams felt deeply the meaning of the years that had taken him from being a draper's apprentice to a wealthy, socially minded leader. The town of Bridgwater responded generously. The mayor made the usual speech; the streets were decorated to welcome a hero. On this trip, however, Williams could not neglect his friends at Dulverton. There he visited his father's grave and recalled the memories of childhood. He also presented a set of stained-glass windows to the Dulverton church he attended as a boy.

As a part of its program the Y.M.C.A. sent missionaries to various lands, for the movement was founded in part to meet the desires of those who wished to contribute to missionary activities. The income of the early years was carefully divided so that some money would support the work of the London association and some would support a missionary program. By 1889, the missionary work was significant—from England alone, nearly fifty young men left for the mission fields. To strengthen the association in other countries, a travelling foreign secretary was appointed. Later, the cost of this effort was assumed by the U.S. branches of the association.

Williams's home life was rich and full, considering the large amount of time that he gave to outside activities. His marriage to Helen Hitchcock was nearly ideal. They had five sons and one daughter; three of the sons joined the family business and eventually assumed its leadership. Of the remaining two, one became a lawyer and one entered the ministry of the Church of England. Williams's daughter, Nellie, was the joy of his life. When she died at the age of nineteen, his heart was broken.

Outside his family as within, Williams tried to apply Christian principles. From an early period he was interested in reducing the number of hours that young men worked. He was one of the mainstays of the Early-Closing Association, formed to encourage employers voluntarily to grant shorter working hours. He did not believe in social legislation as the first means of encouraging or forcing industry to meet the demands of workers. He thought that voluntary action was preferable. He, himself, established shorter hours for the men in his employ and felt that this example, from one of the largest draper's firms, should lead the way. While this move by Williams set a moral standard for many within the industry, it threatened his own financial welfare, for smaller businesses were able to improve their position by maintaining the regular hours of employment. When voluntary action did not solve the problem, Williams did not hesitate to turn to social legislation. He gave loyal support to Lord Shaftesbury and others who sought to remedy the conditions of workers through parliamentary action.

Williams was also a leader in several employers' associations, and for a time he was vice-president of the Linen and Woolen Drapers' Institution. He was a pioneer in the forming of the Cottage Home movement, in which employers established cottages for workers who were retired or hurt on the job. During his lifetime Williams donated two such cottages at Mill Hill, and his firm gave two more. He was concerned with charities connected with his business, but he also worked for many other organizations and contributed liberally to countless agencies. Practically all of the institutions, agencies, and organizations in which he was concerned were specifically Christian and Protestant.

Williams's correspondence was enormous. Many wrote to him from foreign countries about the work of the association. But many persons without official status or without concerns connected with the association also wrote to him. Some had deep personal needs and wrote because of his reputation for helpfulness. For example, a mother wrote him that she had not heard from her son who had come to London. Would Williams look him up to see that he was well and in no mischief? A young man wrote to say that he was anxious to come to London to work and could George Williams give him a job or find him one. Williams did not ignore these personal letters but took them as seriously as any of his obligations. He would take out time from his busy schedule to locate a boy who had failed to write home. He would try to find work for someone. At times it seemed as though he was so wrapped up with his many responsibilities to organizations and individuals that he would not be able to manage his business successfully.

The fiftieth anniversary of the founding of the association, the Jubilee, was held in London in June 1894. Shortly before the date fixed for the celebration, the queen bestowed on Williams a knighthood in acknowledgment of his "distinguished service to the cause of humanity." While he had received several honors previously from private organizations, this was the greatest honor of all. It was characteristic of him to declare openly that the honor conferred on him was in recognition not so much of his personal contributions as of the causes he happened to represent.

Among the many responsibilities Williams had in connection with the Jubilee was making arrangements for guests. He shared even in the smallest details, making sure that all the delegates would enjoy their stay in London. Such details included ordering 12,500 pounds of meat, 24,000 dinner rolls, and 2.75 tons of potatoes, plus other commodities. The Jubilee advanced the spirit and work of the Y.M.C.A. more than any other single conference. Outstanding world leaders congratulated the Y movement and George Williams for their accomplishments. Delegates from all parts of the world gave testimony to the ways the association was catching on. Williams was given the key to the city of London, a rare and noteworthy distinction, and more than three hundred special sermons were preached in the city's churches on the work of the association.

Williams was interested in the work of the Y in the United States, because he realized that, if this great nation would give its time and energy to the idea, it would be given the greatest possible prestige. In 1901, the association in the United States celebrated its fiftieth anniversary. This marked the fact that the idea had been realized successfully and had indeed set a pattern for many other countries.

The relations of Williams with the Y.M.C.A. in America, however, predated the American Jubilee. In 1876, he and an old friend, M. H. Hodder, had visited the United States and Canada as representatives of the London association. Everywhere Williams went in the New World he was met with appreciative crowds.

The Y.M.C.A. in the United States was founded by Captain Thomas V. Sullivan. Shortly before Christmas in 1851, he picked up a religious weekly and happened on an account of how the first Y was founded in London in 1844. A retired Boston mariner, Captain Sullivan gathered a few friends together and proposed that they form an American Young Men's Christian Association. A few weeks later, on December 29, 1851, in the chapel of the Old South Meeting House, the United States Y.M.C.A. was born. Like the London association, the American Y movement spread quickly to other towns. In only seven years Y.M.C.A.s were found from coast to coast. This growth was remarkable in that each association was the result of spontaneous local action to have an organization that would meet the needs of the people.

The American Y.M.C.A. has many "firsts" to its credit. It was the first organization during wartime to aid troops in the field and in prison camps. It pioneered sports and athletics, invented basketball and volleyball, and taught swimming and water safety to large numbers of people. Three quarters of a century ago, it devised a Peace Corps type of service when it introduced its international program of social service. It originated camping as it is known today and developed night schools and adult education. It started the father-son movement and was the first to conduct widespread nondenominational Christian work for college students. It was also the first to extend a helpful hand to foreign students. In these and other ways, the Y.M.C.A. has carried out in the United States, as it has also in many other nations, the spirit of its founder, George Williams.

In June 1903, Sir George and Lady Williams celebrated another Jubilee—their golden wedding anniversary. Presentations were made to them by the association, and a small reception was held in their honor. Though Sir George was in his eighty-third year, he remained active in many of his responsibilities. His statement on that occasion well marked his spirit, "So long as I have any strength left, I will fight. There is still much to be done. God help me, I will fight the Evil One to the end."

But his strength was not what it had been. He gave over to friends and relatives the duties he had carried for so long, and shortly after his eighty-fourth birthday, he died. A memorial service was held at Exeter Hall, and hundreds of his friends were in attendance. Persons came from many parts of the world to pay tribute to George Williams and to the organization he left behind him.

The funeral was conducted from St. Paul's Cathedral in London, and over two thousand people attended the service. On the Sunday following Sir George Williams's burial, a sermon was preached at St. Paul's by Archdeacon Sinclair. He concluded by saying of Williams: "His name stands for the abiding truth that a simple, heartfelt faith in the power and presence of Christ is possible in any age, under any circumstances, to any Christian man."[11]

Notes

Chapter One: Jane Addams

1. A statement by Professor Charles E. Merriam in James Weber Linn, *Jane Addams: A Biography* (New York: D. Appleton-Century, 1936), p. 189.

2. Jane Addams, *Twenty Years at Hull House* (New York: Macmillan, 1911), p. 16. The Hicksite Quakers are the "liberal" branch of the Friends, taking their name from Elias Hicks, a pioneer leader of "liberal" Quakerism.

3. Ibid., p. 64.

4. Ibid., p. 71.

5. Linn, *Jane Addams*, pp. 83–84.

6. Ibid., p. 163.

7. Addams, *Twenty Years at Hull House*, pp. 285–86.

8. Jane Addams, *The Spirit of Youth and the City Streets* (New York: Macmillan, 1909), p. 53.

Chapter Two: Robert Baden-Powell

1. Robert Baden-Powell, *Scouting for Boys* (London: C.A. Pearson, 1910), p. 27.

2. Ernest E. Reynolds, *Baden-Powell* (New York: Oxford University Press, 1943), p. 15.

3. Ibid., pp. 19–20.

4. Ibid., pp. 20–21.

5. Eileen K. Wade, *The Piper of Pax* (London: C.A. Pearson, 1924), p. 111.

6. Reynolds, *Baden-Powell*, pp. 122–23.

7. Ibid., pp. 137–38.

8. Baden-Powell, *Scouting*, pp. 10–12.

9. Ibid.

10. Reynolds, *Baden-Powell*, p. 159.

11. Wade, *Piper*, p. 157.

12. Baden-Powell, *Scouting*, p. 27.

13. Reynolds, *Baden-Powell*, p. 263.

Chapter Three: Samuel Barnett

1. Henrietta Barnett, *Canon Barnett: His Life, Work, and Friends* (Boston: Houghton Mifflin, 1919), vol. 1 p. 76.

2. Ibid., pp. 25–26.

3. Ibid., p. 75.

4. Ibid., pp. 83–84.

5. Ibid., p. 85.

6. Ibid., pp. 302–3.

7. Ibid., p. 310.

8. Ibid., p. 313.

9. Ibid., p. 356.

Chapter Four: William Booth

1. G. S. Railton, *The Authoritative Life of General William Booth: Founder of the Salvation Army* (New York: Reliance Trading Co., 1912), preface.

2. St. John Ervine, *God's Soldier: General William Booth* (New York: Macmillan, 1935), vol. 1, pp. 34–35.

3. Railton, *Authoritative Life of General William Booth*, p. 30.

4. Ibid., p. 43.

5. Ervine, *God's Soldier*, p. 506.

6. Richard Collier, *The General Next to God: The Story of William Booth and the Salvation Army* (New York: Dutton, 1965), p. 76.

7. Ibid., pp. 246–48.

Chapter Five: Dorothea Dix

1. Helen E. Marshall, *Dorothea Dix: Forgotten Samaritan* (Chapel Hill: University of North Carolina Press, 1937), p. 128. A quotation from a letter written by Dix to Mrs. William Rathbone in 1850.

2. A fictionalized account. For original, see Marshall, *Dorothea Dix*, p. 9.

3. Marshall, *Dorothea Dix*, p. 22. The friend was Ann Heath.

4. Ibid., p. 27.

5. Based on an account in Marshall, *Dorothea Dix*, p. 44.

6. Based on an account in Francis Tiffany, *Life of Dorothea Lynde Dix* (Boston, Mass.: Houghton Mifflin, 1918), pp. 72–73.

7. Tiffany, *Life of Dorothea Lynde Dix*, pp. 77–78.

8. Fictional account based on Tiffany, *Life of Dorothea Lynde Dix*, pp. 96–100.

9. Fictional account based on Marshall, *Dorothea Dix*, pp. 102–3.

10. Marshall, *Dorothea Dix*, p. 105.

11. Ibid., p. 115.

12. Tiffany, *Life of Dorothea Lynde Dix*, pp. 288–89.

13. Marshall, *Dorothea Dix*, p. 186.

14. Tiffany, *Life of Dorothea Lynde Dix*, pp. 153–55.

15. Marshall, *Dorothea Dix*, p. 206.

Chapter Six: Samuel Gridley Howe

1. "The Hero," a poem by John Greenleaf Whittier, memorialized Howe.

2. Laura Richards, *Samuel Gridley Howe* (New York: D. Appleton-Century, 1935), pp. 12–13.

3. Ibid., pp. 23–24.

4. Ibid., pp. 93–94.

5. Ibid., pp. 99–100.

6. Ibid., p. 28.

7. Ibid., pp. 173–74.

8. Ibid.

9. Ibid., pp. 192–93.

10. Ibid., p. 230.

Chapter Seven: Frederick Ozanam

1. From an address by the Most Reverend John J. Glennon, archbishop of St. Louis, "Frederick Ozanam: Founder of the Society of St. Vincent de Paul," Columbia Broadcasting System, Sunday, Aug. 29, 1943.

2. Albert P. Schimberg, *The Great Friend: Frederick Ozanam* (Milwaukee, Wis.: Bruce Pub. Co., 1946), pp. 23–24.

3. Ibid., pp. 26–27.

4. Ibid., p. 31.

5. Ibid., p. 32.

6. Ainslee Coates, *Letters of Frederick Ozanam* (New York: Benziger Bros., 1886), p. 19.

7. Schimberg, *The Great Friend*, p. 74.

8. Ibid., pp. 102–3.

9. Ibid., p. 103.

Chapter Eight: Lord Shaftesbury: Anthony Ashley Cooper

1. Edwin Hodder, *The Life and Work of the Seventh Earl of Shaftesbury*, vol. 3 (London: Casel, 1887), pp. 421, 520–21. A statement made by Disraeli while prime minister.

2. J. Wesley Bready, *Lord Shaftesbury and Social-Industrial Progress* (London: George Allen & Unwin, 1926), pp. 18–19.

3. Ibid., pp. 69–70.

4. John Hammond, and Barbara Hammond, *Lord Shaftesbury* (New York: Longmans, Green 1936), p. 157.

5. Hodder, *The Life and Work of the Seventh Earl of Shaftesbury*, pp. 264–65.

6. Bready, *Lord Shaftesbury and Social-Industrial Progress*, p. 149.

7. Ibid., p. 340.

8. Hodder, *Life and Work of the Seventh Earl of Shaftesbury*, p. 421.

Chapter Nine: Mary Kingsbury Simkhovitch

1. Mary Kingsbury Simkhovitch, *Neighborhood: My Story of Greenwich House* (New York: W. W. Norton, 1938), p. 301.

2. Ibid., pp. 29.

3. Ibid., pp. 40–41.

4. Ibid., p. 94.

5. Ibid., p. 220.

6. Mary Kingsbury Simkhovitch, *Here Is God's Plenty: Reflections on American Social Advance* (New York: Harper, 1949), p. 93.

Chapter Ten: George Williams

1. Spoken by the earl of Shaftesbury at the reception given for George Williams by the lord mayor of London in 1884. J. E. Hodder Williams, *The Father of the Red Triangle: The Life of Sir George Williams* (London: Hodder & Stoughton, 1918), p. 198.

2. Williams, *Father of the Red Triangle*, pp. 11-12.

3. From an address given at the opening of a new building of the Y.M.C.A. in Bridgwater. Williams, *Father of the Red Triangle*, pp. 22-23.

4. A story told by M. R. Creese, one of the co-founders of the movement. Williams, *Father of the Red Triangle*, p. 69.

5. Williams, *Father of the Red Triangle*, pp. 80-81.

6. Ibid., p. 99.

7. Ibid., pp. 101-3.

8. A reference to the men of Berea (Acts 17: 11 and 12) who "received the Word with all readiness of mind, and searched the Scriptures daily, whether these things were so." A sect of this name was founded in Scotland in 1773 by the Reverend John Barclay.

9. Williams, *Father of the Red Triangle*, p. 150.

10. Ibid., p. 199.

11. Ibid., p. 276.

Bibliography

Chapter One: Jane Addams

Addams, Jane, *Child Labor Legislation.* New York: National Child Labor Committee, 1905.

_____. *The Spirit of Youth and the City Streets.* New York: Macmillan, 1909.

_____. *Twenty Years at Hull House.* New York: Macmillan, 1910.

_____. *Newer Ideals of Peace.* New York: Macmillan, 1911.

_____. *The New Conscience and an Old Evil.* New York: Macmillan, 1912.

_____. *Democracy and Social Ethics.* New York: Macmillan, 1913.

_____. *Women at the Hague.* New York: Macmillan, 1915.

_____. *The Long Road of Woman's Memory.* New York: Macmillan, 1916.

_____. *Peace and Bread in Time of War.* New York: Macmillan, 1922.

_____. *The Child, the Clinic, and the Court.* New York: New Republic, 1925.

_____. *The Second Twenty Years at Hull House.* New York: Macmillan, 1930.

_____. *The Excellent Becomes the Permanent.* New York: Macmillan, 1932.

_____. *My Friend, Julia Lathrop.* New York: Macmillan, 1932.

_____. "First Impressions." In Edward C. Wagenknecht, ed.

_____. *When I Was a Child: An Anthology.* New York: Dutton, 1946.

Barnard, Harry. *Eagle Forgotten: The Life of John Peter Altgeld.* Indianapolis, Ind.: Bobbs-Merrill, 1938.

Barrows, Esther. *Neighbors All: A Settlement Notebook.* Boston, Mass.: Houghton Mifflin, 1929.

Bowen, Louise. *Open Windows: Stories of People and Places.* Chicago, Ill.: Seymour, 1946.

Carmer, Carl. ed. *Cavalcade of America.* New York: Crown, 1956.

Coit, Stanton. *Neighborhood Guilds: An Instrument of Social Reform.* London: S. Sonnenschein, 1892.

Davis, Allen F. *American Heroine: The Life and Legend of Jane Addams.* New York: Oxford University Press, 1973.

Farrrell, John C. *Beloved Lady: A History of Jane Addams' Ideas on Reform and Peace.* Baltimore: Johns Hopkins Press, 1967.

Ferris, Helen. *When I Was a Girl.* New York: Macmillan, 1930.

Gage, Lyman. *Memoirs of Lyman J. Gage.* New York: House of Field, 1937.

Grant, Matthew. *Jane Addams: Helper of the Poor.* Chicago: Children's Press, 1974.

Hagedorn, Hermann. *Americans: A Book of Lives.* New York: Day, 1946.

Hall, Kenneth. *They Stand Tall.* Indianapolis, Ind.: Warner Press, 1953.

Hamilton, Alice. *Exploring the Dangerous Trades: The Autobiography of Alice Hamilton, M.D.* Boston, Mass.: Little, Brown, 1943.

Harlow, S. Ralph. *The Life of H. Roswell Bates.* New York: F. H. Revell, 1914.

Hurd, Charles, and E. B. Hurd. *Treasury of Great American Letters.* New York: Hawthorn Books, 1961.

Judson, Clara I. *City Neighbor: The Story of Jane Addams.* New York: Scribner, 1951.

Kelly, Florence. *Modern Industry in Relation to the Family, Health, Education, Morality.* New York: Longmans Green, 1914.

Levine, Daniel. *Jane Addams and the Liberal Tradition.* Madison, Wis.: State Historical Society, 1971.

Linn, James W. *Jane Addams: A Biography.* New York: Appleton-Century, 1935.

Maude, Aylmer. *Leo Tolstoy and His Works.* New York: Oxford University Press, 1931.

Mears, Louise W. *They Come and Go.* Boston, Mass.: Christopher, 1955.

Meigs, Cornelia. *Jane Addams: Pioneer for Social Justice.* Boston, Mass.: Little, Brown, 1970.

Morris, Lloyd. *Postscript to Yesterday.* New York: Random House, 1946.

Oakley, Violet. *Cathedral of Compassion: Dramatic Outline of the*

Life of Jane Addams: 1860–1935. Philadelphia, Penn.: Women's International League for Peace and Freedom, 1955.

Paxton, Hibben. *The Peerless Leader: William Jennings Bryan.* New York: Farrar & Rhinehart, 1929.

Schnittkind, Henry T., and D. A. Schnittkind. *50 Great Americans.* New York: Doubleday, 1948.

Taylor, Graham. *Religion in Social Action.* New York: Dodd, Mead, 1913.

_____. *Pioneering on Social Frontiers.* Chicago: University of Chicago Press, 1930.

_____. *Chicago Commons Through Forty Years.* Chicago: Chicago Commons Association, 1936.

Tims, Margaret. *Jane Addams of Hull House: 1860–1935: A Centenary Study.* New York: Macmillan, 1961.

Werner, Morris. *Julius Rosenwald: The Life of a Practical Humanitarian.* New York: Harper, 1939.

Wilson, Howard. *Mary McDowell: Neighbor.* Chicago, Ill.: University of Chicago Press, 1928.

Wise, Winifred. *Jane Addams of Hull House: A Biography.* New York: Harcourt, Brace, 1935.

Woods, Eleanor. *Robert A. Woods.* Boston: Houghton Mifflin, 1929.

Woods, Robert. *University of Settlements: Their Point and Drift.* Boston, Mass.: G. H. Ellis, 1899.

_____. *The Neighborhood in Nation Building: The Running Comment of Thirty Years at South End House.* Boston, Mass.: Houghton Mifflin, 1923.

_____, and Albert Kennedy. *Handbook of Settlements.* New York: Charities Publication Committee, 1911.

Chapter Two: Robert Baden-Powell

Abbott, Evelyn, and Lewis Campbell. *Life and Letters of Benjamin Jowett.* London: J. Murray, 1897.

Baden-Powell, Robert. *Scouting for Boys.* London: C. A. Pearson, 1910.

_____. *Quick Training for War.* London: H. Jenkins, 1914.

_____. *Indian Memories: Recollections of Soldiering, Sport, Etc.* London: H. Jenkins, 1915.

_____. *My Adventures as a Spy.* London: C. A. Pearson, 1915.

———. *Girl Guiding*. London: C. A. Pearson, 1918.

———. *Scoutmastership*. New York: G. P. Putnam's Sons, 1920.

———. *Young Knights of the Empire*. London: C. A. Pearson, 1920.

———. *An Old Wolf's Favorites: Animals I Have Known*. London: C. A. Pearson, 1921.

———. *Pig-Sticking or Hog-Hunting*. London: H. Jenkins, 1929.

———. *Rovering to Success*. London: H. Jenkins, 1930.

———. *Scouting and Youth Movements*. New York: J. Cape and H. Smith, 1931.

———. *Lessons from the Varsity Apostrophe of Life*. London: C. A. Pearson, 1933.

———. *Scouting Round the World*. London: H. Jenkins, 1935.

———. *Adventures and Accidents*. London: Methuen, 1936.

———. *The Handbook for Brownies or Blue Birds*. London: C. A. Pearson, 1936.

———. *What Scouts Can Do*. London: C. A. Pearson, 1936.

———. *African Adventures*. London: C. A. Pearson, 1937.

———. *Birds and Beasts in Africa*. London: Macmillan, 1938.

———. *Life's Snags and How to Meet Them: Talks to Young Men*. London: C. A. Pearson, 1939.

———. *Paddle Your Own Canoe*. London: Macmillan, 1939.

———. *More Sketches of Kenya*. London: Macmillan, 1940.

———. "Tea and a Turk." In K. D. Singer, ed., *Three Thousand Years of Espionage*. New York: Prentice-Hall, 1948.

———, and Agnes Baden-Powell. *The Handbook for Girl Guides*. London: T. Nelson and Sons, 1912.

Batchelder, W. J., and D. Balfour. *The Scout's Life of Baden-Powell*. London: Collins' Clear-type Press, 1929.

Beard, Daniel. *The Boy Pioneers: Sons of Daniel Boone*. New York: Scribners, 1932.

———. *Hardly a Man Is Now Alive: The Autobiography of Dan Beard*. New York: Doubleday Doran, 1939.

Boy Scouts of America. *Thirty Years of Service: Tributes to James E. West*. New York: Carey Press, 1941.

Dimmock, Fred. *Bare Knee Days*. London: Bouswood, 1937.

Fast, Howard. *Lord Baden-Powell of the Boy Scouts*. New York: J. Messner, 1941.

Grinnell-Milne, Duncan W. *Baden-Powell at Maseking*. London: Bodley Head, 1957.

Hillcourt, William. *Baden-Powell: The Two Lives of a Hero.* New York: G. P. Putnam's Sons, 1964.

Murray, William. *The History of the Boy Scouts of America.* New York: Boy Scouts of America, 1937.

Reynolds, Ernest E. *Baden-Powell: A Biography of Lord Baden-Powell of Gilwell.* New York: Oxford University Press, 1943.

Rowe, J. G. *Boy's Life of Baden-Powell.* London: Epworth Press, 1929.

Seton, Ernest. *Boy Scouts of America: A Handbook of Woodcraft, Scouting and Life-craft.* New York: Doubleday, Page, 1910.

_____. *Manual of the Woodcraft Indians.* New York: Doubleday, Page, 1915.

_____. *Trail of an Artist-Naturalist: The Autobiography of Ernest Thompson Seton.* New York: Scribners, 1940.

Thorp, Margaret. *Charles Kingsley: 1819–1875.* Princeton, N.J.: Princeton University Press, 1937.

Wade, Eileen K. *The Piper of Pax.* London: C. A. Pearson, 1924.

_____. *A Boy's Life of the Chief Scout.* London: C. A. Pearson, 1929.

_____. *Twenty-One Years of Scouting: The Official History of the Boy Scout Movement from Its Inception.* London: C. A. Pearson, 1929.

_____. *27 Years with Baden-Powell.* London: Blandford, 1957.

Chapter 3: Samuel Barnett

Barnett, Henrietta. *Canon Barnett: His Life, Work, and Friends,* 2 vols. Boston: Houghton Mifflin, 1919.

Barnett, Samuel. *Religion and Progress.* New York: Macmillan, 1907.

_____. *Worship and Work: Thoughts from the Unpublished Writings.* New York: Survey Associates, 1914.

_____, and Henrietta Barnett. *Practicable Socialism: Essays on Social Reform.* New York: Longmans Green, 1893.

_____, and Henrietta Barnett. *Towards Social Reform.* New York: Macmillan, 1909.

Booth, Charles. *Pauperism: A Picture.* London: Macmillan, 1892.

_____. *Life and Labor of the People of London,* 9 vols. New York: Macmillan, 1892–97.

_____. *Old Age Pensions and the Aged Poor: A Proposal.* London: Macmillan, 1899.

Cambridge House. *The History and Function of Cambridge House.* London: Bowes & Bowes, 1934.

Curzon, George. *Principles and Methods of University Reform: Being a Letter Addressed to the University of Oxford.* Oxford: Clarendon Press, 1909.

Geiger, George. *The Philosophy of Henry George.* New York: Macmillan, 1937.

Henderson, C. R. *Social Settlements.* New York: Lentilhon, 1899.

Henry, George, Jr. *The Life of Henry George.* New York: Doubleday & McClure, 1900.

Hodson, Alice. *Letters from a Settlement.* London: E. Arnold, 1909.

Holden, Arthur. *The Settlement Idea: A Vision of Social Justice.* New York: Macmillan, 1922.

International Conference of Settlements. *Settlements and Their Outlook: An Account of the First International Conference of Settlements: Toynbee Hall: London: July 1922.* London: P. S. King, 1922.

Kennedy-Cox, Reginald. *The Happiest Man.* London: Hodder & Stoughton, 1932.

Lidgett, John. *Reminiscences.* London: Epworth Press, 1928.

Mansbridge, Albert. *Fellowmen.* London: Dent, 1948.

Murray, Clyde. *New Horizons for the Settlement Movement.* New York: National Federation of Settlements, 1944.

Picht, Werner. *Toynbee Hall and the English Settlement House Movement.* London: G. Bell, 1914.

Pimlott, John. *Toynbee Hall: Fifty Years of Social Progress: 1884–1934.* London: Dent, 1935.

Russell, Cyril. *The Jew in London.* New York: Crowell, 1901.

Stocks, Mary. *Fifty Years in Every Street: The Story of the Manchester University Settlement.* Manchester: Manchester University Press, 1945.

Townshend, Mrs. *The Case Against the Charity Organization Society.* London: Fabian Society, 1913.

Zetland, Lawrence. *The Life of Lord Curzon,* 3 vols. New York: Boni & Liveright, 1928.

Chapter Four: William Booth

Barnes, Cyril. *God's Army.* Elgin, Ill.: David C. Cook, 1978.

Begbie, Harold. *The Life of General William Booth: The Founder of the Salvation Army,* 2 vols. New York: Macmillan, 1927.

Bishop, Edward. *Blood and Fire!: The Story of General William Booth and the Salvation Army.* Chicago: Moody Press, 1964.

Booth, Catherine B. *Bramwell Booth.* London: Rich and Cowan, 1933.

Booth, Catherine M. *Life and Death.* London: Salvation Army, 1890.

Booth, Maud Ballington. *After Prison—What?* New York: F. H. Revell, 1903.

Booth, W. Bramwell. *Friends of the Poor: A Birdseye View of the Social Work of the Salvation Army.* London: Spottiswoode, 1901.

_____. *Echoes and Memories.* London: Hodder & Stoughton, 1925.

Booth, William. *Training of Children.* London: Salvation Army, 1888.

_____. *In Darkest England and the Way Out.* New York: Funk & Wagnalls, 1890.

_____. *Letters to Salvationists on Religion for Everyday,* 2 vols. London: Salvation Army, 1902.

_____. *The Vagrant and the Unemployable.* London: Salvation Army, 1909.

Booth-Tucker, Frederick. *The Life of Catherine Booth: The Mother of the Salvation Army,* 2 vols. New York: F. H. Revell, 1892.

_____, ed. *The Salvation Army in America: Selected Reports: 1899–1903.* New York: Arno Press, 1972.

Carpenter, Minnie. *Some Notable Officers of the Salvation Army.* London, 1925.

Chesham, Sallie. *Born to Battle: The Salvation Army in America.* New York: Rand McNally, 1965.

Coates, Thomas F. G. *Prophet of the Poor: Life-Story of General Booth.* New York: Dutton, 1906.

Collier, Richard. *The General Next to God.* New York: Dutton, 1965.

Douglas, Eileen, and Mildred Duff. *Commissioner Railton.* London: Salvation Army, 1920.

Ervine, St. John. *God's Soldier: General William Booth,* 2 vols. New York: Macmillan, 1935.

Friedericks, Hulda. *The Romance of the Salvation Army.* London: Cassell, 1907.

Huxley, Thomas. *Social Diseases and Worse Remedies.* London: Macmillan, 1891.

Lee, Umphrey. *The Historical Backgrounds of Early Methodist Enthusiasm.* New York: Columbia University Press, 1931.

Metcalf, Joan. *God Used a Woman: Catherine Booth.* London: Challenge Books, 1967.

Neal, Harry E. *The Hallelujah Army*. Philadelphia, Penn.: Chilton, 1961.

Nelson, William. *Blood and Fire: General William Booth*. New York: Century, 1929.

Nygaard, Norman E. *Trumpet of Salvation: The Story of William and Catherine Booth*. Grand Rapids, Mich.: Zondervan Publ. Co., 1961.

Potter, Charles F. *Great Religious Leaders*. New York: Simon and Schuster, 1958.

Railton, George S. *The Authoritative Life of General William Booth: Founder of the Salvation Army*. New York: Reliance Trading Co., 1912.

Southey, Robert. *The Life of Wesley and the Rise and Progress of Methodism*, 2 vols. London: Oxford University Press, 1925.

Stead, William. *Life of Mrs. Booth: The Founder of the Salvation Army*. New York: F. H. Revell, 1900.

Steele, Harold C. *I Was a Stranger: The Faith of William Booth: Founder of the Salvation Army*. New York: Exposition, 1954.

Watson, Bernard. *A Hundred Years' War*. London: Hodder & Stoughton, 1965.

Wearmouth, Robert. *Methodism and the Working-class Movements of England: 1800–1850*. London: Epworth Press, 1937.

Wilson, Philip. *The General: The Story of Evangeline Booth*. London: Hodder & Stoughton, 1935.

Wisbey, Herbert A. *Soldiers Without Swords*. New York: Macmillan, 1955.

Chapter Five: Dorothea Dix

Adams, Elmer, and Warren Foster. *Heroines of Modern Progress*. New York: Sturgis & Walton, 1913.

Bennett, Helen. *American Women in Civic Work*. New York: Dodd, Mead, 1915.

Bremer, Frederika. *The Homes of the New World: Impressions of America*, 2 vols. New York: Harper, 1853.

Channing, William H. *The Life of William Ellery Channing: The Centenary Memorial Edition*. Boston: American Unitarian Association, 1890.

Dell, Floyd. *Women as World Builders*. Chicago, Ill.: Forbes, 1913.

Dix, Dorothea. *Conversations on Common Things*, 3rd ed. Boston, Mass.: Munroe & Francis, 1828.

————. *The Garland of Flora*. Boston: S. G. Goodrich, 1829.

————. *Memorial in Behalf of the Pauper Insane and Idiots in Jails and Poorhouses Throughout the Commonwealth: To the Legislature of Massachusetts*. Boston: Munroe & Francis, 1843.

————. *Remarks on Prisons and Prison Discipline in the United States*. Boston: Munroe & Francis, 1845.

Hawthorne, Nathaniel. *Life of Franklin Pierce*. Boston, Mass.: Ticknor, Reed & Fields, 1852.

Heath, Monroe. *Great Americans at a Glance*, vol. 4. San Francisco, Cal.: Pacific Coast Pub., 1957.

Holbrook, Stewart H. *Lost Men of American History*. New York: Macmillan, 1946.

————. *Dreamers of the American Dream*. New York: Doubleday, 1957.

Marshall, Helen E. *Dorothea Dix: Forgotten Samaritan*. Chapel Hill: University of North Carolina Press, 1937.

McKown, Robin. *Pioneers of Mental Health*. New York: Dodd, Mead, 1961.

Roe, Alfred. *Dorothea Lynde Dix*. Wooster, Mass.: F. P. Rice , 1889.

Tiffany, Francis. *Life of Dorothea Lynde Dix*. Boston, Mass.: Houghton Mifflin, 1918.

Washburn, Henry. *The Religious Motive in Philanthropy: Studies in Biography*. Philadelphia, Penn.: University of Pennsylvania Press, 1931.

Wilson, Dorothy Clarke. *Stranger and Traveler: The Story of Dorothea Dix: American Reformer*. Boston, Mass.: Little, Brown, 1975.

————. *The Story of Dorothea Dix: An American Reformer*. Boston, Mass.: Little, Brown, 1975.

Chapter Six: Samuel Gridley Howe

Bass, Edith. *Francis William Bird: 1881–1918: Written for His Children by Their Aunt*. Boston: Private printing, 1924.

Cook, Edward. *The Life of Florence Nightingale*, 2 vols. London: Macmillan, 1914.

Elliott, Maud. *Laura Bridgman: Dr. Howe's Famous Pupil and What He Taught Her*. Boston, Mass.: Little, Brown, 1903.

Goldsmith, Margaret. *Florence Nightingale: The Woman and the Legend.* London: Hodder & Stoughton, 1937.

Holbrook, Steward. *Dreamers of the American Dream.* New York: Doubleday, 1957.

Howe, Samuel Gridley. *An Historical Sketch of the Greek Revolution.* New York: White, Gallagher & White, 1828.

_____. *A Discourse on the Social Relations of Man.* Boston, Mass.: Marsh, Capen & Lyon, 1837.

_____. *A Letter to the Governor of Massachusetts Upon His Veto of a Bill Providing for an Increase of State Beneficiaries at the School for Idiotic Children.* Boston: Ticknor & Field, 1857.

_____. *The Refugees from Slavery in Canada West: Refer to the Freedman's Inquiry Commission.* Boston: Wright & Potter, 1864.

_____. *An Essay on the Separate and Congregate Systems of Prison Discipline.* Boston, Mass.: W. T. Ticknor, 1864.

_____. *Appeal to the People of the United States to Relieve from Starvation the Women and Children of the Greeks in the Island of Crete.* Boston, Mass.: G. C. Rand & Avery, 1867.

_____. *The Cretan Refugees and Their American Helpers.* Boston, Mass.: Lee & Shepard, 1868.

_____. *Causes and Prevention of Idiocy.* Boston, Mass.: Lee & Shepard, 1874.

Jennings, John Edward. *Banners Against the Wind.* Boston, Mass.: Little, Brown, 1954.

Mann, Mary. *Life of Horace Mann: By His Wife.* Boston, Mass.: Lee & Shepard, 1904.

Meltzer, Milton. *A Light in the Dark: The Life of Samuel Gridley Howe.* New York: Crowell, 1964.

Morse, John. *Life and Letters of Oliver Wendell Holmes*, 2 vols. Boston, Mass.: Houghton Mifflin, 1896.

Richards, Laura, ed. *Letters and Journal of Samuel Gridley Howe*, 2 vols. Boston, Mass.: D. Estes, 1909.

_____. *Laura Bridgman: The Story of an Opened Door.* New York: D. Appleton-Century, 1928.

_____. *Samuel Gridley Howe.* New York: D. Appleton-Century, 1935.

Robinson, Mabel. *Runner of the Mountain Tops: The Life of Louis Agassiz.* New York: Random House, 1939.

Ross, Ishbel. *Journey into Light.* New York: Appleton, 1951.

Sanborn, Franklin. *Dr. Samuel Gridley Howe: The Philanthropist.* New York: Funk & Wagnalls, 1891.

Schwartz, Harold. *Samuel Gridley Howe: Social Reformer.* Cambridge, Mass.: Harvard University Press, 1956.

Tharp, Louise H. *Three Saints and a Sinner: Julia Ward Howe, Louisa, Annie and Sam Ward.* Boston, Mass.: Little, Brown, 1956.

Tiffany, Nina M. *Pathbreakers.* Boston, Mass.: Beacon, 1949.

Zarek, Otto. *Kossuth.* London: Selwyn & Blount, 1937.

Chapter 7: Frederick Ozanam

Baunard, Louis. *Ozanam and His Correspondence.* Dublin: Catholic Truth Society of Ireland, 1925.

Broderick, James. *Frederick Ozanam and His Society.* London: Burns, Oates and Washbourne, 1933.

Cassidy, James. *Frederick Ozanam: A Study in Sanctity and Scholarship.* Dublin: Talbot Press, 1943.

Coste, Pierre. *The Life and Works of Saint Vincent de Paul,* 3 vols. London: Burns, Oates and Washbourne, 1934–35.

Derum, James Patrick. *Apostle in a Top Hat: The Life of Frederick Ozanam.* New York: Hanover House, 1960.

Hughes, Henry. *Frederick Ozanam.* London: A. Ouseley, 1933.

Lewandowski, Maurice. *Andre-Marie Ampere.* Paris: Bernard Grasset, 1936.

Maurois, Andre. *Chateaubriand: Poet: Statesman: Lover.* New York: Harper, 1938.

Maynard, Theodore. *Apostle of Charity: The Life of St. Vincent de Paul.* New York: Dial Press, 1939.

O'Connor, Edward. *Secret of Frederick Ozanam: Founder of the Society of St. Vincent de Paul.* Dublin: Gill, 1953.

O'Meara, Kathleen. *Frederick Ozanam: Professor at the Sorbonne: His Life and Work.* New York: Catholic Publishing Society, 1878.

Ozanam, Frederick. *History of Civilization in the Fifth Century,* 2 vols. Philadelphia, Penn.: A. C. Glyn, 1867.

_____. *Oeuvres Completes,* with a Preface by M. Ampere, 11 vols. Paris, 1872–81.

_____. *A Pilgrimage to the Land of the Cid.* New York: Christian Press Association Publishing, 1895.

_____. *Dante and Catholic Philosophy in the Thirteenth Century.* New York: Cathedral Library Association, 1897.

_____. *The Franciscan Poets in Italy of the Thirteenth Century.* London: D. Nutt, 1914.

Renner, Sister Emanuel. *Historical Thought of Frederick Ozanam.* Washington, D.C.: Catholic University of American Press, 1960.

Schimberg, Albert. *The Great Friend: Frederick Ozanam.* Milwaukee, Wis.: Bruce Pub., 1946.

Whitehouse, Henry. *The Life of Lamartine,* 2 vols. Boston, Mass.: Houghton Mifflin, 1918.

Williamson, Claude Charles H., ed. *Great Catholics.* New York: Collier, 1963.

Chapter Eight: Lord Shaftesbury: Anthony Ashley Cooper

Battiscombe, Georgina. *Shaftesbury: The Great Reformer: 1801–1885.* Boston, Mass.: Houghton Mifflin, 1975.

Blackburn, Barbara. *Noble Lord: The Life of the Seventh Earl of Shaftesbury.* London: Home and Van Thal, 1949.

Blugler, Demetrius. *Lord William Bentinck.* Oxford: Clarendon Press, 1892.

Bready, John. *Lord Shaftesbury and Social-Industrial Progress.* London: George Allen & Unwin, 1926.

Frith, Henry. *The Seventh Earl of Shaftesbury.* London: Cassell, 1887.

Hammond, John, and Barbara Hammond. *Lord Shaftesbury,* 4th ed. New York: Longmans Green, 1936.

Higham, Florence. *Lord Shaftesbury: A Portrait.* London: Student Christian Movement Press, 1945.

Hodder, Edwin. *The Life and Work of the Seventh Earl of Shaftesbury,* 3 vols. London: Cassell, 1886–87.

Johnson, Dorothy. *Pioneers of Reform.* London: Methuen, 1929.

Martin, Hugh. *Christian Social Reformers in the Nineteenth Century.* New York: G. H. Doran, 1927.

Newman, A. R. *Dr. Bernardo, As I Knew Him: By One of His Staff.* London: Constable, 1914.

Irwin, Grace. *The Seventh Earl: A Dramatized Biography.* Grand Rapids, Mich.: Eerdmans, 1976.

Pengelly, R. *Lord Shaftesbury: Peer and Philanthropist.* London: National Sunday School Union, 1923.

Rosenbaum, Robert A. *Earnest Victorians.* New York: Hawthorn, 1961.

Trevelyan, George. *The Life of John Bright.* London: Constable, 1913.

Williams, Dorothy. *Lord Shaftesbury: The Story of His Life and Work for Industrial England: 1801–1885.* London: Teachers and Taught, 1925.

Williamson, David. *Lord Shaftesbury's Legacy: A Record of Eighty Years' Service by the Shaftesbury Society and Ragged School Union: 1844–1924.* London: Hodder & Stoughton, 1924.

Chapter Nine: Mary Kingsbury Simkhovitch

Ashley, William. *The Christian Outlook: Being the Sermons of an Economist.* London: Longmans Green, 1925.

Betts, Lillian. *The Leaven in a Great City.* New York: Dodd, Mead, 1903.

Charity Organization Society of New York. *Handbook for Friendly Visitors Among the Poor.* New York: E. P. Putnam's Sons, 1883.

Charity Organization Society of New York. *In Memoriam: Josephine Shaw.* New York: Lowell, 1906.

Daniels, Harriet. *The Girl and Her Chance: A Study of Conditions Surrounding the Young Girl Between Fourteen and Eighteen Years of Age in New York City.* New York: F. H. Revell, 1914.

Duffus, Robert. *Lillian Wald: Neighbor and Crusader.* New York: Macmillan, 1938.

Hawkins, Gaynell. *Educational Experiments in Social Settlements.* New York: American Association for Adult Education, 1937.

Hiram House. *Pioneering on Social Frontiers: 1896–1936.* Cleveland, Ohio: Hiram House, 1937.

Hudson Guild. *The Hudson Guild: Founded 1895: A Brief Record of Twenty-five Years of Service.* New York: Hudson Guild, 1920.

Kennedy, Albert J., Kathryn Farra, and Associates. *Social Settlements in New York City.* New York: Columbia University Press, 1935.

Lawrence, William. *Life of Phillips Brooks.* New York: Harper, 1930.

McConnell, Francis. *Borden Parker Bowne: His Life and His Philosophy.* New York: Abingdon, n.d.

Ovington, Mary. *The Walls Came Tumbling Down: The Story of the National Association for the Advancement of Colored People by One of Its Founders.* New York: Harcourt, Brace, 1947.

Simkhovitch, Mary. *The City Worker's World in America.* New York: Macmillan, 1917.

_____. *The Settlement Primer*. Boston: National Federation of Settlements, 1926.

_____. *The Church and Public Housing*. New York: Department of Christian Social Service, The National Council, 1934.

_____. *Neighborhood: My Story of Greenwich House*. New York: W. W. Norton, 1938.

_____. *Group Life*. New York: Association Press, 1940.

_____. "Self-portrait." In Louis Finkelstein, ed., *American Spiritual Autobiographies*. New York: Harper, 1948.

_____, and Elizabeth Ogg. *Quicksand and the Way of Life in the Slums*. Evanston, Ill.: Row, Peterson, 1942.

Simkhovitch, Vladimir. *Marxism Versus Socialism*. New York: Holt, 1913.

_____. *Toward the Understanding of Jesus*. New York: Macmillan, 1921.

Wald, Lillian. *The House on Henry Street*. New York: Holt, 1915.

_____. *Windows on Henry Street*. Boston, Mass.: Little, Brown, 1934.

Woods, Robert, and Albert J. Kennedy. *The Settlement Horizon: A National Estimate*. New York: Russell Sage Foundation, 1922.

Chapter 10: George Williams

Beardsley, Frank. *A Mighty Winner of Souls: Charles G. Finney: A Study in Evangelism*. New York: American Tract Society, 1937.

Begbie, Harold. *Ordinary Man and the Extraordinary Thing*. New York: Doran, 1912.

_____. *Born in Britain: World Wide Movements and Their Founders: George Williams and the YMCA*. New York: British Information Services, 1945.

Cree, John. *Thomas Kirby Cree: A Memorial*. New York: Association Press, 1914.

Eddy, Sherwood. *A Century with Youth: A History of the YMCA from 1844 to 1944*. New York: Association Press, 1944.

Ellenwood, James. *One Hundred Years and Here We Are*. New York: Association Press, 1944.

Hodder, Edwin. *The Life of Samuel Morley*. New York: A. D. F. Randolph, 1888.

Lentz, E. G. *George Williams: A Tribute to the Founder of the Red Triangle*. Carbondale, Ill.: Illinois Area YMCA, 1959.

Moody, Paul D. *My Father: An Intimate Portrait of Dwight L. Moody.* Boston: Little, Brown, 1938.

Murray, William. *As He Journeyed: The Autobiography of William D. Murray.* New York: Association Press, 1929.

Northcott, Cecil B. A. *Sir George Williams: Founder of the YMCA.* London: The Religious Tract Society, n.d.

Ober, Charles. *Luther D. Wishard: Projector of World Movements.* New York: Association Press, 1927.

Ober, Frank, ed. *James Stokes: Pioneer of the Young Men's Christian Associations.* New York: Association Press, 1921.

Pollock, John Charles. *Pioneers.* Wheaton, Ill.: Tyndale Press, 1951.

Second South East Asia YMCA Training Institute. *Training for Service.* Singapore: YMCA Training Institute, 1958.

Walden, H. A. *Operation Textiles: A City Warehouse in War-time: A Short History of the firm of Hitchcock, Williams and Company, St. Paul's Churchyard.* London: Thomas Reed and Co., 1947.

Warburton, George. *George Alonzo Hall: A Tribute to a Consecrated Personality.* New York: International Committee of the YMCA, 1905.

Williams, J. E. Hodder. *The Father of the Red Triangle: The Life of Sir George Williams.* London: Hodder & Stoughton, 1918.

Index